Waltzing the Magpies

SAM PICKERING

Waltzing *the* *Magpies*

A Year in Australia

For Nicky and Bill and Family, with love,

Sam

UNIVERSITY OF MICHIGAN PRESS ANN ARBOR

Copyright © by Sam Pickering 2004

All rights reserved

Published in the United States of America by

The University of Michigan Press

Manufactured in the United States of America

♾ Printed on acid-free paper

2007   2006   2005   2004   4   3   2   1

A CIP catalog record for this book is available from the British Library.

Library of Congress Cataloging-in-Publication Data

Pickering, Samuel F., 1941–

    Waltzing the magpies : a year in Australia / Sam Pickering.

      p.   cm.

    ISBN 0-472-11377-1 (cloth : alk. paper)

     1. Pickering, Samuel F., 1941—Travel—Australia.

  2. English teachers—Australia—Biography.   3. Australia—

Social life and customs.   4. Americans—Australia—

Biography.   I. Title.

PE64.P53 A3   2004

820.9—dc22   2003015702

Preface

Seven years ago I took a sabbatical year at half pay, and Vicki, the three children, and I lived for twelve months in Western Australia. When we returned to Connecticut, I wrote *Walkabout Year,* an account of our experiences. This past year I had a second sabbatical. For me Time no longer ambles but instead sprints fleet-footed and winged. Consequently I decided to absent myself from teaching for another year. For three months I dallied with going to Great Britain. In the 1960s I attended Cambridge University, and on learning that I had twelve months off, St. Catharine's, my old college, awarded me a scholarship. On snowy winter evenings I imagined visiting classmates and the haunts of greener days. "The spot of ground on which a man has stood is forever interesting to him," wrote Alexander Smith, a nineteenth-century British essayist. "I startle myself with myself at the corners of streets; I confront forgotten bits of myself at the entrance to houses," Smith stated in "On the Revisiting of Places." "In windows which to another man would seem blank and meaningless, I find personal poems too deep to be ever turned into rhymes—more pathetic, mayhap, than I have ever found on a printed page."

I have written essays for so long that I see days as sentences and weeks as paragraphs. In Britain I imagined the past appointing the present. I remembered the evening members of my boat tossed me onto a bonfire, saying, "Let's burn the American," their voices drunken but affectionate. One night I held a party. For some reason stacks of newspaper cluttered the hall outside my rooms. By midnight the paper had migrated into my quarters, and friends had shredded it, creating a pile that rose to our hips, inspiring us to transform ourselves into dolphins. We plunged beneath the newsprint and swam through accounts of South Africa and Southeast Asia, surfacing only when drink ebbed low. At two o'clock someone rapped on my door. I was prepared. I filled a glass with brandy then swung the door open and said, "Dean, where have you been? I've been expecting you." Thrusting the brandy into his hand, I said, "I have saved this for you." The dean emptied the glass and another then said, "This has been splendid. But if the paper is not cleaned up by six in the morning, I will send you down."

The scholarship St. Catharine's awarded me was heavy on honor but light on cash. Daylight burned away sentimental recollection. Friends reported that life in Britain was wildly expensive. Ahead of me stretched a dozen years of college tuition. "What is twelve times $35,000?" Vicki asked. "A sabbatical somewhere cheaper than in England," I said. Moreover, I wasn't sure I'd be welcome at Cambridge. At the University of Connecticut, people tolerate my doings, saying, "Oh, that's just Sam." I was afraid Cambridge would prove stuffy. Three years ago my boy Francis applied to St. Catharine's. The college scheduled Francis's interview for 3:30 the afternoon of December 11. At the time Francis was a senior in high school taking courses at the University of Connecticut. On the eleventh, Francis was supposed to sit two final examinations, and he wrote St. Catharine's saying he could come any day after the eleventh but not the eleventh itself. The college refused to reschedule the interview. Francis took the examinations at Connecticut. The next fall he enrolled in Princeton. "Cambridge might be too hide-bound," Vicki warned.

While I pondered Vicki's warning, I began receiving email from Perth. Earlier I wrote Bob White, a friend from seven years ago and a professor at the University of Western Australia, saying that another sabbatical had rolled around and I was thinking about going to Britain. Bob marshaled members of the English department, and they wrote, urging me to return to Australia. Having people want one is seductive, particularly for a middle-aged man, his hair thin and stomach thick, all sex appeal lost. Almost overnight I decided to return to Australia.

Because Francis was in college and Eliza would be a tenth

grader, the easiest grade in high school to miss, teachers told me, I didn't think the trip would disrupt their lives. I worried about Edward, however. He would miss twelfth grade. Because he had stopped playing sports and had begun taking courses at the university rather than in the high school itself, I convinced myself that the dislocation wouldn't be too bumpy. I worried mostly about his girlfriend Alice. During afternoons she and Edward studied Latin together. "She is the sweetest, nicest girl he will ever date," I told Vicki. "Only a louse would force them apart." "If you don't pack Edward off," Vicki said, "their affection will become love parsonified, and they are too young for marriage." I arranged for Edward to spend the summer working on a cattle station in Queensland. At the end of August, he would join us in Perth. In June, the day after school ended, Edward flew out of Hartford at six in the evening. That morning he and Alice played duets on the piano. She gave him a copy of Shakespeare's sonnets, and he gave her an anthology of French verse in French. After lunch they swam in the Fenton River. Later she sprinkled small red hearts throughout his yearbook. That evening when I drove to the airport, Edward sat beside me on the front seat, tears streaming down his cheeks. "Those tears," Vicki said at home, "were not for little sister and mother and father." That night when Alice's mother returned from work, her daughter was ironing, tears sprinkling the clothes. "What have I done?" I said to my friend Bill the next morning. Bill is provost of a university, and years in administration have toughened him. "Nothing important," he answered. "It's about time Edward's heart had a history."

We did not go to Australia to discover newness or construct a different life. Instead we packed our accustomed lives in suitcases and took them with us. Little aside from my death will make me irresponsible or stop me from worrying about Vicki and the children. Moreover, no matter the abode, once or twice a month I will shout from the bedroom, be the room upstairs as in Storrs or on the same floor as in Australia, "This is it. I'm going to kill myself." And no matter the tenor of my voice, no one will say anything other than, "What?"

Some of my closest friends are fictional. They live in Carthage, Tennessee, and in my essays. Because they make me happy, I couldn't bear to leave them behind, so I took them with me to Australia. Just yesterday I received a letter from Turlow Gutheridge, the mayor of Carthage. This November Hollis Hunnewell brought his carnival to town. The season's leading performer was Androcles Brown, a one-armed juggler. After opening night Thelma Mae Biggles spoke to Androcles. "I see you've lost your arm," Thelma Mae said. "Bless my soul!" Androcles exclaimed, turning his head to peer at the stump jutting from his left shoulder. "I do believe you are right. Oh, my goodness, I wonder where it could have got to."

Now that we are back in Connecticut, Vicki and I find it difficult to believe that we ever went to Australia. Travel does not change the middle-aged. I behave as I have always done. In October I read at a bookstore. When the store manager asked for a quotation to print on the broadside announcing the reading, I made up a quote. "Pickering is," the *Atlanta Constitution* supposedly said, "the King bee of essayists. Sometimes his words sting, but, oh, the sweet honey—Lordy, Lordy, the sweet honey." This fall as usual I donated a carton of books to the local library for the annual fund-raising book sale. As I have done in the past, I inscribed the books fulsomely to myself. From 1922 to 1930 Roy Chapman Andrews led archeological expeditions to Central Asia. On the title page of *Dragon Hunter,* a biography of Andrews, I wrote, "To Sam Pickering, one of our century's great literary adventurers, the man who with his little pencil has unearthed the familiar essay, thus brightening the bedtime reading of countless thousands, in the process saving untold marriages by diverting the frustrated from boredom and resentment." Although I often elevate my literary stature beyond believable fabrication, I don't confine fiction to self-promotion. Last month I received a telephone call from a woman writing an article for the *New York Times.* She had surfed postal codes on Amazon in order to discover what books were popular in different areas of Connecticut. "My idea," she said, "is you are what you read." "No," I responded, "the opposite is true.

People are not what they read about, but instead are what they do not read about. The painfully ordinary read books about celebrities. Rational cowards read about dead heroes. Walking corpses read books about the robust; dumbbells, about intelligence, and the poor, about wealth. Meatballs read about people skinnier than pencils, and the deprived whose intimate lives are more conventional than grape Jell-O purchase books which describe gallivanters partial to caviar and kinky desserts with foreign names." "Goodness," the woman exclaimed, "you must have researched the subject." "Yes," I said. "You are fortunate to have talked to me. Otherwise you would have embarrassed yourself intellectually."

Of course I am not the only person who inhabits a world raised on stretchers. If forbidden to lie, American business would go belly-up. The day after returning from Australia I began receiving letters and telephone calls hawking the fraudulent, not something that occurred in Australia. In 1997, my uncle, Coleman Pickering, died in a nursing home in Houston. He suffered from dementia, and before I managed his affairs, crooks picked his bank account to bones. Christian bookies peddled sad fictions, and oily financiers sold him shares in bottomless pits. Mail confers immortality. Each year since Coleman's death, I have received scores of flyers addressed to him. The week before Christmas, a salesman telephoned and thinking me my uncle tried to sell me stock in a titanium mine. My informing the salesman that Coleman Pickering had been dead for five years only greased the pitch. "I am sorry," the man said, "but that aside, this is a good deal, for you, for him, for anybody." "Time doesn't change much," Vicki said later.

In September I was asked to write a page describing the purpose of an English major. I wrote two sentences. "A major in English ought to brighten students' days by awakening then nurturing a fondness for and an interest in words and reading. English should teach students to read critically, that is, be able to understand not merely how stories or poems are made, but how words can make worlds." Because I didn't teach in Australia, I'd lost touch with academic reality. Once school began in September, students behaved as they have always done. Two days before I returned a midterm examination, a student asked for my office hours. "I want to know your office hours," he said, "so I can come and complain about my grade. I deserve an *A* in this course." The boy made a *B*, and the day after receiving his paper came to my office and complained. One hundred and seven students took the course. The girl who made the lowest grade in the class on the midterm also came to my office. I spent seventy-three minutes explaining how she could improve her work. I urged her to attend class and read the assignments, things she had not done. That afternoon when I returned home an email from the girl greeted me. "I don't understand," she wrote, "why I didn't get a *B*. My friends got *B's*, and they didn't attend class, and I want you to know that I don't appreciate being made fun of."

"Why," I said to Vicki, "did we leave Australia?" Still, words can make worlds. Each semester some few students chase doldrums from classrooms and make teachers delay retirement. One day I lectured on Jane Austen's novel *Sense and Sensibility*. Suddenly Bridget blurted, "Professor Pickering, will you marry me?" For extra credit in a course on the short story, students wrote tales. The stories were mundanely inspirational. A last-second pass won a football game; a grand slam with two out in the ninth won a baseball game; a girl swam personal bests in two events as the university swimming team defeated "its arch-rival Syracuse." Wilt inspired only one out of eighty-six tales. Dan described attending a performance of *Making It,* staged by the drama club at the local junior high school. The narrator's brother was assistant lighting director, a position that required the attendance of his entire family. Dan's story consisted of thirty short paragraphs. "7:36. With thirteen-year old actors on stage discussing unplanned pregnancy, my hands begin to clench the program. Nervously I begin tearing bits off one corner." Sixteen minutes later, the narrator noted, "I find it easier to detach myself from onstage action. The last thing I heard was a soliloquy in which the high school quarterback discusses how his father gets drunk and beats him." "8:05. The parents on stage are trying to force their son to go to business school.

He wants to be an artist. I remember that I need to pick up some loose-leaf paper before I return to college." "8:24. The lights go dark suddenly, leaving a red after-image on my retinas. The temperature is still rising. I remove my sweater. Screaming begins. Why?" Intermission occurred at 8:41, and Dan wrote, "I head for fresh air. In the sky the crescent moon is a dark gold color. Mist is beginning to obscure its features." The play ended at 9:40, and the narrator concluded, "The play was over. The issues. The problems. The conflicts. I could feel life flowing back into me." As the narrator vanished into the night, a cackle of pessimistic laughter rose from my diaphragm, and I, too, felt life coursing through veins flattened by the drumbeat of uplift.

Children are creatures of genes not habit. Edward returned to Connecticut and behaving as if he had spent only a weekend in Australia, telephoned Alice. In September he went to Middlebury College. "I'm taking a course in the eighteenth-century novel," he wrote. "In order to keep up I have to read 62.58 pages each night of the semester." "He is your son," Vicki exclaimed; "Australia didn't affect him." The year in Australia did change Eliza's life slightly. For three years in a row Eliza had been the top Latin student in Connecticut at her grade level. Her school in Perth did not offer Latin, and even though I hired a tutor for Eliza, this fall she dropped Latin and began Russian. In Australia sports are not an important part of secondary school life, and Eliza spent afternoons reading instead of playing. On returning to Storrs, she ran cross-country and made the All-Conference team. In the state meet, she suffered an asthma attack and collapsed after a mile and a half. The Rescue Squad called me at home. There was so much static on the line I thought a telemarketer was speaking to me, and I almost put the receiver down. Like Edward, though, Eliza is a creature of genes. At school other kids don't call her Eliza; instead they address her as, "Oh, that's just Eliza." Still, wonderful things have happened in Connecticut. Although Eliza didn't have a date, she attended the Junior Prom and took pictures in order to raise money for Model United Nations. She wore blue jeans and was glum when I drove her to the dance. Three hours later she returned home smiling. Four girls, strangers really, none of whom were in her class, insisted she enjoy the dance. While one girl curled Eliza's hair with an iron, another lent her a pair of shoes, one and a half sizes smaller than Eliza's foot size but big enough for dancing. For a dress the third girl pinned her shawl around Eliza's waist, and the last girl lent Eliza a red blouse. "Home can be pretty darn good," I said to Vicki.

Of course I miss Australia. We had a wonderful time, the stuff of the pages that follow. Rarely does a day pass during which Australia doesn't come to mind. Two weeks ago Chester sent me an email from Perth. He had just taken a job at an American university, and he wrote in order to give me his new email. By return mail, I sent a note congratulating him and saying that his departure would be a loss to Western Australia. Unfortunately, Chester sent an incorrect email, saying that his new mail began "cgibbon." By noon I had received an email from Charles Gibbon, the "cgibbon" at the address Chester sent. "I don't no you. Remove me immediately from your list." I did so, after which I wrote Chester at his old address. "You had better correct the email," I wrote. "Not only is your cousin Charles a bad speller, but he's a prick." Within minutes I received a response from Chester's email server, saying my note had been forwarded to Chester's new email, "cgibbon," alas, at Charles Gibbon's address. That evening I deleted Cousin Charles's response unread.

Yesterday in the kitchen I put on my old gray windbreaker. In the pocket lay a two-dollar Australian coin, Queen Elizabeth on the front, on the back, a grass tree, a bearded Aboriginal man, and the five stars of the Southern Cross. "Look what I found," I said to Vicki. "I'm watching crows in the back yard," Vicki said, staring over the sink. "Do you think those magpies you fed last year miss us?" she said, turning toward me a moment later. "Miss us?" I said. "Yes, they miss us a lot, and I miss them, but we'll get along all right without each other."

Contents

Bumpy Landing

I spent much of July and June smoothing our arrival in Western Australia. For Immigration I filed a cabinet of forms. Through the University of Western Australia, I rented an apartment for the first two weeks of our stay in Perth. To banish turbulence from the flight, I booked seats on Qantas from Los Angeles to Perth, explaining that I needed an aisle seat because once my legs cramped so badly after a long trip that I almost had "surgery." For the flight from Hartford to Los Angeles, I couldn't book seats, and American Airlines stuffed us into the last row of the plane, practically leading to actual, not fictional, surgery. I cancelled automobile insurance and from our agent obtained a testimonial stating that neither Vicki nor I had caused a car wreck during the past five years. Seven years ago in Perth, I bought a Toyota from Rod Evans at Brooking Mazda. Brooking had closed, but through the Internet, I traced Rod to Mazda City. I telephoned him, and Rod assured me that he'd find a dependable used car and hold it for our arrival. Easily I shifted from automotive to medical matters. I arranged physicals for the family. Vicki and the children were in good health. But I fretted about myself, the condition of a fifty-nine-year-old male being more a matter of chance than pills. Happily, I proved in sustainable shape. After the physical I visited Robert Friedman, a dermatologist, who trimmed me into fleshly topiary, loping off buds that might have bloomed in Australia. A college student, my older boy Francis, was not accompanying us to Australia. Instead he planned to spend the year in Europe, studying in Italy in the fall and Germany in the spring. Because his wisdom teeth were impacted, I arranged for Dr. Grippo to pull them out.

At times days seemed classrooms devoted to educational matters. I enrolled Eliza in St. Hilda's Anglican School for Girls and Edward in Christ Church Grammar School, generally thought the leading schools in Perth. On June 21, Edward flew to Queensland, where he spent the summer working as a jackeroo on Tumbar Station. Because applying to colleges would be difficult enough without having to request forms from Australia, I solicited applications from a gaggle of schools: Oberlin, Carleton, Duke, Sewanee, Middlebury, Bowdoin, Tulane, and Virginia, among others. I telephoned admissions officers. Although application forms were not generally available until the middle of August, officers promised to speed them to me so that I would have them in hand when I left Connecticut. Most schools got the applications to me. Those that did not I nagged, usually successfully but sometimes unsuccessfully. Over the telephone an admissions officer at Amherst assured me Edward's application was in the mail and would arrive "tomorrow, the next day at the latest." Six days later the application had not arrived. "I will mail an application to Storrs this afternoon," the officer then assured me. Nine days later we flew to Australia without the application.

In July Vicki cleaned house and held a tag sale. She cleared $217.85, or 7.46% of a roundtrip ticket from Hartford to Perth. Three roundtrip tickets cost $8,759.45. For its part Edward's ticket to Queensland, including a leg from Queensland to Perth, but not a return flight to Connecticut, cost $1,824.19. To earn airfare, I taught children's literature in both sessions of summer school. Three mornings a week I lectured from 9:00 to 12:15, giving students two six-minute lavatory breaks. By eleven-thirty students were weary, and one day, two hours and forty-six minutes into class, a girl turned to a boy sitting behind her and referring to *Alice's Adventures in Wonderland*, exclaimed, "Are we down the rabbit hole or what?" "Swept down the burrow," I said, "and I am

SAM PICKERING

shoveling in words by the peck." In the haste to earn tickets, I rarely slowed. Moreover, money was seldom out of mind. To pull Francis's teeth, Dr. Grippo charged $1,289, of which I paid $486.31. Francis was in the chair for twenty-one minutes, the expense to me, I told Vicki, "amounting to $23.16 a minute." Because I owned two small dogs, I didn't rent the house. Instead Aaron, a graduate student, occupied the house and in place of rent cared for the dogs, leaving me $3,028.47 to pay in town taxes. Lamentation was not an affordable indulgence. Instead of grinding molars over lost dollars, I hustled. For $3,000, I wrote eleven thousand words describing the life of Gilbert White, an eighteenth-century British naturalist and author of *The Natural History of Selborne.* In June I earned $2,750 for two speeches, traveling to Tennessee for one and making the other in Storrs.

"Enough about money," Vicki said one night at dinner. Alas, purging the balance sheet from days was impossible. Insofar as I calculated, tuition and contributions to "Foundations" at St. Hilda's and Christ Church amounted to $15,000. For Francis's year abroad I expected to pay $20,000. Early in June I handed the University of Connecticut a check for $8,126, charges for the first half of Francis's year. Although writing the check battered my wallet, it did not raise a blood blister on my bank account, as had tuition for Francis's freshman year at Princeton. "At least," I said to Vicki that night, "I won't have to pay Princeton." I was mistaken. The next day I received a letter from Princeton approving Francis's year abroad but informing me that to keep Francis on the roster of active students and to process his transcript from Connecticut the fee was $4,000. That night I wrote Princeton. Tuition for a year at the University of Connecticut, I noted, amounted to $4,282. In responding, a dean observed that I was fortunate that Francis chose the present to go abroad. Next fall, she informed me, Princeton planned to charge students on foreign study full Princeton tuition, from the proceeds of which the university would reimburse schools under whose auspices students studied. "This behavior from a school whose endowment is over seven billion dollars," Vicki said, "lowers academic cash jacking to new depths.

Don't pay a penny." A wearing correspondence then ensued, at the end of which Princeton reduced their lay-away charges to $2,000.

Princeton was only one of my correspondents. For Aaron, I typed twenty-two single-spaced pages of instructions. For the dogs alone Vicki wrote seven pages. Penny, Vicki wrote, "is a wind-up toy. She runs on Energizer batteries. High-maintenance is the word. She likes to play all day. She plays like a cat. She chews a rawhide chip or a squeaky toy. She will bring it to you and wait for you to kick or throw it. She enjoys this while one is cooking dinner—which makes life interesting! Penny suffers from not having a window seat near a picture window. Her other favorite occupation is squirrel watching and chasing. In the kitchen she will stare up at the window into the trees. She will whimper and paw your foot imploring to be picked up and held for a better view. We call this The Elevator. If there are squirrels in the back yard, you can let her out the kitchen door to run around the house after them, or better still, sneak through the garage door for an ambush. The dogs also chase cats off the property, which is fine, only don't let the dogs follow cats into the road. The dogs smell everything, even through closed windows and doors. Quite often at night, they go wild, smelling an animal on the property. Don't let them out right away because the prowler might be a skunk. Twice skunks have blasted Penny."

In the basement Vicki stored a year's supply of dog food, including packages of snacks, "Milkbone Soft and Chewy" and "Alpo Prime Treats." She marked days on the calendar when the dogs should receive heartworm pills and tick medicine, besides dates for vaccinations and license renewals. In case food ran low, she recommended supermarkets. "Pedigree Chunky Beef can be purchased in 22 oz cans from Big Y, Shaw's, or Wal-Mart. Stop and Shop only carries 13 oz cans. Pro Plan can be purchased from Mackey's Home Center on Route 66 in Willimantic. Bags of treats are available from all over. Chew-eez chips come from the grocery store. Don't get the basted kind as they might wreck rugs. Rawhide comes from Mackey's."

Vicki and I ricocheted from chore to chore. One morning we drove to Jiffy Lube in Willimantic and had the oil changed in the Mazda. While the car was atop the rack, we walked to Dunkin' Donuts. We both drank coffee, but while I munched a doughnut iced with chocolate, Vicki ordered a blueberry muffin, only, however, after asking if the berries were real. In addition to the owner, his wife, and their twelve-year-old daughter, six employees worked in the shop, "four and a half people to each customer," I said. "We are the only customers," Vicki said. "Right," I said, "four and a half for each of us." After fetching the car, I drove to Electrical Wholesales on Watson Street, and Vicki bought half a dozen halogen bulbs for the study. From Watson we drove to the Department of Motor Vehicles. Because her automobile license would expire while we were in Australia, Vicki wanted to renew early. "Our computer won't let you do that," a clerk said. Next we drove to Constant Brothers in Franklin, and Vicki purchased a new stove. "What would Aaron do if the stove died while we were in Australia?" she said. "The stove is twenty-six years old and peppy," I said. "Exactly," she said. "Among the elderly pep foreshadows death." On the way back to Willimantic, I stopped at a roadside stand, and Vicki bought six flats of geraniums. "If the house looks good, Aaron will take better care of it," she said. Next we stopped at Winnelson on Moulton Court and bought floats for the three toilets in the house.

Unlike the future, which can loom black and stormy, the past often appeals to people, appearing as a sheltered but sunny haven. I returned to Perth in part because I knew place and people. Not being startled makes books dull but lives pleasant. Seven years ago I had an account at Commonwealth Bank on Stirling Highway. In 1993, I wired a year's money to Perth. "Unbelievably," a customer service representative wrote that July, "your account details were confirmed with us today." Because matters had gone smoothly in the past, I decided to bank with Commonwealth again. Wiring money was more complex this time. I was instructed to wire money to the Bank of New York where it would be credited to Commonwealth then wired to Sydney from which it would be wired to Perth, Branch 6155. On August 16, a certificate of deposit for $70,000 matured at Liberty Bank in Storrs, and I decided to send the money to Australia. However, Liberty needed not only the ABA numbers of the banks along the chain but also the banks' addresses including zip codes. I obtained all addresses except that of the Bank of New York, no employee of the Commonwealth Bank in New York being able to furnish the appropriate address, this despite my telephoning six times. I also discovered that because I did not have an active account in Perth that if I wired money to Perth the money would immediately be returned to the United States. "You have to be in Perth to set up an account," an employee in New York explained.

Thinking there had to be a simple way to transfer money, I telephoned the head office of Commonwealth Bank in Sydney. "Put the $70,000 into an official bank check and carry it with you to Perth," a woman suggested. "How long will the bank take to process the check?" I asked. "Three days for an official check," the woman said. I am meticulous about financial matters, and so I called the New York branch of Commonwealth. "Three days for an official check," a young man said. That afternoon Liberty issued me a bank check. And that I thought was that.

A decade ago I spent a week at Stanford University as guest of the Medical School. On returning to Storrs, I left San Francisco on the night flight to Chicago, the red-eye, as it is called. "Take this as soon as you are in the air," my host said at the terminal, handing me a minute pill. "The flight will pass like a dream." "Is this dope?" I said. "Absolutely," he said, "Grade A, straight from the pharmacy." "Thank you," I said, "but I don't think I'll take it." I am a white-knuckle flyer, and two minutes out of San Francisco, I bolted the pill, muttering "to Hell with water." I awoke in Hartford. "Would that I had a pellet or two for this trip," I said while sipping coffee in the Cup of Sun the week before I left. "I've got what you need," my friend Ellen responded immediately, "and I'll give it to you tomorrow." Three weeks earlier, Ellen's husband Sam died. Sam had been ill for months, and Ellen's medicine cabinet was a cornucopia of painkillers. "These are a going-away present from Sam," Ellen said, handing me a plastic container holding three small pills. I swallowed the first pill as American Airlines flew over Long Island. I took the second off California and the third, a smidgen west of Fiji. "This is the way to fly," I said, tumbling across a vacant seat. For her part Vicki sat straight in her seat across the aisle, insomnia wracking her spine. On the final leg of the trip, the four and a half hours from Sydney to Perth, I felt perky and read, knocking off two books, Patricia Cornwell's *Black Notice* and James Lee Burke's *Heartwood,* wrapping up the butchery just as the plane slid through wind shifting above Perth.

At 12:30 on August 23, Ian Saunders, head of the English department at the University of Western Australia, met us at the airport and drove us to Cooper Street. Sunlight fell in yellow showers. A kookaburra perched on a railing below the apartment, and a wattlebird racketed through bottlebrush, scarlet flowers shaking around him like pompoms. At three that afternoon I crossed Broadway and walked along Stirling to Commonwealth Bank. I handed my check to a teller. "We'll process this immediately," he said, adding, "and you should receive your money in twenty-eight days." Sydney and New York misinformed me. To process a check on a foreign bank, official or not, took a month. The manager of the branch telephoned the head office in Sydney. "Rules," she reported, "are rules." I brought $2,000 in Australian money with me. I also had Master and Visa cards. Charging all expenses on the cards, however, would deplete my bank account at home, and in October I had to pay the University of Connecticut $8,000 for Francis's second semester abroad. Moreover I owed Princeton the $2,000 for keeping Francis on their books. In January taxes for the Town of Mansfield came due, this time $1,523.64. Misinformation smashed careful planning. After two weeks I knew I would owe the realtor in Perth $827, $750 for rent, $70 for cleaning, and $7 tax. Suddenly I was tired. The thirty-three hour trip weighed me down, pills aside. "Should we start processing the check?" the manager asked. "It will go to Sydney tonight." Not thinking clearly, I said, "Yes."

That night I pondered ways to cash the check. I didn't bring the telephone number of Liberty Bank with me to Perth. Even if I called the manager and told her to stop payment on the check and wire money, she couldn't have done so without my signing the order in her presence. Moreover I did not have routing numbers. I considered returning to Connecticut in order to wire the money. All night my mind bounced around like a ball in a pinball machine, notions flipping idea this way and that. "I think I'll kill myself," I said to Vicki the next morning. "That seems extreme," she said. "You'll eventually work this out." "How?" I said. "I don't know," she said. "It's your problem. You are in charge of finances." Shedding worry was impossible. A young man, my friend Josh once told me, rode Barnaby, his mule, to a revival. On arriving outside the tent, the man said, "I'm going to turn Barnaby loose and entrust him to God." "Brother," the preacher leading the revival said, sounding like me, "tie your mule to a tree then entrust him to God."

That morning I described my problem to friends at the university. Within an hour Rosemary in the dean's office fashioned a solution. She instructed me to transfer my check to the university. The university would submit the check to Wespac, its banker, then advance me the equivalent of twenty thousand American dollars. I raced back to Commonwealth Bank. "I don't know if I can retrieve the check," the manager said. "It has already left Perth, but I will try." That afternoon she reported that the check would be back Friday morning. On Friday the check did not appear, and I spent a sleepless weekend, suffering from colitis, diverticulitis, nephritis, all the itises known to man. On Saturday during black early morning, I planned decamping, carrying the whole family back to Connecticut. "If you didn't worry," Vicki said, "you'd have a heart attack." "I'm having one now," I said, flopping down on the bed and covering my face with a pillow. "Horseshit," Vicki said.

Like confession essays are good for soul but bad for reputation. In daylight I reined in concern and appeared rational. Duty does not permit indulgence. Thursday morning after visiting Commonwealth and inquiring about the check, Vicki and I took a taxi to St. Hilda's and registered Eliza for classes. We also bought her school uniform, paying with my Visa card. Friday night Edward flew into Perth from Queensland. Dennis Haskell drove me to the airport. Normally I would have refused Dennis's offer to fetch Edward. But concerned about money, I begrudged paying taxi fare and accepted the kindness. Edward was the only person on the flight who looked Australian. Rangy and tanned from spending six hours a day in the saddle, he wore battered jeans, a checked shirt mended in the back, R. M. Williams boots, and an Akubra hat.

Sunday afternoon the four of us roamed Kings Park. I recognized flowers, the names and colors distracting me from monetary worries: wild violet, pepper and salt, devils pins, and conostylis. Red freckles dappled cowslip orchids, and yellow melted and ran like butter from scoops of red runner. Magpies spiraled into song, and families of twenty-eight parrots burbled through the bush. Freesia bloomed in baskets, and fairy lilies gleamed like cloisonné. Acacia appeared wet with yellow, and sheaves of pink petals hung above the greenish centers of everlasting. I crushed a handful of Geraldton wax and inhaled the tart fragrance. Coral trees exploded, the red petals flaring like flames above a gas burner. "I had forgotten the beauty," Eliza said. "Write about it, Daddy, so I can remember it when I am older."

Because sleeping was difficult, I read through the weekend, hoping that margins would prevent thought from wandering. I read *Songlines,* Bruce Chatwin's book about Australia. For a while Chatwin entertained me, but eventually the book unraveled into cartoon. For sanity I started a biography of Ralph Waldo Emerson. Monday afternoon my check reappeared. The next day I gave it to Rosemary. On Friday she handed me a check made out to Wespac, and that afternoon, I deposited the money. The next Monday Vicki and I took a taxi to Mazda City, and I purchased a 1996 Mitsubishi sedan driven some 74,342 kilometers. The car cost $15,000, stamp duty adding $388.15 to the price and insurance, another $384. I paid the insurance, stamp duty, and $2,000 of the price with Visa. The rest I paid with a check from Wespac, $13,388.15.

If not for pleasure, life would be endurable. Pleasure disrupts.

"If we had stayed in Storrs," I told Vicki, "these last few days would have been calm." "And," I added, "I would not have gotten ringworm." Fungus splotched my arms, the result of sleeping on Qantas and sprawling across seats. "Oh, Lord," Vicki said, "what next?" Once worry subsides, my thoughts drift. Why, since the earth rotated around the sun, I wondered, ignoring Vicki, did Joshua command the sun to be still?

Jawing

I have talked for many suppers. I have talked for tuition, roofing, automobile parts, and home repairs. Twice corporations paid me four thousand dollars for motivational speeches. In Australia I expected to talk for publicity. I hoped publicity would create interest that I could use to barter, say, an article in an airline magazine for a ticket to Melbourne. Modest means impose flexibility upon life. Still, when Dennis Haskell asked me to address the Friends of the University Press of Western Australia on August 25, two days after my arrival in Perth, I demurred, shifting the date to September 1.

Because landing in Perth had been bumpy, I had trouble concentrating on the talk. Nevertheless when Vicki and I walked from Cooper Street to the Hackett Dining Room at the university on the first, I was ready. For speakers buffets aren't fun. The Friends served fish, lamb, lasagna, and chicken curry for dinner. Eructation spoils enunciation, and I ate a smidgen of rice. In Connecticut a driver is legally intoxicated if his blood-alcohol content measures .10. In Western Australia the figure is .05. For a speaker .00 is the only acceptable reading. At any higher content, a speaker is liable to drift over the curb of respectability.

Eighty people attended the meeting, paying thirty-five dollars each to eat then hear me discuss writing for forty minutes. My talk was a success. Afterward the Friends gave me a book published by the press, *Dawn Till Dusk in the Stirling and Porongurup Ranges,* and a bottle of wine, Gnangara Shiraz, priced by Vicki the next morning at Broadway Fair at $11.95. Following the talk desserts appeared, but I ate only half a glass of chocolate mousse. The previous week one of the Friends, Michael Crouch, fetched me from the university and drove me to his home where he interviewed me for the Friends' *Newsletter*. From 1958 to 1967, Michael was in the British Overseas Service, serving in southern Arabia, revolution and assassination peppering the years with excitement. At the interview Michael gave me a copy of his memoir, *An Element of Luck*. Thirty years ago I taught in Jordan for a year. Six years later I taught in Syria. The desert burrows under the skin and gets into the blood where, like malaria, it occasionally erupts, making sufferers thirst for camels and kaftans. After I finished the biography of Emerson, I read *Luck*. "Self-Reliance" and "Nature" vanished from mind, and I dreamed of Aden and sunny checkless days. After my speech Michael reverted to being an overseas officer. He took me by the wrist and led me to a table. Eight minutes later he escorted me to another table. He handled Vicki the same way, and by the end of the evening we had met every person attending the dinner. "That was work," I said, walking back to the apartment. "Yes," Vicki said, "but fun." In 1994, the University Press of New England published *Trespassing*, a collection of my essays. Because I was in Perth when *Trespassing* appeared, the University Press of Western Australia ordered copies. Twenty-eight books remained at the press. At the dinner twenty-five sold, each priced at $5.63 in order to clear the shelves.

I am fond of the University of Western Australia. Members of the English department and administration have been generous to me. Consequently I speak when a member of the university asks me to do so. In truth, though, I'm tired of speaking, seeing myself an aging actor, parodying better days and thoughts. That aside, however, in July, George Core, editor of the *Sewanee Review* and Edward's godfather, spent three weeks in London. One morning in the Pen Club, he met Frank Sheehan, chaplain of Christ Church Grammar School, Edward's school in Perth. While exploring Christ Church, I bumped into Frank. We talked about George,

SAM PICKERING

after which Frank asked me to address two hundred eleventh graders. Subjects of previous talks had been various. One speaker described vicious dogs. Another touted legalizing marijuana while a third praised Hitler's leadership qualities. I decided to avoid controversy and said I would discuss curiosity.

Edward finished eleventh grade in Connecticut. Because Australian and American academic calendars do not dovetail, he entered eleventh grade at Christ Church, coming midway through the year. When a secretary asked if I had any wishes concerning my speech, I requested that Edward be excused from the assembly, explaining he'd heard me lecture breakfast, lunch, and dinner for seventeen years. "He will die a score of deaths listening to me," I wrote by email. "Let him spend the morning playing piano or lifting weights. Daughters love listening to fathers. Sons break out in hives." "Don't worry about Edward," my correspondent wrote back. "He is a big boy now, and there comes a time when he has to be man enough to sit through a talk given by his father." The reply irked me, particularly since I was speaking for free, and I pondered a rough response. "Oh, screw it," I finally said and went for a walk. I ambled along Melvista Avenue and looked at the house we rented seven years ago. At a cost of over two hundred thousand dollars, it had been remodeled, in, as Vicki put it, "Japanese bathroom style." From a paperbark a singing honeyeater called, its song green and optimistic. I strolled beside Matilda Bay. A wagtail wheeled over the grass. Pied cormorants floated off shore, and a pair of pelicans drifted like buoys. Eventually I returned to the apartment on Cooper Street. "What's on your mind?" Vicki asked. "Not much," I said. "Sometimes I walks and thinks. Other times I just walks."

House

The realtor who managed the apartment on Cooper Street limited our stay to a fortnight. "The day you leave," she said, "someone else is moving in." Ten days after we left, the apartment remained unoccupied. In 1993, I rented a furnished house in Nedlands, on Melvista Avenue within walking distance of both the university and shops at Broadway Fair. Furnished housing is difficult to come by in Perth. On the Wednesday after we arrived in Western Australia, I visited seven realtors. All were pessimistic. "Furnished houses," a woman said, "are endangered." One realtor suggested I lease furniture and utensils, the cost for appointing a three-bedroom house running between $150 and $165 a week. Because Nedlands was familiar, I tried to find a place in the area. On Archdeacon Street an unfurnished house was available for $340 a week. Not far from the Swan River and close to shops, the location was good. Unfortunately, the house was in poor shape. Rooms were dark and damp, and paper peeled from walls in sheaves. In the living room cockroaches lay belly-up on the carpet, from a distance resembling hunks of chocolate. Later we looked at an apartment on Park Avenue under the lip of Kings Park. A rectangle, the apartment consisted of three bedrooms, a kitchen, and a combination dining room and lounge. Rooms banged against each other, making escaping other people impossible. A bright blue carpet ran wall to wall throughout the apartment, turning floors into a garish sea, the sight of which made me dizzy. A balcony opened toward Matilda Bay. Unfortunately the roof of a flat nearer the bay blocked view of the water. Moreover the apartment was unfurnished. For a modest price the owner, the realtor said, would return his belongings to the flat.

The realtor asked if we were considering other properties. When I mentioned that we planned to look at a house in Mosman Park, he warned us that crime plagued the area. Public housing, he said, had ruined Mosman Park. Robberies were frequent, and rapes, not uncommon. "Baloney," I thought. The next day Leasing Elite showed us the house in Mosman Park. "This is awfully far from the university," Vicki said, the distance from the front door of the house to Hackett 1, the faculty parking lot near the Humanities Building, being 9.2 kilometers. In Storrs I ride a bicycle to the university, and before seeing the house I loathed the prospect of being coupled to an automobile. I drove to Mosman Park along Stirling Highway. The road was narrow; shoulders didn't exist, and cars inched through Claremont, turning my mood sour. Once I saw The Corner Cupboard, as Eliza dubbed the house, however, my spirits lifted, and the next morning I rented the house.

Set at the corner of Kalgoorlie and Swan, the house is directly behind St. Hilda's School. From the edge of our garage to the entrance of the junior school, the distance is 107 steps. Walking out the front door and around the house adds 53 steps to the walk. From a bus stop near St. Hilda's, Edward catches a bus that takes him to Christ Church in twelve minutes. A white picket fence runs beside Kalgoorlie in front of the house. Along Swan stretches a rail fence, passion vine scrolling over it. Because the fence is high, passersby cannot see into the back yard. Originally a workman's cottage built in the 1920s, the house is brick and painted white. Six glass panels decorate the front door. Stained red, green, and blue, the panels depict roses blossoming amid tufts of leaves. The roof of the house is asbestos, dark and corrugated like tin. Two chimneys poke through the roof, a red pot perched atop each. Inside the house floors are jarrah and bright with red and orange. Running from front door to back terrace, a hall divides the house. Walls are pale yellow and trimmed with white. Halfway down the hall, an arch curves overhead. From each side of the arch, molding hangs rich with bouquets of buds and nuts.

On the left side of the hall are two bedrooms and a laundry room. Edward occupies the first bedroom. The room is sixteen feet square, and one end sinks into a fireplace. The next room is Eliza's. Instead of a fireplace, an enameled stove sits in a recess. Vicki and I share the first room on the right, eighteen feet square with a bathroom and a deep closet opening off it. Beyond our room just down the hall is a second bathroom. Across the far end of the hall, a room runs like the top of a T, the left side, a dining area; the right, a kitchen. Four steps below the kitchen is a carpeted family room, twenty-four by nineteen feet. From the dining area a door opens onto a covered terrace. After breakfast I sit at a table on the terrace and write. Binoculars stand next to my yellow pad, and I'm always ready to drop my pen and look at birds: wattlebirds, laughing and spotted doves, and singing and New Holland honeyeaters. Every morning magpies chortle. Ravens nest in a eucalyptus that leans over the garage. Often the ravens perch on the fence, eyes white-walled, feathers on their necks bursting into ruffs. Lots in the neighborhood are small, and houses close, fences creating the illusion of separation. Throughout the day I hear the calls of women, chatting and exclaiming, talking to neighbors and nestlings. Voices are often high, and I prefer wordless birdsong, singing honeyeaters trilling and white-cheeked honeyeaters whistling.

Some days I sit atop the front steps and count cape daisies weedy in the grass. Behind me windows on the front of the house are leaded, the metal crosshatched. Vines of wrought iron curl around the porch and the edge of the roof. Twenty-one rose bushes border the picket fence, and at the edge of the road, heavy swabs of red hang from a bottlebrush. Behind the rail fence running along Swan are bushes of camellias, a lemon tree lumpy with fruit and flower; three palm trees, tops spread like umbrellas; grevilleas, orange with blossoms; Indian hawthorn; hibiscus; and potato bush, its flowers small blue platters. Birds' nest ferns tumble out of hanging baskets, and from a large blue urn a fig tilts sideways. At the edge of the terrace stands a birdbath, the watering hole of neighborhood cats. Right now my favorite plant is daphne or Victorian box. Its leaves twist like the blades of Saracens' knives, and its fragrance pulls honeyeaters from the air. The back yard resembles a card table. Across the table opposite the terrace sits a green garage, a long metal shed, the narrow mouth of which opens onto Swan.

The new, be it a neighborhood or style of life, rarely appeals to Vicki, and she has not settled as easily as I have. Light rises airy through the house like a soufflé, and once shopping becomes routine, Vicki's spirits will rise. Moreover the doings of days shift attention so fast that one is never quiet enough to sink into melancholy. Yesterday Jay Parini wrote that he'd received a huge advance for his next book of verse, two novels, and a biography— an amount that filled me with envy. In truth, though, not money but vanity keeps my words flowing. One morning I went to the university library. Seven years ago the library owned one of my books. Now they own five, including two copies of *Trespassing*. "Things are looking up," I said to Eliza. The mail that brought Jay's news also brought a letter from Kentucky. For years a librarian in Lexington has sent me silly verse. "Here's one for the anthology," he wrote. "I call it 'High Falutin' Love.'" "Oh, how I planned to make her love me / Longed to call her mine. / But I feared she was above me. / She seemed so divine. / Now, alas, my hopes are broken. / Alone, I must bear reproof / For my accents harshly spoken, / 'Damn you, come down off the roof.'"

In part, not living in Nedlands pleases me. A new book needs a new environment. If we had rented a house on Melvista again, paragraphs would have become comparative, forever measuring the present by the past. Since moving to Mosman Park, we have driven to Fremantle twice. Yesterday we shopped in the fruit and vegetable market. Four rows of stalls run the length of the building, one on each side and two down the middle. At the west end of the building is another row of stalls. The other end opens into the remainder of the market, scores of booths selling snacks, souvenirs, and knick-knacks. Crowds rumble though the market, sometimes clotting aisles, other times staggering forward in heavy clumps. Stall owners hawk produce, shouting and changing prices. Yesterday I bought two heads of broccoli for a dollar, a bag of white mushrooms for two dollars, and late in the day a kilo of strawberries for three dollars. Fruits glowed like the tips of crayons in boxes—string beans, celery, peas, avocados, artichokes, and rumply custard apple, green; mounds of garlic and the hammer heads of leeks, white; eggplant and turnip, purple; mandarins of all sizes, some bigger than fists, others small as cotton balls, all orange; kiwis and pineapples with cowlicks of leaves, brown; tomatoes, apples, radishes, and hunks of watermelon, red. Knobs of ginger looked like joints of pipes; Ord River honeydews lolled in voluptuous piles, and white sweet potatoes resembled plugs dug from sumps. Vicki shopped at several stalls: Johnny's, Ho's, Jack's, Scotty's, Gina's, and Fresh Fair. She bought bananas, carrots, red beans, pears, and three varieties of mandarins. I munched a curry puff then a vegetable samosa, the first costing $1.40, the second, $1.80.

Later we roamed the town, chatting with clerks in stores. At "Into Camelot," clerks were barefoot. On a table stood a diminutive Rhine maiden, bare-breasted and wearing a helmet topped by horns. "She's a witch," a clerk explained. Buskers performed on street corners, most inept, their humor rarely rising above private parts. Youth roiled streets. To escape crowds Vicki and I meandered Mouat and Henry, Leake and Lower High Street. Facades of many buildings are late Victorian, columned with arched windows and fanciful with cast iron balustrades. From a post hung a wad of yellow plastic bags. Stamped in black across the front of the bags was "Doggy Dumpage Disposal Unit." In Mosman Park similar bags are labeled "Poo-ch Pouch." At dusk sunlight trickled pink down the masts of boats docked at the Royal Perth Yacht Club. We ate fish and chips at Cicerellos, sitting outside at a table facing the Fishing Boat Harbor. The chips were too heavy for my middle-aged metabolism, so I took them home. After feeding a handful to the staghorn fern on the rail fence, I tossed the rest into the back yard. Ravens dropped from the fence and fed on them, one of the birds carting a beak full to the birdbath to wash them. Ravens are wary birds, but by year's end I'll be able to lure them to the terrace to eat. "To do that," Vicki said, "you'll have to serve better fare."

Between

Once I was comfortable in the house, I read Patrick White's novel *The Eye of the Storm*. White's intellectual stew is thick, and I can manage only one of his books a year. In the *Eye* characters swirled around the deathbed of an old woman. The novel undermined peace of mind, and suddenly essays bored me. Rarely do I depict anything other than routine. "What are you doing?" Eliza asked me last night. "I'm rubbing zinc oxide into my left heel," I answered, "to prevent skin from cracking." White's characters lived intensely, never dipping into medicine cabinets for chap sticks or baby oil. For an evening or two I regretted being commonsensical. How different, I mused, life would have been if I were capable of religious faith, or, for that matter, any kind of fervor.

Writing tempers zeal and enthusiasm. Forcing happenings, or the absence thereof, into paragraphs orders my days. When I write, I resemble a gardener. I bed nouns and verbs and weed life, so color can riot safely across pages, staining sight but not deed. Would that I were a real gardener. Yesterday while walking I paused in front of the garden at 48 Irvine Street, my favorite garden in Peppermint Grove. The owner was digging near a hibiscus. "Your garden gives people great pleasure," I said. "Thank you," he said. "Those are nice words." "They are only words," I said, "not flowers."

Rarely do thoughts provoked by books endure. Vicki's mother

is dying. She spends days on a couch, unable to rise without help. As I read White, Vicki's mother drifted into imagination, "a beached jellyfish," I thought, "her skin orange, her arms and legs thin as tentacles." Fortunately ravens brayed from the back yard, pushing the picture from mind. Suddenly Vicki, herself, walked into the room. By attaching a spotlight she found in the garage to a broken coat rack, she'd constructed a lamp for the living room.

After feeding the ravens and examining the lamp, I read more, pondering the gap between youth and age. Often news darkens my mood. I long for simplicity, and because I cannot remember the past, I sentimentalize times that never existed. In contrast Eliza and Edward are optimistic and read newspapers eagerly. Complexity appeals to them, and they anticipate the future, imaging days that will never exist. While they dream of cantering over the present into a misty unknown, I mull unhitching myself from the wheel of time and sinking immobile into emptiness. When the children stack improbabilities one atop another, my conversation is cautionary, toppling not raising dream. While I slump over reading, Edward is so active Vicki calls him "Mr. Gonad."

Conversation between youth and middle age is impossible, giving the lie to educators who celebrate "mentoring." Happily before gloom covered me like the top of an iron kettle, Vicki approached. "Quit your book," she said. "The time has come for a walk and a treat." We ambled the shore of Freshwater Bay until rubble ended the path. From the Esplanade nasturtiums tumbled down the hill, breaking orange and green through periwinkle and daisy. Morning glories cloaked dead limbs in purple. Cabbage white butterflies wavered like thin notes, and honeyeaters burst from the shelter of Rottnest Island pine, clouds of pollen trailing caramel behind them. Figs dug into a limestone bluff. Guttered by rain, the bluff looked like a wasps' nest, half the cells broken, the papery tissue burned black and gold. Beneath the bluff wattles bloomed, and perfume from freesia wavered in sheets. A puffer fish seized a fisherman's bait. "Ah, you . . ." the man began as he unhooked the fish. Then he noticed Vicki. "Ah, you, cute little fellow," he continued and tossed the fish back in the bay. Vicki and I walked to Stirling Highway and at Vans on Napoleon Street drank cappuccino and ate cake, Vicki having a slice of blueberry tart, and I, pear and almond pie. The bill was eleven dollars, and we returned the next day. Walking and eating, not talk, binds us together.

On Saturday the four of us went to Cottesloe Beach. I watched boats slide across the horizon, freighters spindly with cranes, tankers, dark tubs. Because waves were thick as barrels, I swam cautiously. A fortnight later a boy drowned at Cottesloe, and at Scarborough Beach lifeguards pulled forty-two swimmers from the water. After swimming we bought lunch at Cott's, an eatery on Marine Parade. Vicki and Edward ate steak sandwiches; Eliza, a pineapple-chicken sandwich, and I, bacon, egg, and tomato. For the family I bought a large container of chips. While Eliza drank chocolate milk, Vicki, Edward, and I divided a bottle of Coca-Cola, each of us jabbing a plastic straw into the mouth of the bottle. I left my watch at home. As we walked to the car, I asked a man the time. "Beer o'clock, mate," he said. We spent the rest of the afternoon in Kings Park. Under brush Vicki found a brown and cream goanna. Next she saw a thin lizard clinging to a twig of smoke bush, a strand of diamonds running fragile down his spine. For my part I collected bouquets of flowers, first arranging them by name: tinsel lily, blowfly grass, blue boy, and Prince of Wales feather. Next I gathered by color: enameled orchids, purple and simonized, petals turning down like the hoods of hot rods; milkmaids, frothy with white; wild gladiola; and granny bonnets, their faces orange sunsets. For the first time I noticed donkey, king spider, and jug orchids. I ran my hand along the cold inflorescence of a grass tree and pocketed nuts fallen from eucalyptus trees. A wattlebird forced its bill into the blossom of a mangles kangaroo paw, bending the flower into a red bow. "This is my idea of a good day," I said to Vicki. "At home," she said, "you'll probably read something that will ruffle your mood." "No," I said, "I've finished *The Eye of the Storm.*" Alas, humans are silly and fretful. Because I was comfortable, I had leisure enough for disruption. The next morning I began thinking about a trip to Exmouth, 1,300 kilometers north of Perth along the Brand Highway. "What is school vacation for, if not travel," I explained to Vicki. "I thought you wanted to rest in Australia," she said. "Travel is exhausting." "Yes," I said, "but if we don't see the country, we'll leave with regrets."

Settling

We have been in Perth for twenty-four days and have begun to settle. In the morning I feed the staghorn fern attached to the fence in the back yard. While the body of the fern looks like a massive cabbage, the horns jut out for two and a half feet, the tips browning then turning gray. In tropical forests refuse tumbles into the fern and rots, providing nourishment. More to entertain myself than for the fern's digestion, I vary the plant's diet, so far having let it sample mandarins, apple cores, banana peels, and French fries, these last seasoned with salt and vinegar. Next to the fern stands a lemon tree, its buds droplets of sugar. Early in the morning the fragrance of almonds hangs over the wedding bush by the side gate. I now recognize birds by wing beat, ravens splashing into flight and the pat of honeyeaters flicking through daphne. At the bottom of a blue coffee can is a clump of eighteen snail shells. Bands of brown and yellow circle the shells. Here and there yellow jumps through brown like a cardiogram. Sometimes while I sit on the terrace, a gray cat weaves between my legs. A silver bell hangs from the cat's neck. The clapper has fallen from the bell, and when the cat appears, I chase away the doves that forage beyond the terrace.

Habit creates contentment. Instead of enticing, newness often disrupts and irritates. Only after Vicki stamps habit upon life is she comfortable. Shopping areas abound in Mosman Park, but thus far, Vicki has not settled, hopping between Coles, SupaValu, and Woolworths. Place makes me happier than routine. Once the yard became familiar, I roamed the neighborhood, east from St. Hilda's School along Mosman Bay then north through Peppermint Grove along the Esplanade to Claremont. Peppermint Grove is Perth's most affluent district. Although streets are wide, driving is difficult because a bark of gardeners' trucks rumples curbs. Aged peppermint trees grow next to sidewalks. The trees are squat, and their trunks are sinewy, looking like rugs rolled and stacked upright. Often the rolls lean sideways and lever the ground up into umbrellas of dirt. Burls bulge in fibrous balls, and exits dug through bark by beetles resemble shot holes. The bark itself is loose, and dark flakes splatter the ground like psoriasis. Sometimes portions of the trunks rot and unroll, so that a single tree often seems two or three saplings, the common lower trunk and roots covered by throws of grass. In September flowers dangle from branches in chains, the blossoms minute and girlish.

On walks I wander north along View, dipping to the shore along the eastern ends of Johnston, Keane, Irvine, Leake, Forrest, and McNeil. Homes jumble eclectic across large yards: 1960s American colonial; French chateau; ranches flat as pancakes; Brighton holiday duplex; Squibb domestic; art deco; bungalows, roofs tin or red tile, their walls dressed limestone splotched with fungus; and Federation Queen Anne, porches wrapping red brick, their railings white lattices, the designs rectangles, transforming exteriors into game boards. Gables and turrets punctuate roofs and expand bungalows. Front doors lurk behind whimsical drawbridges, and scrolls of ornate iron wrap verandas. Bay and picture widows bulge and blink, and Italianate terraces descend to tennis courts. Hedges, fences, and walls protect houses like wallets: wood, iron, gray sheaves of wattle, limestone, oleander, and plumbago, spiked with blue flowers.

After a sixteen-year rest, I have started jogging again. After thirty-five minutes my lungs rasp, and the skin atop my thighs looks blistered. Often I jog alleys winding behind houses in Peppermint Grove. Graffiti pocks walls, letters usually indistinct, fading soon after being painted, as anonymous as the boys who sprayed them, yet threatening, too, not simply to wealth and order, but to beauty and higher truth, threats that walls cannot seal off. Last evening welcome swallows sliced the air above Johnson Parade into flower petals. In the fading light water jingled like silver dollars. A fat woman walked a fat dog. "Come along, Katy, dear," she said. Offshore a boy paddled a yellow kayak. Two mountain ducks gleaned grass, a collar of white feathers around the male's neck, his chest buffed orange and bugling like a samovar. I wanted the idyll to last, and I sat at a picnic table. Painted on the table in letters ten inches high was the word *Fuck*.

Properties mirror owners and like people themselves are inconsistent. While fences repel, gardens invite. From walls in Peppermint Grove hang carpets, soft and grapy with wisteria and yellow with goblets of golden chalice vine. Horns of angel's-trumpet dangle in racks. With leaves cut into costume jewelry, bougainvillea winds through fences. Bottlebrush reaches over stones, blossoms beckoning like red fingers. Daphne is pink, and at the edge of lawns Brunfelsia blossoms in checkers of blue and white. A mottlecah sways over a fence, its leaves silver and green, from nuts stamens bursting exuberantly red and yellow. Between walls and sidewalks geraniums grow hip-high, and nasturtiums float over green leaves like orange lily pads.

I stand in driveways and look at gardens colorful with larkspur, wind poppy, foxglove, azalea, mounds of pale lavender, calla lilies, and roses, stalks thin as pencils, but blossoms clouds of stormy color. Ribbons of Zephirine Drouhin wrap our porch, the fragrance decadently sweet, "summer sunshine," Edward said, "a mixture of dandelion and lilac." "Or," he continued, parodying labels on wine bottles, "cedar basket overflowing with chocolate and cantaloupe, cabbage and blackberry." Gum trees tower over houses, spotted and lemon-scented, trunks smooth, sometimes mottled with red. Galahs racket punk through gums. Yesterday Vicki and I watched a pair of galahs hover about a hole in a gum. "Why," Vicki asked, "do beautiful birds often nest amid opulence?" "Birds of a feather," I began then noticed a blond woman pushing a baby carriage. "That woman's husband," I said to Vicki,

SAM PICKERING

"is twenty-eight years older than she is." "How do you know?" Vicki said. "I know about such things," I said.

Although covetousness heats an economy, its grounds sour contentment. As I leaned against a limestone wall, I imagined my books rioting though bookstores, blooming in royalties, gathering honey enough for me to buy a house along the Swan River. "Affluence is more easily explained than a modest talent like yours," Vicki said. "Be satisfied with what genetics doled out." Happily for calm of mind, brick does not interest me so much as leaf and feather. This afternoon I wandered scrub below the bluff at Bay View Park. Acacia was blooming, the flowers bouncing in the heat like popcorn—at the tip of the bluff, summer-scented and down the slope, coastal wattle, branches smooth and pale gray, stretching like rubber tubes. Small-leaved clematis rumpled over stumps, and sand plain lupin colonized open patches, its flowers blue saucers. Fountain grass sprayed upward in clumps, inflorescences purple, silver wrinkling frosted across them. Honeyeaters foraged parrotbush. A ring-necked parrot perched on a dead limb, bill curved like a nut, white against its purple cheeks. A pelican bobbed in the water, and eleven pied oystercatchers stirred along a spit of sand while a male darter dozed on a piling, plumage falling dusty and golden down its back.

Eliza and Edward have settled into school. Last week in religion Eliza's class lay on the floor and meditated. "The teacher told us to empty thoughts from our minds and watch colors falling in waterfalls through our heads." "At first I saw a blue meadow," Eliza recounted, "but then I had to bite my cheeks to keep from laughing. Common sense is a burden." There is not so much busywork in Australian schools as there is in Connecticut. Last Saturday Eliza and sixty members of her class left for a week's camping along the Margaret River. The girls spent days hiking, rappelling down cliffs, and climbing ropes threaded through trees. "The activities will challenge the girls," the director of outdoor education told parents. "Reasonable people avoid challenges, and sane people avoid cliffs," I told Vicki.

Eliza will spend the first week of next term on "work experience." An advisor at St. Hilda's suggested she volunteer in an art museum. Instead she'll work at Nedlands Veterinary Centre. Anton Ottenhoff, the vet, discouraged Eliza. "Work experience is disastrous, at least for me," he said. The last girl Ottenhoff took on worked for a day then spent four days at home, calling in sick each morning. The previous girl was "unbelievably lazy," and he'd "fired" her after two days. Eliza is persistent. Ottenhoff instructed her to return the next day and talk to Sharon, his assistant. "No," Sharon said the following afternoon, "I don't want another work experience student." Eliza left the building but then returned. Ten minutes later she had the post. "I wanted that job," she said that night at dinner. "You would have gone back, too, Daddy." Not only is the female of our species tougher than the male, but she has a better memory. Next door to the clinic is a small shopping center, housing Martineau's, my favorite bakery. Seven years ago I bought croissants there. While Mr. Ottenhoff interviewed Eliza, I went to the bakery. I hadn't visited the bakery since arriving in Perth. "Did you finish your book?" the wife of the owner said as I strolled through the door.

One or two bumps have disrupted schooldays. Eliza planned to run track, but during the first fortnight of school, she was not able to meet the long-distance coach for a time trial. As a result she didn't participate in September's athletic meet. In truth I suspect Eliza avoided the trial. The meet was the only race of the term. "It's not fair," Eliza said at dinner, "for me suddenly to appear and displace a girl who trained all term. That wouldn't be right, and I'd feel guilty." Eliza wears a uniform to school, something she both likes and dislikes, at times delighting in the dress, at other times saying it inhibits personality. Each morning she puts on a light blue shirt; a blue necktie, bands striping it, each band consisting of dark blue sandwiched between yellow; a gray V-necked sweater with four stripes around the neck, two light blue and two yellow; thick gray knee-socks; clunky brown "school shoes," Clarks bought at Betts and Betts with rubber soles pressed into deep treads; a gray beret; and a light blue blazer, on the pocket of which is emblazoned the school crest—a yellow shield, three gold chambered nautiluses beached upon it. Below the shield waves a banner. Stamped in gold upon it is the school motto, DOMINE DIRGE NOS, God Guide Us. Edward's uniform is similar: gray flannel trousers, gray socks, black school shoes, a white shirt, a striped necktie, and a dark blue blazer, the school crest again over the left pocket, this time a blue shield quartered by a red cross and topped by a miter, in the upper left quarter of the shield a black swan pasted to a gold wafer. Meticulous attention is paid to uniforms, even to exercise shorts and athletic warm-ups. Despite the religious affiliation of both schools, doctrinal matters receive little attention, reflecting the Anglican Church's reasonable accommodation with the world. In class academic matters are often informal. A radio plays during art at Christ Church, and teachers tell jokes. Homework assignments are not arduous, giving Eliza and Edward time to read and write, to educate themselves, something neither had the leisure for in Storrs.

Eliza likes her classmates at St. Hilda's and has more friends than in Connecticut. "Most are rambunctious and don't worry about studies," she said, "but they are nice." The "Year 11 Dance" was held last week at Christ Church. "Smoking will not be permitted," a letter from the senior master stated. At the dance tablecloths hung to the floor. When boys wanted to smoke, they crawled under tables into tents formed by the cloths. Edward had not planned to attend the dance, but one night Tanya, a student at St. Hilda's, telephoned. Having seen his picture, she invited him to his dance. Edward accepted. Tanya's mother drove the couple to the dance. In Connecticut Edward began driving three months before his sixteenth birthday. In Australia a boy cannot get a driver's license until he is eighteen. Although none of his friends were driving, Edward wanted to drive to the dance. During the three months he spent in Queensland, Edward drove about Tumbar Station. The outback by day is not Perth at night. "You will be driving down the opposite side of the street from America," I said at dinner two nights before the dance. "I am not going to let you risk the life of someone's little girl." That night I slept fitfully. I dreamed Edward shot a man and was sentenced to twenty-eight years in prison, becoming eligible for parole only after he served twenty years. "How terrible," Eliza said at breakfast. "Edward's youth will have vanished by the time he is released, and he is so good-looking." That morning I telephoned Christ Church. "Edward should not drive," the senior master said. "No student will drive himself." "Good," I said.

Edward likes Christ Church. He doesn't study much, however. "Even Asians don't work hard," he said. He pondered playing Cricket IIIs with a group of friendly, unathletic boys. "We'd just hack around and laugh," he said. Eventually, however, he decided to play basketball, reckoning that being on the varsity would help applications to college. "Too bad Edward cannot escape the pressure of college admissions even in Australia," Vicki said.

Settling transforms the new into the ordinary. Eliza has visited an orthodontist and had her braces tightened. We now have a telephone. The first day the phone was installed, we received two calls, the second day, one; the third, three, two of the calls this last day for Edward, the other for Eliza. I have agreed to make four talks, none for money. I spend nights in the library searching for stories to plant in essays. So far I've dug up only one, a Greek tale. In August Monroe Dowd found a twenty-dollar bill on Spring Street in Carthage. "Are you going to advertise the money on the Lost and Found page of the *Courier*?" Vester McBee asked Monroe. "Of course," Monroe said. "I'm as honest as the day's long. But to save time I used the money to buy a new trough for my hogs. Next Friday I'll advertise the trough." On Tuesday I received a second letter from the librarian who collects battered verse. "In Australia you won't stumble across anything like the enclosed," the man wrote, adding, "what a discovery!" "'I am dying, Darwin, dying!' / Said old Pongo at the last. / 'You're ill, eh, my gorilla?' / Uttered Darwin, half aghast. / 'Yes, I'm ill, eh, your gorilla; / I am dying— yes—I think,' / Groaned old Pongo, then departed / Like a good old missing link."

We are so comfortable that I have planned a dislocating trip. Three days after Eliza returns from Margaret River, we drive north to Exmouth for a week of snorkeling and bush-walking. Because the car drops into low gear with a thud, last week I took it to Mazda City to be serviced. While mechanics tinkered with the gears, Vicki and I spent the day downtown. Streets were familiar, Hay, Murray, and St. George's. Vicki explored Target, and I bought a book in Dymocks, *Wildflowers of South Western Australia*. "Not an unexpected purchase," Vicki said. We drank cappuccino at a sidewalk café and split a date muffin. I told a clerk at R. M. Williams I would return to the store when Americans received discounts. "I'd wear the boots in Connecticut," I said. "Think what good advertising that would be." The Carillon Arcade charged twenty cents to use the lavatory. "Do most people get their money's worth?" I asked the attendant. "Ninety-nine out of a hundred are satisfied," she said. "The bathrooms are safe and clean." Late that afternoon I drove Eliza to the university so she could type a paper about Charlotte Brontë. As I drove, we listened to "Drive" on the radio. At 5:58, the station played "The Battle Hymn of the Republic." "Here we are riding north on Stirling Highway at dusk singing a Civil War song," Eliza said. "What fun!"

Exmouth

In July Edward wrote from Queensland. "We have to visit Exmouth," he urged. "For 160 miles Ningaloo Reef runs along the North West Cape. Tourist brochures call Ningaloo West Australia's Great Barrier Reef." In the United States I'm not much traveler. New York City is three hours from Storrs. During the twenty-two years I've lived in Connecticut, I've visited New York twice. Nevertheless, soon after arriving in Australia, I began planning trips. In part I wanted to travel for the afterward, memories which in later years would make me think life had been exciting. For two decades I've roamed Storrs, describing hill and field. The plant I miss one spring will probably be there next spring. In contrast my time in Australia was finite, and I wanted to pluck moments before they withered and vanished.

On October 5, three days after Eliza returned from the St. Hilda's camping trip, school vacation began, and we left the house at eleven minutes after seven in the morning. The car was loaded. In addition to duffels bulging with clothes, Vicki stuffed an Eski in the trunk, cramming it with bread, cheese, nuts, dried and fresh fruit, soft drinks, and liters of water. Exmouth is 790 miles north of Perth as maps calculate, but 851 miles as I drove. We arrived the next afternoon at 4:36. On the road I hoped to escape the Olympics and youth wrapping itself in flags, looking like uncooked, and unseasoned, tortillas. The drive crossed sundry landscapes. Just beyond Perth grapes stamped gridirons across the

Swan Valley. After the grapes shrank to heeltaps, horses glistened in fat green fields. Cattle grazed red as boulders, and sheep clumped together like patches of fungi. Eventually, however, rich land became sand plain. Time leached nutrients from the soil, leaving behind quartz crystals, bits of iron and aluminum, and white kaolin. Atop the sand the surface hardened into pans of ironstone, known as duricrust. Afterward floods boiled across the land and sweeping the ironstone away sliced deep into the pan, exposing gashes white as suet. In plains north of Perth, many plants, including harsh hakea, firewood banksia, and parrot and woolly bushes, formed cluster roots, brushes composed of masses of small roots which brewed chemicals enabling plants to pull otherwise insoluble nutrients from the ground.

Landscapes interest me. They resemble the ages of a man, flowing into one another, differences at first not noticeable but then suddenly marked. Although highways north were two-lane and roughly-paved, I studied the country as I drove. Traffic was light, consisting mostly of four-wheel drives, many pulling campers; a few sedans; utes, Australian pickup trucks; and road trains, these last growling across the land, some of the trailers boxes, others scoops for minerals. When drivers approached, they raised three or four fingers off the steering wheel, as if acknowledgement could lessen loneliness. Beyond Carnarvon, where we stopped the first night after driving 593 miles, the highway was frighteningly empty. For me workings of machines are mysterious. When I was a boy in Nashville, my father and I often stood near the bridge that crossed West End Avenue just beyond Fairfax and watched steam engines pulling roads of cars. I marveled at pistons fisting and big wheels rolling, long bars thrusting about them like arms. The sight did not lead to workaday knowledge, however, only dreams steamy with words. Throughout the drive to Exmouth I worried that the car would fail. If it did, all I knew to do was stand beside the road. Grandfather Pickering never learned to drive, and Grandfather Ratcliffe didn't keep a car longer than a year, warning family members that after a year cars became death traps. Here I was driving a car four years old. I didn't even know the location of the jack and spare tire. Before leaving Carnarvon on the second morning, I stopped at a filling station to purchase gas and have the oil checked. The previous day had been hot and long, endlessly throbbing, the sort of driving to burn oil, I told Vicki. Unfortunately the station was self-service, and after releasing the latch beside the steering wheel, I couldn't figure out how to lift the hood. Ineptness embarrassed me. Instead of asking the woman pumping gas beside me how to raise the hood, I decided to drive to the next station, Minilya Roadhouse, 94 miles north. At Minilya I pulled under a gum and after tugging right and left and up and down raised the hood. The engine needed oil. "I don't have oil," the attendant said. "I'm supposed to get a shipment tonight. You could wait here until the shipment arrives, if it arrives, or you could drive to Coral Bay."

Coral Bay was 64 miles away, the last 8 miles west off the Coastal Highway. "They might have oil there," the attendant said, "but you never know." "Try the grocery store," a man eating a ham sandwich said. The man and his wife were from Adelaide and had been on the road since May. Sitting beside them at a picnic table was a friend who had been traveling for eleven months. "You'll make it," the friend said. "I always make it." On the trip I usually drove between sixty-eight and eighty miles an hour. On the road to Coral Bay, I never drove faster than fifty-five, my eyes serving as governors, studying the dashboard, alert for a red light. In Coral Bay twenty plastic bottles of oil sat on a shelf close to sliced bread. I bought two liters of British Petroleum's Visco 2000, "20W—50 Multigrade Engine Oil," priced at $6.70 a liter. Neither the store nor the gas station had a funnel, so Vicki poured the oil into the engine. She held the bottle a foot above the engine and didn't spill a drop. Afterward we hurried to Exmouth and the next gas station, 85 miles north.

Beyond Coral Bay the road was empty, and we met only six cars. Not once during the 2,114 miles I drove during the vacation did I see a policeman, this despite signs warning that speed was "monitored." In addition to oil I worried about brakes. At times they seemed loose, and when I slapped my foot on the pedal, they knocked. "If I have to stop suddenly, we are goners," I said to Vicki. "Goners," I repeated a dozen times during the trip, enough to disturb Vicki, particularly since animal carcasses littered the road: kangaroos, emus, sheep, pigs, goats, and then small creatures, foxes and rabbits. In the Gascoigne, where many stations were not fenced, cattle and sheep clumped dead on shoulders, decay raising hind legs into racks. At roadhouses people warned me not to drive after dusk. "Last year," a woman said, "my girlfriend hit a steer. She survived but lost her right leg." On the road north of Perth, traffic flattened goannas, pressing them thinner than the soles of leather shoes. Instead of avoiding cars goannas faced them, opening mouths and exposing blue tongues. What intimidated predators in the bush failed on the pavement. Farther north lizards replaced goannas. Because lizards raised their heads and backs, they were easier to see than goannas, and I swerved around a score of them. Throughout the trip feathers waved from mounds, looking like semaphores. Most dead birds were ravens and magpies, but occasionally an emu collapsed like a damp bale of hay. Beyond Carnarvon I scanned the bush on either side of the road, looking for sheep and cattle that grazed the scrub in jittery groups.

Dead euros lay thick along the Yardie Creek Road running from Exmouth into the Cape Range National Park. On shoulders of the road shags of kangaroo bunched in carpets. From bloated bodies legs stuck out wooden. Intestines dried and blowing around bones masked them like tape. Ribs and spines clutched the air, grasping futilely, and pools of black blood splotched the pavement. The fragrance of decay hung heavy, oiling the breeze. To escape the smell I switched on the air conditioner. Although scores of euros bundled across the road in front of the car, I did not hit any. "Tourists," a park ranger said, "don't hit euros. They are hit by people from Perth who don't care." Eventually the dust mops of bone and skin beside the road made me wince. Bodies of sheep and cattle did not affect me the same way. Because their carcasses were larger than those of euros and could flip a car, sight of them brought vulnerability to mind, not sentiment.

For me plants cure mood, the greenery absorbed by eye not swallowed by mouth, however. According to the Australasian Flower Essence Academy, a belt of smoke bush "helps to re-integrate the subtle and more physical aspects of your being into a functioning whole again. Helpful also in cases of difficulty in concentration, fainting and after anesthesia to promote quick recovery of mind/body connections so important for the healing processes. For anxiety, vagueness and feeling caused by the mind and body separating in times of extreme stress." None of the clamps stapling my mind and body together have broken. Still, sight of plants growing along the Brand Highway tempered the stress of driving. Smoke bush blossomed in sand plains north of Perth. From the car window the bushes looked like boulders. Above and on either side of them, banksia grew like molding, leaves hard and sharp, amid them fruits rising ornate: Menzies banksia, its cones dry and gray; lemony slender banksia; then Hooker's banksia, orange sherbet atop vanilla. After Geraldton I noticed Ashby's banksia. Here and there solitary fruits ripened orange and red.

Quilts of clematis bunched over scrub, and brushes of yellow swept the roadside: spears of grevillea, single blossoms left high by the ebb of days; and pools of feather flowers, yellow morrisons in heady sprays, amid the sprays, pads of pink. Beyond Geraldton hills wrinkled into fields, many patches purple and yellow, the latter canola, the former Paterson's curse, sometimes known as salvation weed because in hard times cattle eat it. Throughout the trip mulla mulla bloomed in pillows: silvertails; green pussytails, featherheads yellow and green melting into silver; and then at North West Cape, purple mulla mulla, its flowers tall and cool, swizzle sticks stirring the heat. Hummocks of green leaves erupted from the trunks of grass trees. Amid leaves inflorescences rose spiked. The trees, or clippings from them, the Flower Academy said, nurtured "the maturing of the male principle or the man within." For me the trees smacked of an ancient past enduring vital into the present, not Freud, his views having fossilized, preserved in the sediment of battered textbooks.

SAM PICKERING

Throughout the trip groves of trees flourished on the slope of vision: shaggy coastal woolly butt; flooded gum, trunks gravelly, upper branches smooth; wandoo, and salmon gum, its branches crocheting the horizon. Beyond Carnarvon river red gums swung out from the banks of the Gascoigne then curved upward in white bows. Below the trees the river oozed red; and sand banks shimmered like fat. Near Kalbarri rails of white-plumed grevillea fenced the roadside. For some people the fragrance of the grevillea smacks of old socks. For my part I think the aroma bubbles clean as bath soap. In truth almost no fragrance repulses me, and I forever snuff air for place. North of Geraldton, for example, dusk was grevillea season, and in the rising dark, air swelled creamy, almost whipped.

Land that at first glance appears barren appeals to me. The frothy gardens of Peppermint Grove eventually plug sight and sap energy. In contrast the open beckons and awakens. Although I know that all landscapes are complex and infinitely alluring, the appearance of simplicity attracts me. Wandering the open creates the illusion of escaping organized living, that baroque existence in which days are masquerades, the appointments of years ornate but during which inner lives are so thin that to endure crowds manufacture entertainments—wars or circuses like the Olympics that in their lightness become reassuring metaphors affirming the importance of diversion.

On the North West Cape land pushed the Olympics from mind, and appreciation rather than bile rose to the craw. Near Coral Bay termite mounds turned the bush warty. Spinifex termites harvested grass and constructed the mounds, the insects' underground galleries sometimes farming outward for 150 feet. Mounds looked like ricks of red hay, here and there sheaves loosening and shifting sideways into round knots. Birds perched atop mounds and sprayed droppings out and down in white cowlicks. Midway up the cape the plain bunched into a limestone ridge known as the Cape Range. Sun baked the ridge into hard colors, pink in the morning, orange and brown at midday, and purple at dusk.

One morning Vicki, the children, and I hiked Mandu Mandu Gorge in the park, forty-two miles from Exmouth along the western side of the Cape. The entrance to the gorge was at the end of a dirt road, as were entrances to all beaches in the park. Roads were corrugated and awash with sharp stones. When I drove, the drive shaft clanked, shaking the steering wheel and making my nerves thump. At Mandu Mandu we walked the north side of a canyon carved by an ancient river. Stone slabs formed walls of the gorge. When a slab lost moorings and slipped the wall, it crumbled into cinnamon rock, leaving a dark untidy cavity behind. Along the path spinifex grew in lumps between limestone settings. Blades of the grass bent over and intertwining formed sharp cushions. Amid the grass lurked snakes and mice. While grass on the periphery of hummocks was green, that in the center died and collapsed into purple and black. For a moment the dead blades made me melancholy. "An emblem of modern life," I said to Vicki, "the skin green but the heart dead." "Don't be silly," Vicki said, adding, "Watch your step. Wind and water have honed this limestone into razors." Amid rocks lay the knuckle-sized droppings of euros. Near a boulder a perentie tilted backward, stared at us then slid away, body rolling leathery through curves. A brown falcon soared along the lip of the gorge. On slopes grevillea bloomed in pale, tentative fingers. To return to the car we descended into the canyon and walked west in the riverbed. The bed resembled a rumpled white terrace. Acacia thrust weedy through stones, and baskets of figs hung from walls, bony roots prying into cracks. The hike invigorated me, and at the end of the walk, I fetched the Eski from the car, and we ate lunch in the riverbed, a Cape Range mallee rising in an umbrella above us. That night I plucked an engorged pepper tick from my calf. The tick looked like a minute blood blister. I wanted to think the tick hooked my calf at lunch when I dozed under the mallee. In truth it clambered on me in Mosman Park, a gift from a neighborhood cat.

Without work vacations become laborious. Doing something when one is not obliged to do anything satisfies, and so I collected furnishings of the cape: sand hibiscus, margins of petals wrinkled in the heat; potato bush; dead finish, a prickly acacia, pods wrung tubercular; Kanji bush, sunlight pooling on leaves; and Cape Range kurrajong, a squat tree, its trunk a swollen ankle, heavy and yellow with fat. On the shoulder of Yardie Road, Sturt's desert pea blossomed, the flowers flaring gaseous from leaves flat as stove tops. Instead of black as in other parts of Australia, bosses of the flowers bulged red. Hundreds of wood white chrysalises hung from coastal caper looking like droppings. On a six-inch twig I counted eleven chrysalises. After hatching, the butterflies swirled about the caper in a breeze of white petals. Concentrating on one thing brings other things to the eye. Beneath a bush behind the butterflies, two euros lounged in a dirt bowl. Beyond the kangaroos three emus plodded slowly along.

At Mangrove Bay parakelia dyed the ground purple. At dusk white-breasted wood swallows whirled above inlets. Ruddy turnstones skipped the shore, and reef herons stalked mud flats. Behind the mangroves a pair of bustards strode stately, heads high, bills raised. Above the sand plain a kestrel stuttered like a question mark. Near Exmouth a wedge-tail eagle stood atop a dead sheep, the bird's great talons rooted in wool. Behind the shore corellas caught the wind and blew spinning until shrubs snagged them, transforming them into white rags. Outside our room in Exmouth zebra finches flocked nervously through bushes, and yellow-throated minas belled and whistled.

Because Exmouth was too far from Perth for a day's driving, I idled miles, stopping first at Badgingarra, two and a half hours after I left Mosman Park and 141 miles north of Perth. At roadhouses along the highway picnic tables huddled under trees. After buying gas we snacked. I munched apricots and prunes and drank a Coke while Vicki, Edward, and Eliza drank chocolate milk and ate cheese and crackers, topping off the snack with Snickers bars. For the trip gas cost $475.05, prices ranging from $.94 a liter in Perth to $1.18 in Exmouth. The manager at Badgingarra was genial, in contrast to most employees along the highway. Near Perth, at least from a Western Australian perspective, he probably didn't think himself isolated. At other roadhouses employees were sour. Perhaps, though, they chose to separate themselves from community, and their moods reflected personality, not job. On the other hand maybe the thinness of weeks beside the road tainted lives. Perhaps contemporary westerners can only be happy in crowds. On the cistern in the lavatory in Badgingarra, two names appeared, written with a dark marking pen, Travis Hill and Darryl Ride. The white surfaces of lavatory cisterns invited prose. At Billabong someone wrote, "If You Can't Flush Me, Don't Use Me. Punishment: God Will Send You Back As A Toilet Cleaner." Employees at Billabong were addicted to capital letters. Beneath the cash register hung a white sign. "Please Do Not Ask For Water," red letters cautioned, "As Refusal May Offend."

From the shade of picnic tables, I studied travelers. A bus crammed with Japanese tourists bound for Monkey Mia stopped at Billabong. A rented Volkswagen bus spilled American college students. At Dongara a man said he once worked at Exmouth. "Three years of prawning, then five years at the naval base." Sixty kilometers of tunnels, he said, wound beneath the base. "Nobody knows if they are still used," he added, "or if they are, what they are used for." Exmouth was established in 1967 in order to support the Holt Naval Station, a joint Australian and American venture. Although military doings have been pruned, the town rooted. Population now numbers 3,100 people, many involved with tourism. In fact part of the base has become the Sea Breeze Resort, "the only 3 Star Hotel inside a navy base," advertisements claim.

The first day we ate lunch in Hampton Gardens, a town garden in Northhampton. For my part I ate cheese and crackers and two mandarins. For herself and the children Vicki bought sandwiches at a BP Roadhouse, a chicken burger for Eliza, for Edward, a steak burger, and for herself, cheese sausage. The garden was a small rectangle. Around the border petunias and icy white roses bloomed. The day was hot, and we sat on steps shaded by a eucalyptus. For two minutes a small boy wearing a red shirt and eating vanilla ice cream stared at us. On leaving town we passed the bowling club. Twenty women in white caps, skirts, blouses, and white shoes were bowling. "Escapees from the loony bin," Edward said. "Only the insane go out in such heat."

In Exmouth a woman told me she drove to Perth three times a year. "You get used to the drive," she said. Like the road the day stretched interminably, and by 3:50 when we reached Billabong Roadhouse, 428 miles from Perth, I was ready for ice cream. I ate a Magnum Classic, dark chocolate poured over vanilla. While I sat and ate, a crested pigeon foraged tired grass. I talked to the roadhouse caretaker. He'd spent decades in the Kimberley, retiring south to Billabong, he said, shaking a lid of ash from a cigarette. His skin sank into gullies, and muscles had peeled from his arms. The word *Billabong* appealed to Vicki, and she bought eleven tea towels as presents for friends in Connecticut. The towels cost $7.15 each, and Vicki selected three designs. On one a pair of parrots perched in a wattle, yellow blossoms flickering about them like fireflies. Sturt peas stretched across another towel while on the third an aviary of cockatoos clung to a gum tree: gang-gang, little corella, palm, cockatiel, pink, sulfur-crested, and both yellow-tailed and red-tailed blacks. Scrolling across the bottom of the towels was "Greetings from Billabong Western Australia."

During the trip Vicki did not buy many souvenirs. At the tourist center in Exmouth, Edward purchased a blue short-sleeve shirt with a collar. Stitched across the left breast was a lion fish with a gold body and spines. Circling the fish was a bowl of words, these, too, in gold, "Ningaloo Reef" around the sides and top and "Exmouth" forming a stable base. For her part Eliza purchased a laminated poster. Twenty-nine by nineteen inches, the poster depicted Australia's "DANGEROUS SNAKES." Among snakes curled like puddings were the king brown, tiger, and death adder. For herself Vicki bought two patches, Sturt peas appearing on one, angel fish on the other. She also bought a yellow T-shirt. Sewn on the left front were the words CAPE RANGE NATIONAL PARK, WESTERN AUSTRALIA, the first two words turquoise, the next two, silver, the last, orange. Over the words the sun rose into a spiky red crown. I didn't buy anything for myself, the tourist center's having sold out of extra-large shirts.

The first day we reached Carnarvon at five o'clock. An hour later we settled. Initially I explored the town and looked at motels. Eventually we booked into Fascine Lodge, the brochure for which advertised "luxury units." Luxury meant gray rooms with linoleum floors. Before going to Fascine Vicki inspected a room at the Gateway Motel. The unit was adequate, but the room had been doused with insecticide, and the fragrance made me dizzy. Throughout the trip I paid corporate rates, explaining I was in the book business, $110 in Carnarvon, $93 in Geraldton on the way home, and $125 instead of $137 in Exmouth.

At the Fascine the room consisted of a large square containing a double and two single beds. A small kitchen filled a corner; adjoining it was a shower and lavatory. Early the next morning I drove to Woolworths, and Vicki bought orange juice, cereal, and milk for breakfast. Grocery lists expand in stores, and Vicki purchased other items: mandarins, bread, plastic bowls, and cutlery, the bill coming to $22.67. Throughout the trip we ate breakfast in our rooms and for lunch packed picnics. Preparations always included trips to the grocery. Exmouth contained two groceries, and every day we visited both, Foodland and Super Market. In Exmouth we stayed in Unit 50 on the edge of Potshot Resort. The unit consisted of two dark bedrooms, a small living area which combined kitchen and sitting room, and then a bathroom. On the drive back to Perth, we stopped at the Batavia Motel in Geraldton. At nine that night Vicki sent me out for breakfast milk. After roaming downtown for forty-eight minutes and finding only bars open, I returned to the motel and at the front desk bought a pint of milk.

A good meal drives bile from the mind. Family trips are ordeals. Because people are jumbled together, tempers flare. "Never again will I go on a trip with this family," Edward said the first day after an hour on the road. "Damnation," I said and gripping the wheel, mumbled, "my God, you are ungrateful." Food nurtures the sentimental imagination, however, sweetening bacterial hours. In Carnarvon we ate pizza on a terrace outside the old post office. Wind swept palms along Robinson Street, rustling fronds, making them sound like plastic bags speared by barbed wire. Buoyed by the meal, we strolled downtown, in the process purging asphalt from our systems. The next day we walked the one-mile jetty splintering into the Indian Ocean. A toy green and yellow train called the Coffee Pot took tourists and fishermen to the end of the jetty. Because a long drive loomed ahead, we meandered the jetty. I counted thirty-two fishermen. While I watched, a boy pulled in a mulloway, silver and blue and looking like a serving dish.

I took the South River Road out of town, and we stopped for a snack at Munro's Banana Plantation. Amaryllis and impatiens bloomed in beds; red and purple quilts of bougainvillea draped over fences; and seedpods swung from poinciana in black scabbards. A terrace twisted through a grove of palms. White plastic tables and chairs clustered like mushrooms. In the middle of each table, a yellow napkin holder spread into six points, each point a banana. Under a white throw of bougainvillea was an aviary bright with budgies. A second aviary housed parrots and cockatoos: a pair of northern rosellas, a galah, corellas, and red-winged parrots. Birds should be free, and I want to cut the wires of almost every aviary I see. "Suppose," Eliza said, "we were confined to a living room and couldn't walk but were forced to crawl." "Look what I have," a little girl said as I studied the birds. The girl pushed a red metal truck through sand. In the back of the truck lay a dead frog, dirt clinging to it in fingers.

As a traveler spins across miles, he rolls through mood, one arm of road soon muscled from mind by the next. I've reached the age at which irritation seldom undermines digestion. Turning away from the girl, I sat at a table and ordered a banana-mango smoothie. Vicki ordered avocado scones, and Eliza, corn-asparagus scones. Edward said he would sample our leavings. There were none. After the snack Vicki and Eliza fed crusts to the birds, their favorite, a galah. "He's lonely," Vicki said. The smoothie was so tasty that when Vicki shopped for groceries in Exmouth, I scampered to the Continental Café and wolfed down smoothies. On the way back to Perth, I stopped at Munro's again. This time I ordered mango pancakes soaked in mango syrup and topped with dollops of mango ice cream. Despite being behind schedule we dallied long enough to eat, even Edward who downed a platter of mango chicken nachos.

Family travelers exist on high-fat, low-intellectual diets. Instead of backpacks parents shoulder responsibility. No matter a day's doings parents cannot drift from food. Instead of standing a course and biting the bullet, as threadbare expressions put it, parents sit and bite muffins. On discovering the Minilya roadhouse was out of oil, Vicki popped the trunk and pulled out the Eski. Under a river red gum she spread cheese cloth, and we almost ate ourselves out of concern, snacking on bread, ham, cheddar and swiss cheeses, black olives, peanuts, prunes, and mandarins. A flock of corellas floated in a curtain along the river. A crab spider pressed itself into a crease on the gum, and I tossed bread to a magpie.

After unloading at the Potshot I drove about Exmouth, piddling along Murat, Nimitz, Learmouth, Kraft, and Skipjack. I studied restaurants. Edward and Eliza are not adventuresome diners. Penurious moods occasionally sweep over me, and I begrudge seasoning weary ends of days with money and watching the children pick at expensive meals. The first night we ate at the Rock Cod, a restaurant that was for sale, a fact I learned the next day while reading real estate advertisements. The second night I purchased take-out at the Fancy Fish. The waitress did not write our order down. As a result she forgot Edward's dinner. Vicki gave Edward her dinner and at the Potshot ate a bowl of Wheaties. "Nights will be long," I said. I was wrong. The next evening we ate at Whalers behind the "Shopping Precinct." Bolts of cloth hung over tables and chairs, creating the appearance of chintz. Above a terrace stretched an awning. Food was splendid. I ate snapper stuffed with cheese, spinach, and mango. Vicki and I split a bottle of Mad Fish wine, with, strangely enough, a turtle depicted on the label. The wine cost $22.50. In the Potshot liquor store the price was $19. At Broadway Fair in Perth the price was $17. The bill for dinner came to $107.50. Two nights later we returned.

On the thirtieth, my birthday, we went to a Chinese restaurant,

　　　　　　　　　　　　　　　SAM PICKERING

the Golden Orchid. That morning Vicki bought a Sara Lee mud cake at Foodland. "We'll eat dessert in the room," she said, "and celebrate your birthday." At Whalers we waited forty-eight minutes for our meal; at the Orchid, fifty-three. I ordered Szechwan chicken, Mongolian lamb, Peking duck, and a platter of the house rice. We finished all the dishes and were so full Vicki didn't cut the mud cake. The night before we returned to Perth, I ordered takeout from the Orchid. "How," Vicki asked, "can a little town beyond the end of the world have two good restaurants?"

We ate lunches in the national park. Vicki crammed the Eski and the trunk of the car with food. Every morning she sliced carrots and celery and prepared chicken and ham sandwiches. In the Eski she stuffed bottles of water, apple juice, and soft drinks; slabs of cheese; loaves of bread; and candy bars—Bounty, Mars, and Snickers. In a plastic bag she put salted peanuts. She also packed a jar of Kraft peanut butter, the "crunchy" variety. In a box she put dried packages of Angus Park prunes, Sanitarium apricots, and Meriam Breakfast Plus, this last a blend of bananas, raisins, and nuts. In the box she also packed Uncle Toby's Muesli Bars, usually four varieties, three of them "crunchy," one containing "Coconut Chocolate Chips," another "Apricots," and a third "Nut Crumble." The fourth variety contained strawberry yogurt. In addition to the groceries the shopping center on Maidstone Crescent housed a liquor store, newsagent, pharmacy, bakery, real estate agent, and the Continental Café. On returning from the beach we always stopped at the center. Most automobiles in the parking lot were four-wheel drives. "Close Encounters Does Not Mean Ramming Me In The Ass," warned a sticker on the back of a Land Rover, its paint the color of a rotten orange peel. While Vicki picked up supplies for breakfast and I belted down smoothies, the children perused magazines and bought postcards from the newsagent. In the pharmacy Vicki purchased sunscreen and four straw hats, labels on the fronts of the hats reading BLACK ICE. The hats were made in China and cost $12.95 each. One morning I set my driving glasses on the seat of the car. After buying a newspaper I forgot the glasses and sat on them when I returned to the car. The frames twisted, and both lenses fell out. I asked a man on the street what to do. He told me to take them to the pharmacist. The pharmacist repaired them and didn't charge me. Thus the only crisis of the trip passed easily, not a single four-letter word marking its appearance.

We went to Exmouth to snorkel. I rented masks and flippers at the Exmouth Diving Center behind the Potshot, for two days paying the backpacker rate of $6.60 per person or $27.40 a day for the family. After the first two days a new clerk charged me the tourist rate of $13.60 a head or $54.40 a day. For $17 I bought a year's pass to the national park, number 028899. We snorkeled at three spots in the park, Lakeside, Sandy, and Turquoise Bay. Sun burned like iron, and temperatures ranged between eighty-eight and one hundred degrees Fahrenheit. The first day I rolled sunscreen over my face, shoulders, and legs, including my calves. I was careless and missed the sides of my back. That night they boiled, rising into red feathery wings. My ankles swelled, and patties of flesh hung over the bony knobs on the sides. To sleep I swallowed three aspirin. The next morning I bathed in sunscreen and wore a long-sleeved shirt in and out of the ocean. As soon as I got out of the water, I removed mask and flippers and put on the hat, blue jeans, socks, and over my damp shirt a sweat shirt. "You look like you are dressed for the Arctic," Vicki said.

Sand around the bays was starched, and water, silver and blue. Beaches rose into a collar of dunes. Beyond the dunes land flattened and peeled scrubby back to the range where it crumpled into ridges and canyons. At Sandy Bay we walked north along the beach and looked at fossils bedded in sandstone. Some fossils twitched into screws; others fanned into wheels. Twice we ate lunch at a picnic table behind the Milyering Visitor Center. Kangaroos dozed under acacia, and corellas tumbled through the air. For Edward the trip was a camera safari, he being the object of the shutter. During five days at the beach, Vicki took twenty-seven pictures of Edward.

I did not escape worry at the beach. Riptides jerked along the shore like ropes. Edward and Eliza swam far from beaches, and I tired myself reeling them back. Gray reef sharks wrinkled across the bottom. Sight of the sharks thrilled Edward, and when a shark shunted aside and slipped away, Edward pursued him. I warned the children about blue-ringed octopuses, sea snakes, stonefish, and cone shells. No parent, of course, can warn children against youth itself. Happily small irritations drove worry from mind, such things as sand getting inside my flippers or water seeping under and fogging my face mask.

Of the three places we snorkeled, my favorite was Turquoise Bay. Bombies were a short swim away. Slightly farther from the shore rose ratchets of staghorn coral. Here I drifted wantonly, beneath me groves and bowers, seraglios, caverns, evenings of rose red twilight, golden sunrises, and fish, looking like birds one moment, the next petals ticking through the air. Plate, cabbage, lichen, and brain coral slipped luscious beneath me, pink and blue, sometimes hard-shelled, other times downy. A green turtle paddled past. A moray eel wound through stone, its skin pale lattice. A blue-spotted ribbontail ray cruised the bottom like a whisper. A potato grouper lounged in shadows. Nearby black-spotted snappers congregated in a crevice, waving like seaweed, the yellow lines along their backs delicate fronds. A blue-spotted sting ray fluffed the bottom and disappeared into tracery. A many-stripped puffer looked uncooked. A starfish splayed red across coral, and black sea cucumbers oozed along the bottom, sand dusting them. When my shadow drifted over them, giant clams snapped shut, their mantles green and blue ruffles.

While dumpling squid backed away from me, trevallies slid past in a shower of silver splinters. Amid the coral fish blossomed like water flowers. My eyes picked bouquets. In one vase stood two stems, a yellow trumpet fish and a cornet fish, green and silver. Damselfish smiled like daisies—neons, blue and purple; sergeants, black and white; lemons; and brown western gregories. Parrotfish bowled through the water, most green and pink. Looking like palettes splattered with paint, triggerfish hovered about me: particularly the humuhumu, its sides streaks of damp paint, blue, yellow, brown, and black. Sweetlips hid under ledges, and cardinal fish wrapped themselves around coral. Nearby anemone fish rode currents like leaves the air in fall, orange and black. Butterfly fish patrolled bombies, many yellow, others yellow tarnished with black. "Rock daffodils," Eliza called them. "Rays," Edward added, "are nettles, and the small neons, periwinkle." "What are parrotfish?" I asked. "Iris," Eliza said, "ornate hybrids."

Driving home I suggested spending three nights at Kalbarri, four hundred miles north of Perth. Seven years ago we spent five days in Kalbarri. Snorkeling had tired the family, however, and they vetoed my suggestion. Instead of turning off the highway, I pushed ahead to Geraldton. Because we reached town after dark, we ate Whoppers and french fries at Hungry Jacks. Inside Eliza's meal was a coupon, awarding her a milkshake. Unfortunately the milkshake machine was broken. At two-fifteen the following afternoon we were back on Kalgoorlie Street. "Where are we going next vacation?" Eliza asked as I unloaded the car. "Maybe south to the Porongurups," I said. "No," Edward said, "let's go to Malaysia. That wouldn't cost much." The week in Exmouth cost $2,834.59. We were gone from Perth for eight nights. At $955.10 lodging was the big expense. In restaurants we spent $414.30, or $51.79 a night. Groceries cost $228.17, and gas, $475.05. Other expenses were smaller, at Claremont Sports, the day before we left, for example, $119.85, for bathing suits for Vicki and Eliza. "Our next trip will be more expensive," Vicki said. "I know it," I said, "but why not?"

October

In Connecticut spring begins in April. The school year wilts, and as days lengthen into flower, purpose sifts away. I slip the shackles of duty and wander field and ridge. In October freedom from paragraph weighs heavy, and I bustle into the academic year, pencils sharp and date book open. Travelers cannot escape pattern. No matter where the traveler goes, he eventually forces place into the familiar. By October days in Perth were routine. The trip to Exmouth seemed summer vacation, and I began to stir, no matter that in Australia October brought spring.

After a long absence Turlow Gutheridge wrote from Carthage, reporting that Artemus Shugrue died, the second time Artemus died in my books, a fact that startled me, the significance of which I haven't fathomed. "Before attending the funeral," Turlow reported, "Billie Dinwidder ate four Mars bars. As the choir sang 'In the Sweet By and By,' Billie got sick, splattering Hoben Donkin, sitting in the pew in front of him. 'That just spoiled the whole funeral,' Hoben said later in Ankerrow's Café. 'After Billie threw up, I didn't have no fun at all.'" I read Turlow's letter to Vicki. "What does Carthage have to do with Australia?" Vicki said. "A lot," I said. On the afternoon of the funeral, Posthumous Blodgett wandered into the café. "Posthumous," Googoo Hooberry said, "I've been thinking about your Christian name. I know that you were named Posthumous because one of your parents died before you were born. But was it your mother or your father?"

Old friends are good tonic. After perusing Turlow's letter, I studied the children's doings, something I do every fall. Eliza spent the week beginning October 9 on Work Experience. She worked for Mr. Ottenhoff, a veterinarian. She started work at eight and finished at five. During the week Eliza saw a spaying and a castration. A young bull terrier was operated on for a hernia. During the operation the puppy stopped breathing, and Mr. Ottenhoff brought him back with artificial respiration. For the most part Eliza's work was janitorial. Every morning she cleaned cat cages. Then she washed litter boxes and food bowls. She emptied garbage and hung up clean towels. She washed and dried syringes and surgical tools. Every day she mopped and vacuumed the building. She dusted shelves and books and collapsed cardboard boxes. The week passed slowly. Occasionally Mr. Ottenhoff chatted with her, about money not animals, however. He had attended a "Wealth Creation Seminar" and owned a library of self-help books. At week's end Eliza filled in a form for St. Hilda's. "The down-to-earth gritty aspects" of the job, she recounted, "disagreed with me—the endless cleaning, the technical parts, such as dispensing medication and ordering supplies." "Even the surgical experiences were tiresome." In answer to the question, "Are you still interested in this career?" she wrote, "NO." "My view of veterinary medicine was unrealistic. I love animals and enjoy playing with them. But that is not vet medicine. Vet medicine is based on facts and numbers. It is not imaginative or creative enough for me. For me the environment was sterile. My career will have to be fanciful and less factual. The chemical and symptomatic minutiae bored me. I'm disappointed that I couldn't muster interest in the job." "One career down," Vicki said, "five hundred more to go."

In October Edward began college applications. He considered applying to Princeton. "I don't have a chance of getting in," he said, "but Francis is there, and I love him." The statement startled me. Never have Francis and Edward been affectionate to each other. This past spring when Francis came home for vacation, the boys quarreled. Applying to college from Perth was difficult.

Applications demanded midterm reports. Three weeks after Edward entered Christ Church, the term ended, and school adjourned for a fortnight. In Australia school tests pale in importance to the Tertiary Entrance Examination, a national test which determines college admission. During his short time in school, Edward took no tests. To compensate for the lack of a midterm report, Edward wrote an essay describing the summer he spent in Queensland on Tumbar Station. "Beginning on July 3," he wrote, "we mustered each paddock in succession. Tumbar was divided into thirty paddocks, separated from one another by barbed wire fence and grids and distinguished by natural features that gave them names: Burnt Yard, Top Sunday, Tent Mountain, Tillman's, Eight Mile, and Gidyea, among others. The landscape had once been forested, but Bevan [owner of the station] had cleared great swaths to accommodate stock. The bush that remained presented an array of greens, some shaded blue, others olive and gray. Gidyea bush and eucalypts were confined to narrow alleys along fences, where cattle found shade. Even areas left uncleared were remarkable for openness; trees, broad and thin-leaved, never formed a canopy. Trunks tilted at odd angles and well-spaced from each other created a fabric whose depth seemed both false and inviting." "Bliss was it in that dawn to be alive," I muttered as I read, quoting William Wordsworth, my favorite poet, "but to be young was very heaven."

"The names of the men," Edward continued, "will remain with me, wonderfully short and lilting: Will Gray, Malcolm Brown, Kelly Alexander, and Mark Walsh. Years of mustering and droving had shaped their personalities. Often quiet and reserved apart from the saddle, they jumped to life on horseback, responsive to subtleties in stock and weather that I could not see. All had been raised in the rugged Kimberley ranges. All competed in rodeos, as bull riders, bronc saddle riders, or both. None had finished school. Kelly, my age, was illiterate by his admission. Yet he could play the guitar by ear and could recall scores of tunes from memory. The men accepted me and taught me a great deal. Theirs was a world of rodeos and outback pubs, small towns and distant stations—a world in which I had been unsuspectingly tossed but which I came to appreciate, even love."

Particular memories stood out. "The Jordan River ran through Brett's Paddock, dry and dust-laden. Dense bushes crowded the banks nearest the yards and spread outwards. Here, cattle hid warily, motionless and alert, fading into leaves. It was a thrill to chase them, weaving along faint tracks at a trot and dipping madly down banks. . . . Walking cattle home became a familiar routine. The unpredictable nature of a morning roundup contrasted with the relatively straightforward task of bringing cattle to the yard before nightfall. The dying light in combination with so much dust, kicked from the heels of the mob, created a golden filter, through which the forms of Will and the others lost detail and distinction. Once cattle were in the yards, the horses unsaddled, fed, and washed down, the working day was done." "Gosh," I said to Vicki, "I wish I'd spent a summer on horseback. Then I'd have a real book." In Perth Edward enjoyed Christ Church. One night at dinner he reported that a teacher dismissed class, saying, "Okay, gentlemen, piss off." Athletics in Perth were more relaxed than in Storrs. Edward dislikes competition and in Connecticut had given up sports. At Christ Church he played basketball. "We only practice two afternoons a week," he said. "That keeps things in perspective."

Small doings drizzled across October. I spoke to five classes at the university. After class a teacher told me that at night her brother often read the Sydney telephone book. "The white pages," she said, explaining; "he is a statistician and enjoys numerical patterns. 'Do you know how many people named Hargreaves live in Sydney?' he asks. 'Or do you know the number of times consecutive entries live on the identical street, excluding multiple listings for the same address?'" Unfortunately the teacher did not remember the answer to this last query. For a moment I considered studying the Perth telephone book and counting the times consecutive entries lived on the same street. I jettisoned the idea. The Perth directory contained 1,575 white pages, five columns to a page, approximately eighty-four entries to a column. At least the second column on page 1056 running from "Nelli RW & DF" living at 3a Valiencia Court in Alexander Heights to "Nelson BL" at 120 Lesmurdie Road in Lesmurdie contained eighty-four entries.

One afternoon I spoke to creative writing students at the university. "Nonfiction frees writers from truth," I said, "unlike fiction, which forces writers to embrace truth in order to create character and landscape." "In general nonfiction is more fictional than fiction." "That's baloney," Eliza said at dinner that night. After chapel I addressed eleventh graders at Christ Church. In the talk I warned students against people my age bent on becoming their friends. "Couldn't you be our friend?" two boys asked later. "No," I said. "I could be your teacher. That's better."

A week later I spoke to the Center of Ethics at Christ Church. After the talk Frank Sheehan, the school chaplain, and I chatted. At a funeral service of a friend, Frank recounted, an old man gave a brief testimonial. Instead of a wordy tribute, the man walked to the front of the church, rested his right hand on his friend's coffin, and said, "See you soon, John." The man then turned around, walked back to his pew, sat down, and died. At midnight one evening a woman telephoned from North Dakota and interviewed me for an Internet magazine. Four days later the host of a radio show interviewed me, calling during dinner, chicken Kiev being the main course, the wine, a Shiraz from the Barossa Valley, costing sixteen dollars, seven dollars more than I usually plunk down for grape juice. That Sunday when I left my office at the university, I counted seven photographers taking pictures of wedding parties. One bride posed cradling her new baby. In another group three out of four bridesmaids were talking on cellular phones. Parties arrived in white limousines: Bentleys, Rolls-Royces, and Cadillacs, steering wheels of this last switched from left sides of front seats to right. The next weekend while I wandered Kings Park, a wedding party sped past in a pair of red Mustangs.

Near the end of October iceberg roses lining the fence in front of our house burst into bloom. One hundred and fifty-eight blossoms covered the bush nearest the mailbox, bending stems and looking like hands and shoulders of snow. One morning after parking the Mitsubishi at the university, I noticed a tail dangling from beneath the hubcap of the right front tire. Pinched beneath the cap, a small lizard had traveled from Kalgoorlie Street to Hackett Drive, enduring nine kilometers of spinning. I forced a twig under the hubcap and pressing upward freed the lizard. I carried the lizard into the Great Court and turned it loose under a fern, first glancing about to make sure a kookaburra was not watching. Next I noticed a crowd near the Moreton Bay Fig at the corner of Saw Promenade. A ten-year-old boy had climbed the trunk of the tree then shimmied along a limb that reached across the brick walk. Going was easier than returning. Suddenly becoming frightened, the boy froze, locking arms and legs around the limb. "I'm not going to move," he said, his words a blend of tears, exasperation, and laughter. "You'll be fine," a gardener said. "I've sent for a cherry-picker."

When I returned from Exmouth, a university official informed me that my check had not cleared. Forty-two days having passed, I telephoned Liberty Bank in Storrs. "Your check was processed on September 5 by Bank One in Bedford, Texas," the manager told me. "Oh," the university administrator said. "I didn't think the check would clear so quickly. I'll bet we've had your money for a month." Two days later I received the money. Alas, when the check cleared, the Australian dollar was worth 57.5 cents. Now it is worth 51.9 cents. "How much have we lost?" Vicki asked. "9.74 percent, or 6,817 American dollars. I'm good with numbers." "But not with money," Vicki said. In truth the luck of international exchange aside, I handle money well. October awakened my entrepreneurial instincts. *Walkabout Year* went out of print in the United States in August. I brought the last five copies of the book with me to Perth. In October I sent a copy to P & O Cruises, offering myself as lecturer aboard the *Pacific Sky,* my preference being the "Tropical Christmas" cruise. Sailing from Sydney on December 18, the cruise lasted ten nights and called at four ports: Noumea and Isle of Pines in New Caledonia, Lifou on the Loyalty Islands, and lastly Vila on Vanuatu. To Ansett Airlines I sent my second copy of *Walkabout Year,* offering to barter articles for their in-flight magazine for tickets. I suggested that they fly us to Darwin. From there we could explore Kakadu. As an alternative I mentioned Melbourne. I said we would explore the city then ride horses through the High Country. Next I telephoned Bogong Horseback Adventures and Stoney's Bluff and Beyond Trail Rides and requested brochures. Bogong and Stoney's were in Victoria and in December and January, school vacation months, offered five-day trail rides. "Not long enough," Eliza said. "You are a wordsmith, Daddy. Convince them to take us for ten days." Alas, my anvil has cooled. Six weeks have passed, and I have not heard from either Ansett or P & O.

I devoted much of the month to Edward and Francis. Although Francis was in Italy, he was not out of mind. Early in the month I received a letter from the University of Connecticut, saying that because the university had not received records of his immunizations, he would not be allowed to take courses second semester. Francis is a student at Princeton. Although he is spending the year in Europe on a foreign-study program administered by the University of Connecticut, he is not a student at Connecticut. Francis has, of course, endured wards of immunizations. Obtaining records from Princeton would not be easy, as telephone calls to Princeton get shunted onto a telephone tree where they collapse in a nest and addle. Consequently I emailed Michael Kurland, a friend and head of health services at Connecticut. "I took care of Francis's problem," Michael answered. "It's a bureaucratic glitch in the system. He is the first case that has come to my attention for this particular issue. The system interprets him as a full-time student here, subject to the State of Connecticut's regulations. However, he is not taking courses on Connecticut soil. To fix matters, I put him in the system as 'compliant.' We have a set of codes that we can use for an override. I chose the code 'religious exemption' because there is no code for administrative override or 'other reasons.'"

Michael's common sense perked me up. Still, solving Francis's difficulty took a morning. To Edward I devoted a score of evenings and afternoons. I don't have a computer at the house. When

Edward types an assignment or a college application, I drive him to the university. He uses the computer in my office. While he works, I remain at the university, often five or six hours. Members of the English department do not have their own printers. Instead they use a common printer, locked in the department's mailroom. When Edward wishes to print an essay, I must unlock the mailroom and switch on the printer. During Edward's writing sessions I wander back and forth from library to office to mailroom.

In Storrs in October Vicki and I attend the Mansfield Town Fair, the horticultural show at the university, and the open house at the high school, among other events. In Perth routine did not change. On October 6, Vicki, Eliza, and I went to the Royal Agricultural Show at Claremont. Edward stayed home and worked on college applications. We got to the agricultural show at ten in the morning and left at five-twenty that afternoon. Cattle calm me, and we spent the morning wandering "Cattle Lanes." Names of breeds curdled into stanzas: Swiss Brown, Devon, Limousin, Red and Black Angus, Simmental, Belted Galloway, Dexter, Hereford, and Brahmin, Marie-Anjou, and Shorthorn, Charolais, Blond d'Aquitaine, Braunvieh, Holstein, Guernsey, and Square Meater, this last bred for hamburger. Murray Greys clumped heavily together looking like silver boulders. Over Belgian Blues white and black shimmered cloudy, behind the clouds blue roan, turning the cattle into mottled chunks of sky. While Salers were thought descendants of ancient Egyptian cattle and had only recently arrived in Australia, Illawarra arrived in the eighteenth century as food for settlers. Above three stalls hung a sign. "Grinkle Park Jerseys," the sign stated, "Peter and Wilda Tallentire. East Road. Gidgegannup. WA." "Only in Australia would you see such names," Vicki said.

Goats lounged in cattle sheds: Toggenberg; British Alpine; Boer, horns screwed into circles; and Anglo-Nubian, the breed developed from goats transported to Britain on troopships in order to provide milk for soldiers and families. Silver ribbons hung above Marigold and Saanen from Danlalee Park, the first an award for "Doe with Best Udder," the second for "Supreme

Champion Daisy Doe." "Let's take another spin through the stalls," I said after two hours. "No, please," Eliza said, "I've seen enough cows." On Mitchell Avenue I bought a lamb burger. After one bite fat coated my tongue like lanolin, and I tossed the burger into a garbage can. For fifty cents at Woolworths I bought a barbequed mushroom and then for two dollars, an avocado stuffed with guacamole. To promote bananas the store distributed small cups of banana smoothies. I drank two cups.

We roamed the show, wandering Viveash, Hardey, Saunders, and Whitenoom Avenues. Of the dogs on exhibit Eliza and I liked Longcoat Chihuahuas best. Only at exhibitions do I see poisonous snakes: tiger, king brown, and dugite, the skin of this last silver and brown, dappled with olive, camouflaging the snake amid bark and leaf. A rock wallaby dozed through a presentation devoted to salinity. The poultry pavilion contained 991 metal cages, the chickens in them crowing and growling. Combs and wattles on white leghorns and black Australorps glowed like embers. Feathers on frillback pigeons curled into papier-mâché while those above the feet of Dutch tumblers flared into dusters. At three o'clock pigs raced around a small oval. The race lasted eleven seconds. Bacon Bone won, followed by Pork Chop, Hambone, and Porky Pig. In a freezer four carcasses hung from hooks, three sheep and one goat, two of the sheep white Dorpers, the other a white Suffolk. Another freezer contained capretto carcasses, a capretto being an unweaned goat eight to twelve weeks old.

In a small field stood a score of steam engines, most fired up, wheels revolving, belts pulling, and arms heaving and pounding. My favorite was a "Rushton Proctor Portable No. 6 PSC," manufactured in Lincoln, England, in 1904. Until the 1950s the engine drove a chaff cutter at Devils Creek near Mullewa, seventy-five miles east of Geraldton. In the late fifties the engine was sold for scrap. Happily it proved too difficult to move and was abandoned "complete with all its brass fittings," the present owner told me. "It needed a new boiler and crankshaft when I began working on it in 1990." Not until late afternoon did I explore the sideshows. Eliza threw two balls into a basket, but they bounced out as I predicted. A miscellany of rides whirled about us: Kamikaze, Zipper, Mega Mix, Python Loop, Sizzler, Superturbo, Gravitron, and Hurricane. Eliza and I rode the Ferris wheel, but even that frightened me.

The next morning Vicki and I went to the Wildflower Festival at Kings Park. "Having spent too many unpasteurized hours in the cow sheds," as Vicki put it, Eliza stayed home with Edward. The festival took place in the botanic garden. Tents housed caravans of goods: plants, art, souvenirs, tourist brochures, and scientific studies. In the garden Ashby's banksia smelled like hay, and from bull banksia, candelabras of lemon cones rose into the blue light. People spread blankets on the ground and from hampers extracted cheeses, baguettes, and bottles of champagne and red wine, brie and Stilton being the most popular cheeses. While I imagined munching other people's lunches, Vicki shopped. She bought me a T-shirt, "the souvenir you didn't purchase in Exmouth." Across the chest of the shirt, a grass tree spread black over red soil. For herself Vicki purchased a potpourri bowl made from jarrah. She also bought a small painting of eucalyptus cassia, the Silver Princess. Fruits swayed behind a curtain of green leaves, four sealed, caps slipping from two, spilling fountains of pink stamens, their tips yellow. For the dining room table she bought two candleholders, both carved from the fruits of bull banksia, follicles open and puckered.

Two weeks later Vicki and I attended the Nedlands Kite Festival on the foreshore at Matilda Bay. Edward stayed home to work on an application to Middlebury while Eliza read *Middlemarch* and fretted about the fate of Dorothea Brooke. At the festival junior and senior choirs from Nedlands Primary School performed, Edward's and Eliza's old school. Girls wore navy blue skirts, white blouses, blue neckties, and high white socks. Girls with long hair bound it with white ribbons. Boys wore blue trousers, blue neckties, and white shirts. The choirs sang rounds, but there being no shell to contain the music, sound quickly evaporated into silence. Sambanistas snaked through the festival playing samba music. They wore blouses embroidered with bouquets of imaginary flowers, baseball caps topped with ostrich feathers, vests bright as butterfly bushes, and velour trousers, hoops at the ankles turning legs into purple pipes. "The costumes," a band member said, "knock us out of our comfort zones." When Vicki and I arrived, small kites schooled the bay. Large kites lay becalmed on the ground: a green octopus, a fish with bulging eyes, and a train of twelve black and white box kites coupled together. Unfortunately the afternoon drifted into the doldrums, and even the krill of small kites sank to the ground.

Under a tent used books were for sale. On the title page of Wilhelm Reich's *The Function of the Orgasm,* I wrote, "This is my favorite book, and I will always be indebted to my beloved husband Johnnie for this wonderful anniversary present." I signed the inscription, "Mary Magdalene Jones." I placed the book atop a stack of dull novels. Hands of several customers paused above the cover, but no one seized the book. "People sense that the inscription is old-fashioned," Vicki said. "You should have written, 'I will always be indebted to my partners, Kate, Sally, and Henry.' Get with the new innovative domestic program." The manager of the stall rarely smiled. Indeed she glared at me when I inscribed Reich's book and did not buy it. For fifty cents, however, I bought L. M. Montgomery's *Rainbow Valley.* Montgomery is remembered for novels describing Anne of Green Gables, one of my favorite characters, wholesome and so old-fashioned that she could never have imagined the quartet Vicki mentioned glibly. I handed Vicki the book, saying, "Someday you might inscribe the title page, writing something like, 'This is my favorite book. I will always be indebted to my beloved husband Sam for this uplifting present.'"

I suspect Vicki will not inscribe the book. Actually I bought the book because it was already inscribed. Pasted inside the cover was a label, three and a quarter inches wide and five and a quarter tall. Printed on the label in red, almost Gothic, letters was "Presented to." Beneath the words were four lines, on which was written in cursive, "Ruth Stubbings for attendance Special Prize 100% R. F. Thomas, Supt." A reprint which appeared in 1949, the book was fifty-one years old. "It was a clear apple-green evening in May," the first paragraph began, "and Four Winds Harbour was mirroring back the clouds of the golden west between its softly dark shores. The sea moaned eerily on the sandbar, sorrowful ever in the spring, but a sly, jovial wind came piping down the red harbour road along which Miss Cornelia's comfortable, matronly figure was making its way towards the village of Glen St. Mary." *Rainbow Valley* was a safe book to give to a bright ten-year old girl. If Ruth Stubbings received the book in 1950 or 1951, she would be sixty. Why, I wondered, did the book appear in the secondhand tent? Had she died? Maybe she moved to a small apartment and friends or children helped pare possessions. The reprint was cheap. Pages were yellow and brittle, and none were marked. The person who never missed a day of school, probably Sunday school, wouldn't have doodled across margins, in or out of books, and perhaps, I thought, would have been a spinster. I found five Stubbings in the Perth telephone book, A., J. D., L. P., and P. and S. K., but no Ruth. The book listed three R. F. Thomases, one of them in Mosman Park. Superintendents of Sunday Scholars are always male and of a stature and age, forty-five at the youngest, making Mr. Thomas ninety-five or so if he were alive. "Ruth would have slipped between cracks in his memory," I said. "Not," Eliza said, "if he married her eight years after giving her the book." "Which," Eliza added after a pause, "he did." "Was the marriage happy?" I asked. "Oh, yes," Eliza said, "despite the age difference. By the way he wasn't forty-five but thirty-one when he was superintendent. Ruth and Bob had three children, two boys and a girl. The boys are lawyers, but the girl Anne is a famous herpetologist, an expert on skinks." "Is she married?" I asked. "Yes," Eliza said, "to an entomologist with red hair. The children were terribly upset when their mother died last year, and they had to move their father to retirement community. Cleaning out the small house took a week. Memories made them pause over each possession. Anne remembered her mother reading *Rainbow Valley* to her when she was six years old."

Along the foreshore stalls sold food: cherry and orange Popsi-

SAM PICKERING

cles, hamburgers, ice cream sandwiches, and pink tufts of fairy floss. To the festival Vicki brought a packet of celery and carrot sticks. For lunch she ate the slices, drank a Coke, and split a hot dog with me, a two-dollar dog buried in onions and ketchup. Vicki and I eat through days. Two mornings a week we have coffee and scones at Cappuccino by the River. Afterward Vicki feeds crumbs to wagtails, and we amble the shore beneath the Esplanade. Under the limestone ridge chenille honey myrtle has started blooming, and along streets in Peppermint Grove lilac trees have burst into blue stars. Last Thursday we walked to La Palm D'Or off Napoleon Street and split an apricot tart. Afterward we studied shop windows. In imagination Vicki bought a pearl necklace. The pearls were natural and lumpy. Some were silver while lemon coated others like tartar. I glanced into the window of a shop that sold expensive used clothing. "Cottesloe's Salvation Army," I said to Vicki. "Certainly not," a woman said and entered the store.

Living in Mosman Park may not be good for character. Roaming sometimes makes me covetous, and momentarily my plenty doesn't seem enough. Sometimes I become irritated that other people have extraordinary means. "Coining money takes gumption," Vicki said. Vicki is right. Not only do I lack gumption but also the discipline to devote days to tasks I think insignificant. On better occasions, however, covetousness awakens imagination, and I return from walks certain something marvelous will happen, usually that one of my books becomes a bestseller. "Good news is coming," I tell Vicki, "coming tomorrow."

In Perth tomorrow brings good times, not news. Last Wednesday Vicki and I went to SupaValu on Wellington and at the deli counter purchased sandwiches. Afterward we walked to Green Place Reserve, eating lunch at Chidley Point. Along the bluff above the river, rose banjine bloomed. Awls of wild oats jabbed my ankles, forcing me to remove my socks four times. Parked in the lot above the point was a ute. Attached to the ute was a small trailer; painted on the side of the trailer was "A Farmyard on Wheels." Below the words a circle fenced the heads of six barnyard animals: a pig, sheep, goat, cow, horse, and chicken. Beside the trailer "Farmer Mick" tossed a yellow tennis ball to a sheep dog, passing time before he drove the barnyard to Iona Presentation College. Inside the van and under a tarpaulin covering the back of the ute were goats, pigs, sheep, a donkey, chickens, and rabbits. During the school year Mick visited six hundred classrooms. On weekends he entertained birthday parties, sometimes six birthdays a weekend, he said. During school holidays he took the barnyard to shopping centers. Mick lived in Armadale. Before purchasing the Farmyard, he'd been a plasterer, managing an eight-man crew. "It was terrible," he said. "I couldn't count on men to show up for work, and many contractors were dishonest and did not pay me. I'd always liked animals, and when the chance came to buy this business, my wife urged me on. She teaches school, and for the first year or so, her salary kept us in feed. But now I'm doing well." Vicki and I talked to Mick for three-quarters of an hour. Afterward we walked the bicycle path along the river toward Stirling Bridge. We returned home at four o'clock that afternoon. "A good day," Vicki said, putting the kettle on the stove. "The best," I said.

By the end of the month, Edward completed applications to Princeton, Sewanee, Virginia, Carleton, and Middlebury. Saying that the rest would be easy, he accompanied Vicki, Eliza, and me to the Art Gallery of Western Australia. The person who knows only home does not know home, and so I study landscapes. Like longing blue flowed through Arthur Streeton's *The Barren Gorge and Sugar Plains*. A peak turned gray above Eugene von Guerard's *Fern Tree Gully, Cape Otway*, the pale stone softening the crisp details of stream and forest. In Hans Heysen's *Droving into the Light*, a horseman slouched into a yellow glaze, gum trees on both sides of the man rising like columns, transforming hard, ordinary work into the holy. "Your taste is as tightly buttoned by the past as Anne Shirley was in her dresses," Vicki said. Vicki was right, but that was fine with me. For a long time I studied Frederick McCubbin's old chestnut *Down on His Luck*. In the painting a weary bushman sat on a log, his left arm bent, elbow resting on his right knee, his hand pressed against his forehead. His right arm fell across his right knee; from his hand a stick dangled loosely. With it the man listlessly stirred the embers of tired fire. Behind the man rose the weighty trunk of a big tree. Except for a weedy sapling in the right front of the painting, the background was smoky. "He is a writer, not a bushman," I said to Eliza, "and he is tired of driving paragraphs day after day." "What is the smoke then?" Eliza asked. "Words," I said, "pale syllables, ghosts of ideas." "That's too glib," Vicki said.

Many paintings delighted me. Trees in John Glover's *Patterdale* writhed upward through curves, leaves at the top bunched into fingerprints. The painting that appealed to me most was not a landscape, however, but Lucien Freud's *Naked Portrait.* A nude woman sprawled in a brown chair, the chair so nondescript it could have been a La-Z-Boy. Drab gray curtains hung behind the woman. Dots crossed the curtain in waves, four lines of dots in each wave. The woman was middle-aged, and she sat splayed, her right leg pulled up and bent, her heel digging into a soiled red cushion on the chair, her left leg thrust to the side, then turning back at the knee, forcing her foot under buttocks. Her posture thrust her pelvis forward. Initially the pose directed observation to the woman's private parts. Sheen clothed the woman, however, softening her anatomy. Quickly my eye shifted from her pelvis to patches of skin as colors pooled and dried, pink, green, and orange. That night at dinner Eliza and I discussed the painting. "Pornography," Eliza said. "No," I said, "Freud's skin is as wonderful as that of Bronzino." "Rubbish," Vicki said, "you just like to look at vaginas." Outside art galleries I am prudish and cannot even whisper the last word Vicki said. To end the conversation, I opened *Rainbow Valley.* "Miss Cornelia was rightfully Mrs. Marshall Eliot," I read, "and had been Mrs. Marshall Eliot for thirteen years, but even yet more people referred to her as Miss Cornelia than as Mrs. Eliot. The old name was dear to her friends."

"The primary object of a student of literature is to be delighted," wrote Lord David Cecil, the British critic. With luck and work delight enriches readers' days. Cecil's statement also applies to painting, albeit delight does not necessarily broaden.

Not all paintings in the gallery appealed to me, of course. "The decadent rag-tail end of the South American political mural," Edward said, looking at Juan Davila's *Stupid as a Painter*. "Stupid represents the disenfranchised, raging with angst," Vicki said. On the wall loomed cartoons, characters' private parts throbbing. A bat bulged woody in a sailor's trousers. "Tedious," Eliza said. A man lubricated another man's anus with an oil can. An androgynous figure had the physique of a male bodybuilder and the privates of a female, these last a red maw sharp with canines. "It should visit the orthodontist," Vicki said. The cartoon was the visual equivalent of inarticulate language—a brew of sound that conveyed emotion not thought. "That's prim," Vicki said. "I am prim," I answered, standing outside the gallery. "Listen to those boys." Three boys rumbled past, their speech rising then falling, punctuated not by grammar but by vulgar exclamation, the sounds confounding the speakers, but not observers like me who knew what the words were and what the boys would always be.

I have lived in Connecticut for over twenty years. No matter how I bustle through October, doings slip into pattern. In Perth bustle remained, but occasionally juxtaposition rather than pattern stamped the month. We visited the art gallery on Saturday. Sunday we went to the zoo. Like clumps of daisies in a garden, yellow speckles adorned the back of a splendid tree frog. When looked at from above, fairy penguins bulged like blue string bags. Crowds were thick, and I longed for the open woodlands of Patterdale. A woman stood on a bank and shook a suspension bridge while her mate of the moment crossed. "You cute little shit," he said, reaching the bank and throwing his right arm over her shoulders. Instead of making people tolerant zoos reinforce tribalism. One of the most beautiful animals at the zoo was the sun bear. The bear's rump was white, the rest of its coat blacker than deep water. At the end of its paws, nails curved in long blue arcs. The bear is endangered. Hunters kill it for the gall bladder that, like tigers' paws, is used in eastern medicine. "Damn the Chinese," Vicki said, admiring the bear. Because so many species are endangered, zoos make me melancholy. "In zoos," Vicki said, "I lose hope."

SAM PICKERING

Although I strolled the bushwalk, visited the Butterfly and Nocturnal Houses, and roamed the Rainforest and the African Savannah, I spent much of the afternoon looking at birds. A barking owl swallowed a mouse headfirst. A grass owl stood motionless in a bower. Torres Strait pigeons cried "you." Peaceful doves bubbled, and the chatter of red-collared lorikeets smoothed into weeping. Noisy pitas wore trails through brush, and bush thick-knees stood motionless in profile, single blue eyes staring. Apostle birds clustered in cup-shaped nests, feathers sticking out like slivers of decorative chocolate. Bills of long-tailed finches seemed the clearest orange I'd ever seen, and the blue adorning fairy wrens was so bright the sky seemed white-washed. For a few moments I forgot cages, but then a Muir's corella stared at me, cocked his head, and said, "Hello."

That night a reporter telephoned. In hiking through forests south of Perth, a group of doctors had been upset by logging. Predictably lumbermen urged the doctors to confine themselves and their words to hospitals and leave the woods to industrial experts. "What do you think?" the reporter said. "Plumbers, laundrymen, waitresses, lawyers, thieves, mechanics, even college professors should roam forests. The only people who should be banished are those carrying chainsaws and moneyed folk who pay others to carry saws for them," I said. "Good for you, Daddy," Eliza said when I put the receiver down. "That caps October," Vicki said.

Shelves

Voluna Hardaker studied librarianship at David Lipscomb College in Nashville for a year. As a result when the new library opened at Cross Keys, Voluna was appointed librarian. Voluna was a member of Malachi Ramus's Church of the Chastening Rod and as a creationist believed science undermined Christian living. At Cross Keys she catalogued books according to library morals, not library science. She scrapped the Dewey decimals, saying that evolution had corrupted the system. For the sake of the new generation, she told Tiny Ramus, Malachi's wife, she shelved books according to the sex of authors, separating those written by women from those by men. "Just think what thoughts might rise in the head of one of our precious little angels if she saw a book written by a man pressed hard against one written by a woman." "Voluna is on to something," Turlow Gutheridge told the crowd at Ankerrow's Café. "If *Childe Harold* had leaned against *Jane Eyre*, Charlotte Brontë's heroine would never have fled Thornfield."

All sorts of arrangements order living. Last Wednesday morning Vicki and I munched apple tarts at La Palm D'Or. We ate on a terrace. On steps behind us sat two green pots, moth orchids spraying out on thin flails. Blossoms hung above my head, not a single moth fluttering about them, or me. "My light has dimmed," I said to Vicki. Before strolling home I explored Collins Bookstore across the street. None of my books were on the shelves. "Whose books?" the clerk asked when I mentioned my name. "Forget books, and be satisfied with magpies," Vicki said later. At least four times a day I feed two magpies, a male who perches on the urn on our back porch and whom I have dubbed Urn Bird, and then Bird of My Bird, a fledgling female. Every morning at ten minutes after six, the birds land on the terrace and warble. As soon as I hear them, I get up and feed them scraps of bread and hunks of ground beef. Before I began feeding the fledgling, the bird was ratty and thin, no parent ever caring for it. Now the fledgling is plump. "Your baby," Vicki calls it. Occasionally raids on the breadbasket irritate Vicki. "Feeding these birds is the most important thing I'll do in Australia," I explain. For some inarticulate reason I believe the feeding important. Throughout the day I glance into the back yard to see if the magpies are there. "Don't write about the birds," Vicki said yesterday. "Readers want excitement." "Maybe," I said, "but feeding birds is what people really do."

Anonymity does not bother me. Having written fifteen non-sellers, I am beyond disappointment. In October I wrote Ansett Airlines, offering to barter writing for flights. "Thank you for your letter addressed to Ansett Airlines detailing the opportunities available to us through the sponsorship of your event," a Sponsorship Development Specialist replied seven weeks later. "Your event whilst unquestionably significant does not meet our strategic objectives or provide the wide scope of benefits we seek in being involved as a sponsor. Therefore, we will be unable to assist you with the support requested. On behalf of Ansett Australia, I wish you the best of luck." "What event did you propose?" Eliza asked at dinner. "Dad is the event," Edward said.

The mail that brought the letter from the Development Specialist also brought the table of contents for *Our Fathers,* a collection of fifteen essays written by sons describing relationships with fathers. The book contained one of my essays. The farther I am from the appointments of home and the touchstones of my history, the more prone I am to melancholy. As I looked at the contents, I suddenly missed Father and Mother. I did not have the leisure to miss them long. "Some day I will have to write about you and the magpies," Eliza said, interrupting and leaning over my right shoulder. That afternoon Edward showed me an email he'd received at school. Geoff Dorr, a friend from Storrs and a student at Carleton, wrote the email. "ed, i gotta tell u," Geoff wrote, "there's nothing like doing ur own laundry. i love the whole process . . . no one to tell u when to warsh ur clothes, u can wash them as long or as short as u like . . . mix colors together to get cool stains on white t-shirts. it just doesn't get any better than this. plus you can put in as much detergent as u want! for experiment, i dumped a can of beer plus 7 cups of detergent in . . . wanted to see if detergent overpowers beer. it doesn't really. oh, yes . . . and i was thinking maybe if i put in some shampooh it might help. who knows? and all because i get to do my own laundry."

"What do you think?" Edward said as I looked at the email. "Geoff had better take a composition course," I said, "what spelling!" "Dad, Geoff's being funny," Eliza said. "Oh," I said then added, "I received a letter from Turlow Gutheridge today. Let me read you a paragraph." "She laid the still white form alongside those that had gone ahead. No groans issued from her throat. No tears furrowed her soft cheek. For a moment she stood quietly. Suddenly, though, she leaned backwards, craned her neck toward the blue heaven, shut her eyes and let out a cry that shattered the stillness, making echoes sob through the air. The sound seemed to issue from her giblets—her very soul, heart, and liver. Twice she repeated the cry. Then she looked at the ground, turning her eyes this way and that, and all was silent once more. Tomorrow she would lay another egg." For a moment Vicki, Eliza, and Edward roosted silently on their chairs. Then Vicki said, "Steady on, Sam."

Time has changed my reading. In Australia most books I've read have been nonfiction, generally English essayists: Auberon Waugh, Raymond Mortimer, Jeanette Winterson, and my favorite Proteus, author of *The Changing Year,* published in 1983 and consisting of short descriptions of country matters. I read essays, not for technique or idea, but for common words that I rarely use on pages—prim, tang, malodorous. I collect phrases, "coffins to last a lifetime" or the description of a man who "liked meat better than any other vegetable." Occasionally I copy sentences into a commonplace book. "Many years ago," Walter De La Mare wrote, "in that once upon a time which is the memory of the imagination rather than of the workaday mind, I went walking with a friend. Of what passed before we set out I have nothing but the vaguest recollection. All I remember is that it was early morning, that we were happy to be in one another's company, that there were bright green boughs overhead amongst which the birds floated and sang." The memory of the imagination is the essayist's landscape. Morning rarely folds into dim afternoon, and instead of drying and cracking, green glistens throughout the year.

Dull books have readers, and dull days contain pleasures. While walking home from Napoleon Street, Vicki glanced at me and said, "You are showing your cakes and cappuccino." That evening I started jogging again, an activity I began early in the fall but stopped after three arthritic weeks. The second night on a sidewalk above the Swan River I almost stepped on a rat. The next evening two black shouldered kites hovered above Mosman Bluff like whirligigs. Last Saturday I accompanied Eliza and Vicki while they shopped in Claremont. Manikins in Esprit had wooden hands and jointed fingers. I started to bend fingers of a manikin into a rude gesture. "Daddy," Eliza said, jerking me away. "Playing with manikins is perverse." In the shop Eliza bought a black blouse that was too small for her and a blue jean skirt that had been scrubbed out of crispness and color. "At the Salvation Army that shirt would cost a dollar," I said. "The skirt is fashionable," Vicki said. "One hundred and nine dollars is too much to pay for fashion," I said. That afternoon two Jehovah's Witnesses came to the house. Eliza answered the door, and they gave her a small book, *Knowledge That Leads to Everlasting Life*. One hundred and ninety-one pages long, the book was a guide to "Godly Life." The book contained nineteen essays, each responding to a statement or question, among others: "What Happens To Our Dead Loved Ones?" "These Are The Last Days," "Resist Wicked Spirit Forces," and "When The Knowledge Of God Fills The Earth."

I read *Knowledge*, learning that only 144,000 people "will be resurrected to heaven." The rest of humanity "will be resurrected to a paradise on earth." "Global warming," Eliza said, "is liable to make earth hell not heaven." Never had I heard of the Nephilim, the offspring of fallen angels who satisfied "their lust for sexual relations with earthly women." Nephilim became "violent bullies." Happily they perished in the Flood. "A godly life frees us," I learned, "from the often burdensome celebration of worldly holidays." According to Luke, *Knowledge* explained, shepherds were living outside at the time of Christ's birth. In Israel late December is chilly and rainy. As a result shepherds would have kept their sheep and themselves in shelters overnight. "Actually, December 25 was set aside by the Romans as the birthday of their sun god. Centuries after Jesus was on the earth, apostate Christians adopted this date for the celebration of Christ's birth. Consequently true Christians do not celebrate Christmas or any other holiday based on false religious beliefs." "How rough the prose," I muttered, "how crude the thought." Strip music away, and the Lord of the Dance will disappear. Bits of hymns suddenly rang through my mind, first Christina Rossetti's wondrous "Love Came Down." "Love came down at Christmas, / Love all lovely, Love divine; / Love was born at Christmas / Star and angels gave the sign." I wondered if the makers of *Knowledge* had ever imagined "the first Noel" or shepherds watching "their flocks by night." Replace the manger and "little Lord Jesus asleep in the hay" with a silent night of contentious reason, then not sleep but waking hours will be dreamless.

Photographs and colored illustrations appeared throughout *Knowledge.* With Christmas damned I lost interest in words and studied pictures. In them appeared thirty-two light-skinned Caucasians; twenty blacks; six people of Korean or Chinese ancestry; eighteen people from the subcontinent; two Persians, one of these a seductress devoted to spiritualism, jewelry scaling over her, a crystal ball before her; forty-eight South Sea Islanders, thirty of these a church congregation; thirty-nine stick figures of no discernible ethnicity; and lastly seventeen Semitic people, the men bearded, long robes billowing about them, the women with their heads covered. In one illustration two women unwrapped Lazarus like children opening a Christmas present, his funeral clothes wrinkled but still white, his beard trim despite the nap. At the conclusion of the book appeared a peaceful valley, the paradise on earth which all people would inhabit except, of course, the damned and then the select who would live in heaven itself. Behind the valley stretched a blue fence of mountains. Along the left front of the drawing, fifteen stalks of gladiola bloomed in a rainbow of color, pink, yellow, orange, purple, and pale blue. A stag posed atop a knoll. A doe and a lioness drank from a stream. Two cattle grazed a yellow field. At the foot of a terraced slope men raised a hall. Behind the gladiolas a woman knelt amid ranunculus, her right arm lifted, her hand extending a pink flower to a man holding a hoe. To the woman's left a mother showed her son a squash. At the edge of the illustration, father appeared, a happy man pushing a wheelbarrow overflowing with fruits and vegetables: watermelon, green and purple grapes, corn, lettuce, cauliflower, apples, eggplant, potatoes, green peppers, peas, cantaloupes, cucumbers, lettuce, and artichokes.

Two days later politics lured me from the peaceful valley. At eight in the morning I drove to the Melbourne Hotel to watch the results of the American presidential election. The Consulate General in Perth invited resident Americans and interested Australians for morning coffee. Atop bagels stuffed with cream cheese and smoked salmon, small American flags waved from toothpicks. Doughnuts lay across a table, some of the doughnuts iced red, others blue, the remainder white. An apostate oilman repeated the Businessman's Prayer. "Our Industry, which art in national parks, hallowed be our stock options, our dividends come, Standard and Poor's be done, in domestic markets as well as abroad. Give us tax relief. Forgive our pollutions as we forgive those whom we bribe. Lead us not into litigation, but deliver us from the Greens. For ours is the White House, the Senate, and House of Representatives, now until global warming fries the world. Amen." Another man tried to persuade me Bush was a better candidate than Gore. Eventually I said, "You are right, and I am wrong, as I suspect you generally are." "What?" the man said.

At noon I left the Melbourne. "The Republicans are coming; the Republicans are coming," Eliza said at dinner that night, adding, "how could so many people vote for George Bush?" "Lots of folks don't think like we do," I said, "but then I don't know why. Maybe Jehovah's Witnesses are right. 'These Are The Last Days.'" "Still," I continued, "Turlow Gutheridge wrote me from Carthage. Because Hink Ruunt's wife Almeda died in Clarksville, people were confused about the date of her death. When Hink returned to Carthage, Googoo Hooberry asked him when Almeda died. 'Well, Googoo,' Hink said, rubbing his brow, 'if the Lord had blessed Almeda and she had lived until tomorrow, she'd have been dead two weeks.'" "Holy cow," Vicki said. "At Dad's age," Edward said, "the fast lane is slow."

Solvitur ambulando, as the Latin advises, "it is solved by walking." Walking distracts me from the momentary. In the presence of bird and tree, I forget politics. The next morning Vicki and I explored Bold Park, 440 hectares of bush, just east of City Beach. A series of trails—Zamia, Possum, Hovea, Thornbill, Sheoak, Banksia, and Camel Lake—twisted through shrub land and dune, limestone bearded with heath, and eucalyptus and peppermint woods. Four and a half kilometers long, Zamia was the longest trail. For two mornings Vicki and I wandered the park. From the summit of Reabold Hill, we watched freighters breast the Indian Ocean. Banksia bloomed through the bush, slender, yellow; bull, cones thick enough to plug ironstone jars; and Ashby's, spikes cool and orange, six inches tall and three and a half in diameter. Fruits on rose banksia looked like pine cones, scales warped and swollen. On dried cones of firewood banksia follicles gapped toothless. Instead of growing straight most banksia staggered, trunks proud with lumps. Leaves swung from branches in fists, and mallets of witch's broom bent limbs into scythes. Mists of bees swarmed around grass trees, and Fremantle mallee blossomed. On the same limbs as the flowers, brown nuts turned around each other in sludgy clusters like rusty bearings. Beside paths zamia shattered into sharp fronds, and fingers of chenille honey myrtle thickened into flowers, sometimes nine or more rubbing uxoriously against

SAM PICKERING

each other. Bush flies clung to my face in pads, probing my eyes for water, forcing me to wear wrap-around sunglasses. Painted ladies had just hatched, and the butterflies spun across gravel. Hare's tail grass grew beside low paths, its inflorescences cottony, minute orange hairs sticking out. Wild oats bristled, and perennial veld grass spread through the park in thick blankets, smothering native plants, its fibrous inflorescences shredding into seed.

Although spring was browning, blossoms lingered on stink-wood. Pigface, buttercups, and evening primrose were yellow. In dusty clumps leschenaultia linarioides flowered, pods of red pressed together like hands in prayer above pale yellow petals looking like surplices. Pixie mops unraveled into threads. Unlike the threads the styles glowed, green brushes topping swollen red disks. Rainbow lorikeets crinkled tinny through the scrub. Ring-necked parrots tore seed from rose pelagonia. A flock of white-cheeked honeyeaters foraged one-sided bottlebrush. A silver eye winked amid banksia, and a rufous whistler sang from a marri. A kookaburra snapped its head, breaking the back of a centipede in its bill. Two little corellas stared from a cavity in a dead tuart. Blue swirled beneath the birds' eyes, making the birds look weary. Honey bees colonized another tuart. Honey bees drive Australian bees away and by preventing pollination may contribute to the decline of native plants. In grass near Camel Lake the shell of an oblong snake-necked turtle resembled a large keyhole. In lowlands near the Old Turf Farm, a tiger snake slid under a log.

Throughout the walk we caught bobtails or shingle-backed lizards. The lizards' heads were shaped like arrows, and they stored fat in their nobby tails. Ticks burrowed into their hides and swelled as big as granola. I plucked clusters from the lizards. I also fed the lizards hunks of apple. I held the apple in front of their jaws, and when one lunged at my fingers, I slipped the apple under its tongue. One lizard enjoyed apple so much that it opened its mouth and stopped striking. Shingle-backs give birth once a year. Young are born alive, usually two at each birth. I was tempted to bring a small lizard home. "What a naturalist you are," Vicki said. "You talk about preserving habitat; yet, you want to keep a bobtail as a pet." Before returning home Vicki and I strolled around Perry Lakes. A grey butcher-bird rattled above us. A great egret and a white-faced heron stalked shallows. A rufous night-heron moved like a mime, two long white plumes sweeping down his back. Sacred and straw-necked ibis plodded muddy inlets. A dusky moorhen begged for a handout, and mallards, coots, and mountain ducks drifted over the ponds, occasionally filching food from bottoms.

The next day I roamed the university. Nine rainbow lorikeets spun about a limb on a weeping fig. Canary island date palms were so big they seemed wise. As I stared at the palms, a professor of Hebrew interrupted me. Old and from Sydney, he needed to use a lavatory. I unlocked the humanities building for him. On coming out of the building, I noticed orange combs on silky oaks. Blossoms on pincushion plants created their own halos. I walked slowly, rubbing my palm across pleats of bark on cork oak. A ring-tailed parrot gnawed a marri nut. Red blossoms on oleander sank darkly into themselves. On getting into my car I noticed that someone had bashed my right front fender. "Backed into the car and didn't leave a note," Vicki said. "Aren't you furious?" "Not really," I said. "Look at this pod from a jacaranda." Gold as honey, sides beveled, the pod resembled a change purse, two and a half by two and a quarter inches. When I turned the pod over in my hand, color seeped and flowed, the honey browning then lightening into peach and apricot.

Emptiness

"An empty chapel," Alexander Smith wrote, "is impressive; a crowded one, comparatively a commonplace affair." A fortnight ago I found Smith's collection of essays *Dreamthorp* in the university library. In idle moments I explore libraries, plucking old books from shelves. I'd never heard of Smith, and I borrowed *Dreamthorp* because no one had checked the book out since 1911. Oddments lurk in neglected books. Between pages fifty-eight and fifty-nine of *Dreamthorp* lay a bookmark, a newspaper clipping six inches long and two and a quarter wide. Acid leached from the clipping staining the inner halves of pages fifty-eight and fifty-nine brown. Printed on one side of the clipping was a letter to an editor, discussing the poetry of Ernest Dowson. Dowson was an English aesthete who wrote at the beginning of the twentieth century. The writer of the letter condemned Dowson as "weak, and mentally and spiritually anaemic." Nevertheless the correspondent admired Dowson's poem "Vesperal," a copy of which followed the letter. All four of the poem's stanzas ended with the line, "Sufficient for the day are the day's evil things."

More interesting to a family man was the list of amusements appearing on the reverse of the letter. On Sunday, February 12, 1911, Ernest Marklew lectured twice at the Bradford Labour Church on Peckover Street, initially at three in the afternoon, then at 6:30 in the evening. Also on Sunday at 6:30, this time the date's being given as February 11, Hilaire Belloc was scheduled to give a

"Limelight Lecture" at the Metropole Theatre. One of the Glasgow Clarion Scouts Winter Lectures, Belloc's talk was entitled "The Nation's Wealth." Reserved seats cost six cents. "Admission to other parts by silver collection." While on Friday at 8:15 in "Rooms" at the Farnworth I.L.P. and Labour Church, Mr. Parry Gunn was going to discuss "The Art of Oscar Wilde," at 6:30 on Saturday, M. J. Toole of Salford would be lecturing on "Present-day Atrocities." "Eliza," I said that evening, "the last time this book was read was 1911 and in Scotland, not Australia." "Inspector Morse dies tonight," Eliza said referring to a television program. "Now that you are a detective, you could replace him."

I liked Smith's essays. "We do not love a man," he wrote in "On Vagabonds," "for his respectability, his prudence and foresight in business, his capacity for living within his income or his balance at his banker's." "The things that really move liking in human beings are the gnarled nodosities of character, vagrant humours, freaks of generosity, some little unextinguishable spark of the aboriginal savage, some sweet savour of the old Adam." "Yes," I thought, "barky characters attract us." The next day I returned to the library and read about Smith's life. Born in Scotland in 1830, Smith was the son of a lace pattern designer. Despite being apprenticed to his father's trade, he became a poet. In 1853 his first book of verse appeared. On the basis of the one hundred pounds the book earned, Smith set off for London. His next two poetry collections were not so successful. *Dreamthorp* was published in 1863. In 1866 two novels appeared. The next year Smith died from typhoid. Biographical commonplace served the man poorly who wrote, "If you wish to make a man look noble, your best course is to kill him." I returned to the essays. In pencil on the title page, an owner of *Dreamthorp* listed writings by Smith, five essays and a poem in the *Argosy* and three poems in *Good Words*. On a whim I busied myself with the handwriting. The writer began capital *E* to the left of the letter, eventually loping right and forming an oval at the top of the letter. Unlike small *e*, which he always linked to the letter that followed, capital *E* stood alone. Likewise the second *s* in a pair of s's never joined the next letter. Thus the owner of the book wrote, "An ess ay on an Old Subject" and "An E ss ay on Sidney Dobell."

Alexander Strahan published *Dreamthorp,* and sixteen pages advertising Strahan's list followed the essays. "Now ready" was "The Fourteenth Thousand" of the "Popular Edition" of *The Recreations of a Country Parson.* While the third chapter of the *Recreations* was entitled "Concerning Two Blisters of Humanity: Being Thoughts of Petty Malignity and Petty Trickery," chapter 7 was "How I Mused in the Railway Train: Being Thoughts on Rising by Candlelight, on Nervous Fears, and on Vapouring." Just printed was the "Fifty-fifth Thousand of *The Pathway of Promise; or, Words of Comfort to the Christian Pilgrim.*" Nineteen chapters guided the pilgrim's wanderings, including, among others, "Preparations for the Journey," "The Bow in the Cloud," "Carefulness," and lastly "Rest." "One of the most fascinating books we have ever seen for the rising youth of the fair sex," a writer in the *Eclectic Review* wrote, praising Sarah Tyler's *Papers for Thoughtful Girls.* The *Morning Herald* agreed, declaring the *Papers* to be "one of the most charming books of its class that we have ever read. It is even superior to Miss Mullock's well-known work, 'A Woman's Thoughts about Women.'"

For the essayist empty is often full. Life thrives in hedgerows and along fences, and coveys of sentences hunker amid brambles. What strikes the corporate as unproductive grows crops of verbs and nouns no matter the season. "Plenty of people live on the other side of the hill," as the old saying puts it. "What does that mean?" Eliza asked. "A great deal," I said, picking up *Dreamthorp.* "When the writer expresses his thought, it is immediately dead to him, however life-giving it may be to others." I spent the following three days seining the manuscript of my next book for errors. "A snapshot of Vicki, the children, and I," I had written, "appeared on this year's Christmas card." After changing *I* to *me,* I boxed the manuscript and mailed it to the United States. Aside from the weeding I enjoyed the book. "I've felled another word lot," I said, "and shrunk the green future." "Don't be silly," Vicki said; "writers are their own echoes."

"Yes," I answered, adding, "fair stands the page for Carthage." On arriving in Carthage I read the *Courier,* the weekly newspaper. In the upper left corner of the front page was the logo of the paper, a globe, an *N* resting atop the Arctic, an *S* beneath Antarctica, to the left on the Pacific Rim an *E,* and to the right in mid-Atlantic a *W.* Read from the top, counterclockwise to the left then across the equator to the right and finally to the bottom of the globe, the letters spelled *NEWS.* "From the four corners of the globe," Levi Crowell, the editor said, "but still from Carthage." "A serious young man," a notice in the classifieds stated, "who wishes to retire from the world and live in some convenient spot near water is willing to engage with any large farmer who is desirous of having a hermit on his land. Will bring bible and can milk." Among the death notices was the obituary of Acamech Wedderburn. "The spinster Acamech Wedderburn," the notice stated, "age eighty-three, weight 172 pounds, height five feet, six inches, eighteen and three-quarter inches across the shoulder blades, shoe size seven wide, and nineteen teeth still in her mouth." Acamech lived in the hills outside Carthage with her bachelor brother, Abesasum, a cacographic archaeologist who adorned speech with bony old words, calling squirrels, nest dreys; bats, rattlemice; and mushrooms, mushrumps. In Abesasum's speech tipplers wroxled, not staggered. Colors that flashed before the eyes of sick people were flickets. Instead of cankered wood was snail-shelley.

Hollis Hunnewell's "Players" just completed a run in Carthage, staging *The Comedy of Nero, The Life and Death of Habbie Simpson,* and on the last night *Hamlet. Hamlet* was a great success. At the end of the performance, the crowd gave the players a standing ovation, Hink Ruunt clapping louder than anyone else and shouting, "Author, author." According to Turlow Gutheridge spirits boosted Hink's enthusiasm. Earlier in the evening, Hink told the dinner crowd at Ankerrow's Café, a rattlesnake attacked him. A human hand grew out of the top of the snake's head. "I thought I was a goner when the snake struck," Hink recounted. "But instead of biting me the snake ducked its head, and the hand seized me by the throat." The grip was so strong that the snake pulled itself off

SAM PICKERING

the ground and swinging its body back and forth lashed Hink across the shoulders. The beating shredded his shirt, and the rattles bruised Hink's right cheek. Despite the explanation most people in Ankerrow's attributed Hink's battered appearance to poisonous alcohol not snake venom.

As usual theological doings caused a ruckus, the preachers in town, as Turlow put it, "pulling in opposite directions despite being joined like Sampson's foxes tail to tail." In October Malachi Ramus, pastor of the Church of the Chastening Rod, compiled a songbook, *Sweet Tunes of Israel High Above the Cumberland.* "My God," Loppie Groat said on thumbing the book, "there ain't nothing like this in Shakespeare, Wesley, or even the Episcopal Hymnal." Many songs were memorable, the fourth hymn beginning: "What is now to the children the dearest thing here? / To be the lamb's lambkins and chickens most dear. / Such lambkins are nourished with food which is best. / Such chickens sit safely and warm in the nest."

Blunt observation is usually sharp. "Malachi," Slubey Garts said after perusing the *Tunes,* "resembles the poet who hung himself on a line." The remark reached Malachi. That Sunday he delivered a sermon entitled "The Spiritual Nursery Weaned." "Evil people," he warned, "creep on all-fours, cackling, formic acid dripping from their beaks, poxing beauty like the red marks left on litmus paper by the feet of ants." "How can you lard pages with such lies?" Vicki said after I described the *Tunes.* "Readers won't believe anything you write." "Yes," I said, "my essays will make people distrust nonfiction. One of the greatest dangers to peace is that mobs believe historical events actually happened."

"A man's books," Smith wrote, "may impoverish his life." My head is musty with rhyme. "Blamed be the man," I thought, "that first invented ink, / And made it easier to write than think." On returning from Carthage I foreswore scribbling. That afternoon Vicki and I went to the Fremantle Festival. Tents circled the Esplanade Reserve, smoke rising from them and people milling about purchasing food. Most dishes originated on the subcontinent. I grazed, some names sticking to memory, Bombay chaat and Bengali gazaar halva. I bolted green pancakes swollen with coconut. I ate a platter of chick peas and potatoes awash in yogurt and mango sauce. Later Vicki and I stood in shadows along Essex Lane and watched the parade. The day was hot, and we crushed mandarins and drank the juice. Scores of children pedaled past on tricycles, ribbons streaming from handlebars. Sikhs danced, and Portuguese sang. A naked man pranced by, body painted blue, private parts horned into a yellow wooden shoe. Six women strolled along, stovepipes atop their heads. Four men pulled a papier-mâché giantess. Chains jangled from her nipples, and from her ribcage six arms spread like claws. Sambanistas drummed up the street, their costumes mélanges of attic, African plain, and Middle Earth. Driving home on Stirling Highway, I passed a red Rolls-Royce. In Connecticut I rarely notice the supercharged world of high-horsepower consumption. Aside from literary reputation I covet little in Storrs. Affluence is conspicuous in Perth, and here I occasionally hanker for the swanky.

As Smith thought writing stained "the inner man with ink," so living off the cusp of Peppermint Grove has drenched vision with wealth. The year won't stain me, however. Story always blocks the spread of envy. For a decade Scutt Measor tried unsuccessfully to join First Presbyterian Church in Nashville. Finally Scutt asked the Lord for help. The Lord heard Scutt's prayer and answered, saying, "I'm afraid I can't help you much. I've been trying to join that church for thirty years. Each time I apply, the congregation turns me down." Peppermint Grove and trendier parts of Mosman Park perch on limestone above Freshwater and Mosman Bay. "Wealth, height, and health," my friend Nigel said, "have long been a ménage à trois. As wordsmiths put it, 'only sickly valleytudinarians inhabit malarial bottoms.'"

During empty hours Vicki and I meandered the neighborhood. From "The Bank," a formidable brickyard at the corner of Johnson and View, we strolled down to the Esplanade. Along the Esplanade houses loomed, architectures thumping cacophonously together: Burma Road, Casino, and Hacienda. "House and land ought to blend harmoniously," Vicki said. "Homes in Peppermint

Grove should be built out of limestone. Rising like shoulders of earth, they wouldn't jar and call attention to owners' wretched tastes." After dismantling a mall of houses, we sipped coffee at Cappuccino on the River and watched poplar leaves twirl in the breeze. Nearby blossoms transformed a Norfolk Island hibiscus into a crazy quilt of pink.

Flowers lance criticism. Throughout Peppermint Grove gardenias bloomed in hedges, and blossoms circled magnolias, turning trees into lazy Susans. Honeysuckle hung slack from the tops of walls, and petals dropped from jacaranda and sliding to the ground, rippled into purple pools. An illawarra flame tree burned bright as the northern lights. Blue buds rolled over agapanthus in balls, and Italian cypress glowed chartreuse. Across walls hollyhock stared bloodshot. Weeping birch, sweet gum, and plane trees veiled houses in green. Aside from magpies, ravens, and doves, birds that thrive around humans, few birds appeared in yards. Some honeyeaters and wattlebirds foraged through grevillea planted at the edges of yards. Rainbow lorikeets bustled tinny high in eucalyptus, and galahs perched on thick limbs. Still I had to crane and peer to find birds. Most garden plants were not indigenous, and birds that had evolved to pollinate indigenous plants inhabited the bush not gardens. Except for cabbage whites no butterflies drifted through the air. Gardens resembled mantles decorated with Spode, Meissen, and Staffordshire—lovely with knickknacks, collectables for the eye. One garden reminded me of an eighteenth-century Worcester pot. Medallions of gilded decorations glittered atop blue scale, brush strokes of parrots and mélanges of peacocks and pheasants. Tails swished green and purple, and from the heads topknots fell in streams of red and yellow. In my mind I set the pot on a sideboard. No one is consistent, however. Despite regretting the absence of native birds, I enjoyed the painted enclosures.

On November 26, Vicki, Eliza, Edward, and I attended Fair Dinkum Fair, a fund-raiser at St. Hilda's. Crowds roamed the school. Maybe Smith was wrong about emptiness; only the unobserved is commonplace. "Last night, my cousin John," Nigel remarked on meeting me, "said he thought he was an agnostic but knew he was an Anglican." The campus was a souk, small stalls turning open space into courtyards: Beads Bazaar, The Beauty Parlour, Santa's House, The Looking Glass, Astrology Charting, Quilters Corner, Designer Cards, Fabulous Flowers, Kindly Cookies, Candy Carousel, and the Fracture Clinic. For two dollars at this last stall, children could have casts attached to their wrists. Before I noticed the stall, I'd seen four children with what I assumed were broken arms. "The danger of skateboarding," I concluded, fancying myself a detective.

Lucky jars cost $3, and Devonshire teas, $2.50. I bought a mystery envelope for $5 and won a certificate redeemable for $50 worth of schoolbooks at Woolridges. At the silent auction parents bid on prints, arrangements of dried flowers, and, among other things, "A Luxurious Full Body Massage and Hydrotherapy Tub with Black Mud" donated by Escape in Claremont. By afternoon four people had bid on the massage, only signing their first names. June bid $21; Cathy, $27; Michelle, $30, and finally Fern, $35. A flock of several thousand yellow plastic ducks bobbed in the school swimming pool. Printed on the bottom of each duck was a number. At the conclusion of the fair, the person whose duck was pulled from the water won $5,000. I purchased Duck 0427 for $5. I did not win. I spent three hours at the fair. "If you wander away again," I heard an exasperated father tell his small son, "you will have to find your way home. And how will you do that?" Some families avoided mishap by using cell phones. "We are at the top of the steps looking at the Oval," a man near the gymnasium said to his wife. "Can you see us?" On the Oval people could ride motorcycles, a merry-go-round, donkeys, camels, these at $3 a ride, and a bucking machine called the Mad Cow. They could paint plaster plates or throw balls at coconuts, china, and a parent sitting in a dunking machine.

A menagerie filled a courtyard. Baa-Baa-Rella's Sheep Escort Agency supplied a barnyard: fourteen geese, two goslings, four emu chicks, two deer, a rock wallaby, a fox, six sheep, four goats, sundry ducks and ducklings, two hens and nine baby chicks, two

SAM PICKERING

sheepdogs, six kittens, and a litter of sheepdog puppies, eyes still closed. While one of the dogs circled the courtyard herding animals, a goat nibbled rose bushes into twigs. A boy in a yellow shirt dumped a duckling into an enclosure containing a white Wyandotte and her chicks. Immediately the hen tried to wring the duckling's neck. Another boy saw the attack and grabbing another duckling dropped him into the enclosure. A rabbit nipped the index finger of a girl wearing a blue playsuit. The girl shrieked and dropped the rabbit. To calm her daughter, the girl's mother handed her a puppy.

For two hours Eliza worked, minding children whose mothers manned stalls. For lunch I ate potato salad and a mutton roll made from Toodyay Valley lamb. From the Hop and Grape Bar, I bought a Carlton beer. Later I bought a slice of chocolate cake, the meal costing me $10.50. For $200 I could have purchased a case of wine. I declined. At the Fair the family spent $126.70. In the Second-Hand Store Eliza purchased a necklace, blouse, belt, and four shirts for $5.50. For $22, Vicki bought ten cupcakes, a carrot cake, and two chocolate cakes. Eight bottles of condiments cost $24: pear and ginger jam, nectarine chutney, apricot jam, strawberry sauce, cumquat marmalade, peach chutney, plum jam, and Seville orange and coriander seed marmalade. For Vicki I bought Elspeth's Huxley's *The Mottled Lizard*, the sequel to *The Flame Trees of Thika*, a book Vicki read the last time we were in Australia. A garland for Eliza's hair cost $2.50; a tea towel, a cartoon depicting the fair printed in blue upon it, $5; and a Christmas fruitcake, $20, reduced at day's end from $25. The fair tired me. That night at home I read the hymnal used at St. Hilda's, *Together in Song: Australian Hymn Book II*. The anthology was superior to that compiled by Malachi Ramus. "God moves in a mysterious way," William Cowper wrote, "His wonders to perform; / He plants his footsteps in the sea, / And rides upon the storm." Even an empty life is too busy for pondering mysterious ways. The best I could do was savor poetry.

Controversy about the presidential election in the United States filled a pew of time. "Republicans," my friend Josh wrote from

Connecticut, "view democracy as an impediment to grasping. They hide lust for power behind piety." "The presidency resembles the top of a pyramid, accessible only by eagles and reptiles. Never has George Bush been thought a high-flyer." On December 3 in Greenmont I presented prizes for short fiction to winners of the Katharine Susannah Pritchard competition. Before doling out checks I described my most recent accolade. Two years ago my friend Jay Parini telephoned. "Sam," he said, "I read in a magazine that you won the Redbud Prize for writing." No one had told me about the prize. "What's that?" I said. "I don't know," Jay said, "but the notice said you will receive a plaque and cash. Who knows how much?" After talking to Jay I discovered the prize on the Internet. That evening I wrote *Redbud* magazine and inquired about the prize. When I did not receive an answer after six weeks, I called the magazine, reaching a telephone tree in Michigan. The trunk split into four branches, the first, the Redbud Bed and Breakfast, the second, the Bud and Bloom Gardening Center, and the third Petals, a bookstore selling used books. The last branch was the magazine. "If you are calling about a submission to *Redbud*," a recording stated; "we are not taking calls. We are several hundred submissions behind in reading. Feel free to submit your article elsewhere." That was the closest I got to the prize.

The following week I spent three mornings in Fremantle attending a conference celebrating the work of Australia's leading environmentalist, George Seddon. George has held chairs in four subjects: English, geology, environmental science, and history and philosophy of science. Never had he frittered time away celebrating emptiness. After breakfast each morning I rode the train from Mosman Park to Fremantle. At the dock a freighter rode black and low in the water, seven layers of animal paddocks stacked on the deck, one paddock atop another hot as bricks. "Bound for Saudi Arabia," a man sitting next to me said. "I wonder how many sheep die on the way—not that it makes much difference except to sharks. Once the sheep disembark their throats will be cut." In Australia sheep farmers are called pastoralists. "Agribusiness," the man continued, "has nothing in common with the pastoral, its green fields, kindly shepherds, and ditties lilting through the air." Religion demanded that the sheep endure the harsh voyage across the Indian Ocean and be slaughtered by the faithful, rather than by infidels in Australia. "Only God can save a person from the superstitions of believers," the man said, as the train left the freighter behind.

Eight times during the past month, I took Eliza to Life Care Physiotherapy at Challenger Stadium. She injured her right foot running. A bone on the bottom of her foot slipped out of a groove in a tendon. I waited while the therapist manipulated Eliza's foot. Magazines in the lobby were terrible. Bare-chested lads appeared on the covers of six consecutive issues of *Men's Health*. "The editor has a tit fixation," a woman said. On eight other occasions I drove Eliza to the stadium so she could swim in the pool. When not driving Eliza, I urged Edward to complete his college applications. "Those who refused to be ruled by the rudder will be ruled by the rock," I said. I proofread Edward's essays and made suggestions for improvement. He didn't thank me. "Kittens," Vicki said, "don't bring mice to cats."

People who meander hedgerows wrote me. "Reading Milton is like dining off gold plate in a company of kings," Smith wrote, "very splendid, very ceremonious, and not a little appalling." Several correspondents sent poems, none Miltonic, most nosegays weedy with life. "Thought these lines might perk up the outback," my librarian friend wrote from Kentucky. Enclosed in the letter were excerpts from Mary Mackey's *Scraps of Nature* published in London in 1810. Mackey's husband died when she was forty-five years old, leaving her a small annuity which she sold to underwrite the *Scraps*. Albeit not profitable the verse was memorable. "I never learned to write or spell, / Although I read and write so well," she stated mysteriously. In the preface to her book, she provided a biographical sketch, calling herself "Nature." "The husband of poor Nature," she recounted, "was a gentleman and an honest man, made a fortune and spent it nearly, in which his wife had no share, for that he governed and ruled the roost is well known to many: he had a noble and generous soul, but always kept poor

Nature's talents under a bushel, where they shall never go again. He was old enough to be her father, and ever treated her like a child."

When Nature overturned the basket, her talent stumbled. In one scrap she compared herself to a pony. "For since she has been free by the death of her / Late owner, the poor thing has been a scamperer, / And often has known the want of a good meal; / For she was highly fed in her old master's lifetime. / But he, alas! Sleeps in peace, and peace be to his soul. / He was a good master and a real gentleman, / And left his little trotter to a merciless world: / She is gentle by Nature; but the poor thing's heart / Is now breaking, yet by kind treatment she might / Be made one of the most valuable and amusing / Things in Nature. She is a little foundered, but not to hurt / Or retard her movements; she is of some mettle and / High spirit, notwithstanding her hard fate, / She will even kick if roughly handled / Nor would she suffer a dirty hand to touch her."

"That is the worst poetry I've ever read," Eliza said. "Terrible but wonderfully memorable," I said. In an empty chapel one slips the crowd. Yesterday I studied Smith's *Poems*, the fourth edition published in London in 1856. A bookplate pasted to the front cover noted that Mrs. W. Fawcett presented the book to the university. On the opposite page H. A. Odell wrote his name and the date, August 5, 1863. On the title page H. B. Jackson wrote his name in ink. Stamped on the title page was an oval, an inch tall and one and three-quarters inches wide. Circling the oval was "W. C. Rigby * 64 King William St. Adelaide." In the center of the oval were the words "Bookseller, Stationer, and Newsagent."

Summer

The last week in November school ended, and summer vacation began. In the United States Edward would have spent summer in Maine working at a boys' camp. Eliza would have attended summer school, perhaps studying a language, Russian being the choice of the moment. In Perth hours swung about us like horse collars. Edward shut the door to his room and read. At six every morning Eliza left the house and ran for forty minutes. Afterward she closed her door and played the keyboard. Despite living in a city throbbing with event, the children did not muster imagination enough to leave the house. Even worse, none of my suggestions appealed to them, spending days in Fremantle or exploring the Darling Scarp. If a sign of greatness is the capacity to forget, then I became petty, the children's lack of enthusiasm a barb tearing hours into irritation. To purge bile, I ran. The exercise failed. I am fifty-nine, and my abdomen resembles a washboard, not one rippling with muscles but one warped into a bow. Instead of running I shuffled, my head bent toward the ground. Still nothing is endlessly bleak. One afternoon I found five cents in the left lane of Wellington Avenue. Generally, however, I collected discouraging encouragement. "You can make it, old fellow," a man shouted one morning just after I began jogging.

Some afternoons I carted Edward and Eliza to Cottesloe Beach. Years have eroded my enthusiasm for body-surfing, and the waves made me feel fragile as bone china. Rarely did the beach cheer me.

The population of Perth is so young that older people feel out of place. As a result plastic surgeons thrive as the aging try to hide furrows dug by Time. Once Time has blown topsoil away, though, youth fades. One afternoon at Cottesloe a young woman frolicked bare-chested. For a moment the sight invigorated me, but then I noticed a man my age hunched in the sand, resembling a cooking pot turned upside down. Warily the man cranked his head up. From the batter around his middle, he extended arms thin as tongs. In his hands he held a camera. Surreptitiously he snapped a picture of the girl, then smirking rolled his head back down and hid the camera beneath folds of a red and blue towel, the colors the same as those on the towel in my backpack.

The next day was Friday, and Vicki, the children, and I went to the Fremantle Market. Vicki bought beans, apricots, and carrots. For $2.50, I purchased two pounds of peaches. "Don't buy them," Vicki advised; "they'll be woody." Vick was right; the peaches resembled pressed wood. After shopping we ate fish and chips. Watching people entertained Vicki and me. The children were bored, however, so we bolted the meal and wandered the town. I found the local Target store. "A triumph," Vicki exclaimed. "What?" Edward said. Vicki suggested coffee and cake at a sidewalk café. "A great idea," I said. "Eliza and I will go to a bookstore while you eat," Edward said. "No," Eliza said, "my stomach hurts. Let's go home." Eliza refused to eat fish and chips, so Vicki bought her lentil balls. Alas, the balls had begun to roll.

To push the children out of mind, I checked Anthony Trollope's novel *He Knew He Was Right* out of the university library. As my life slows, my reading has sped up, and the distraction lasted only two nights. Next I sampled television. Every night SBS shows an artsy movie, usually a film from Central Europe, the Iberian Peninsula, or sometimes from Latin America. Reviews in the newspaper make the films intriguing. "A charming unpretentious wry adventure," an advertisement typically says, "sweet with vignettes of life as it is lived and delightful, sometimes wistful, peregrinations. A man loses his orange galoshes and goes a-searching, until, lo, he finds them in a rose garden, worn in places and patched, but still good enough to make him whistle and skip through sunshine and rain." The discrepancy between advertisement and arty reality is vast. When I switched on the movie, the galoshes were not in sight. Instead a dozen naked people greeted me. Tossing about like the ingredients of a salad, they were up to something, heads shaking like broccoli; their toes, okra; here and there doodads wavering, radishes and seedy slices of tomato, the dressing imported, too exotic for my taste.

Four to six times a day I fed Urn Bird and Bird of My Bird. They stood on the terrace and yodeled. "They whistle, and you trot like a puppy," Vicki said. "How long is this going to continue?" I did not answer. The temperature was ninety-four degrees Fahrenheit, too hot to forge declaratives about ground beef and stale bread. Still backyards nourish more than birds. They help people escape themselves. If a person notices magpies, then days become enjoyable. "Daddy," Eliza said, interrupting the flutter of thought, "do you know why the giraffe has a long neck?" "No," I said. "The giraffe's head is so far from its body that if the two are going to be connected, the animal has to have a long neck."

Birds and corny jokes won't cure pinkeye, but they can soothe viruses that numb genial spirits. Crumbs satisfy me. Recently an editor sent me a book of poetry. "This is the author's second volume of posthumous verse," the editor wrote. "I like it better than the first. The lines are muscular and alive. With each book he grows stronger." Yesterday I received a letter from Turlow Gutheridge. He enclosed an advertisement from the *Courier*. "Gout, Catarrh, Unseemly Odors?" the ad began. "Well, you don't have to worry any longer. Visit Obadiah Flant's Gospital in sunny Maggart, Tennessee, and let the Lord work for YOU. For only $5.00 a day, we use the healing power of the Good Book to turn your ailment into a Pillar of Salt. So the next time you are sick, don't be hospitalized. BE GOSPITALIZED!"

Teenagers have heartier appetites than adults. Tidbits that satisfy me leave them ravenous, so I manufactured entertainment. One Saturday during vacation I drove to Perth Oval. Perth's professional soccer team the Glory played Newcastle United. The previous week a small crowd watched the Glory. On this occasion 11,386 people crowded the Oval. By the time we arrived all seats had been taken, and we stood at the north end of the field. We left at the half, Perth ahead four to nothing and Vicki's legs aching. The following Saturday we went to the races at Ascot. Vicki packed the Eski with sandwiches, soft drinks, apples, celery stalks, and carrots. We sat in the grandstand and watched seven races, the eighth being cancelled because of a spill that sent six jockeys to the hospital and broke a horse's neck, the second horse destroyed during the afternoon.

Signs hung on the railing facing the grandstand, advertising Myer, a department store, Mercedes-Benz, Qantas, Burswood Casino, Channel Nine, and Curtin Radio, 927 AM. Under a pavilion to the right of the grandstand bookies set up tables: James St. John, Russ Cooper, B. J. Page, among others, taking bets not only on races in Perth but on those in Melbourne, Sydney, Adelaide, Mt. Barker, and Toowoomba. Punters were middle-aged men, their figures shaky with cellulite, their pocketbooks, however, sinewy with hundred dollar bills. Scattered about the grounds were smaller pavilions serving food and drink, most people drinking beer, not spirits. Beyond the pavilion stood a half-circle of stalls, horses in them waiting to be called to the track. A woman in an orange dress and pink hat stroked the neck of Classic Lady. I bet $2 on Classic Lady to win and lost.

Vicki, the children, and I each bet $2 every race, thus wagering $56 during the afternoon. By day's end we had lost $14.40. While Eliza always picked horses to place, I bet only on winners. We chose horses named Double Blue, Highwood, Ballet Girl, Magic Edge, Lottila Bay, and Done with Mirrors. Edward enjoyed the best afternoon, his picks finishing 1, 3, 2, 8, 1, 12, and 2. Old Comrade, Eliza's choice, won the afternoon's big race, the Fruit 'n' Vegetable Stakes, collecting a trophy and $202,600. Because she picked Old Comrade to place, however, Eliza only won $3.20. Old Comrade was Eliza's best pick. Her other selections finished 16, 15, 14, and 8, with two of her picks failing to finish. Two of my selections won, one paying $9.40, the other, $6.20.

Petunias and calla lilies bloomed in the warm-up ring. Before each race we milled about the rail surrounding the mounting area. Horses looked like long barrels, and jockeys' silks shimmered neon in the sunlight. In contrast jockeys' faces sank into creases. "What a nice day," a jockey in orange and green said to an outrider. Occasionally an announcer spoke over the public address system. "Allison Lynderwood," he once said, "your little son Tommy is in the Administration Office, and he is very upset." Around the railing women held stems of champagne and wore hats topped with flowers, daisies being most popular. Above the grandstand behind the seats was an air-conditioned room in which punters ate lunch and placed bets. Old women congregated around tables. Make-up basted their faces, and flowers sprouted from hatbands. In front of them stretched narrow boxes, betting cards slotted in categories: Win, Place, Double, Trifecta, and Quenella. Each card measured two and five-eighths inches by three and a quarter inches. Five columns divided the front. Under "Meeting" I shaded in an oval beneath *P*, standing for Perth. Under "Race" I shaded the number of the race, say, 3 for the third race, and under "Selection," the horse's number. Under "Win" and "Place" a bettor could choose between several bets, one-, two-, three-, four-, five-, ten-, twenty-, and one-hundred-dollar bets, plus multiples of both ten dollars and a hundred dollars. Once I marked my card, I handed it to a clerk who ran it through a gadget that looked liked an adding machine. On the back of the card, the machine stamped the type and amount of bet, *Win* or *Place,* there being no *Show,* the racecourse, the number of the race, the date, and the name of the horse. In the first race, 16 Dec 00, P, R1, Eliza bet two dollars on Inveritas to place. Inveritas finished last. "When can we come back?" Edward asked as I drove home to Mosman Park. "I'm not returning," Vicki said. "I have seen enough blue fences." Workers raised a hedge-sized blue fence around fallen horses, so the crowd couldn't see animals destroyed.

A day at the races evaporates quickly. By night the children were bored and to pass time named the furniture in the living room, the two couches dubbed Fiona and Mervin; the chairs, their children, Adrian and Natasha. While the coffee table became Peabody, the ceiling lamp was Adolph, and the standing lamp, Quasimodo. For its part the television was Satan. Summer was not restful. On Monday I carted the family to Penguin Island. An hour south of Perth and seven hundred meters off the shore from Rockingham, the island was small, consisting of 12.5 hectares. Vicki packed a picnic lunch: brie and cheddar, Greek olives, French bread, carrots, grapes, soft drinks, watermelon, and fudge cake. We ate at a table near the "Interpretation Facility." Kings skinks shimmied over the grass and begged handouts, becoming, Eliza said, "wingless gulls." The skinks fancied watermelon and pinched hunks from my hand.

Penguin Island rested sandy atop limestone. I followed paths and circled the island three times. Along the western edge limestone rose into Gothic spires. Dirt daubers plastered nests to the spires, and pigeons perched on rocks looking like gray gargoyles. Snails peppered basins, and brindled terns grasped acacia, their heads slicing the wind. Occasionally the terns barked. Silver gulls surfed air currents then slipping were slung over the water like stones. Pelicans colonized the northern tip of the island. Adults raised their heads sharply, from a distance looking like remnants of a white fence. Lignum climbed thick through acacia; long-leaved spinifex withered into spikes, and in the water a blue manna crab threaded ribbon grass. While thick-leaved fan-flower bloomed in purple clusters, clematis split into down. I chewed native rosemary and followed a pair of pied oystercatchers along the beach. On the beach I found the dried body of a young silver gull. The nestling was two and a half inches wide and five inches tall. The bill was frozen open and looked like heavy tweezers. I took the bird home. "Why do you pick up such things?" Vicki asked. "Life and death interest me," I said. "Yes," Eliza added, "and the bird looks like a small canteen."

No one can avoid his own company, but he can be distracted from others. Because the family enjoyed the excursion to Penguin Island, I began planning a trip the next morning. The workings of memory are various. In part I planned the trip in hopes that in after-years, it, not boredom, would mark summer in Perth. Four years ago I gave the graduation address at Montgomery Bell Academy in Nashville. For weeks before the talk Edward had been moody. To raise his spirits I took him with me to Tennessee. After the talk we spent six days roaming the state. One afternoon we visited the Civil War battlefield at Chickamauga in Georgia. The day quickly slipped my mind. Edward, however, remembered it, and when the University of Virginia asked him to write two paragraphs on "The Past is Never Dead," he described the afternoon.

"Several years ago," Edward wrote, "I accompanied my father to Nashville where he gave a graduation speech. Later we rented a car and drove to Chattanooga. I suggested we visit Chickamauga, the Civil War battlefield in north Georgia. Dad and I spent the day wandering fields and wooded battle lines where northern and southern armies had once faced each other. Although it was spring, dead leaves from the previous fall littered the forest floor. The length of the battle lines marked by a series of monuments surprised me. Stone memorials stood ten or fifteen feet apart, each honoring a different regiment. Though Dad and I walked together, we rarely spoke. At one point Dad broke the silence, indicating a memorial that honored a regiment from Ohio. 'Your great-great-grandfather Pickering fought with them,' he said, 'under General Thomas, the Rock of Chickamauga.' Somewhere along the opposite lines, another great-great grandfather, Gerald Griffin, had fought in a regiment from Georgia."

"The line of battle emerged from trees onto a long, sloping hill at the top of which stood a gray obelisk. The path climbed gently upward, framed by a fringe of trees on the right and on the left by a crumbling stone wall alive with grasshoppers. The trip to Chickamauga was my only trip to Georgia. I have forgotten much detail. Still that day is fixed in my memory, emblematic of the past's living force. Chickamauga slept, as if lulled by the sounds of birds and insects. But as a place and an event, it was not 'dead.' Nor is it even 'past,' so strongly does its impression stay with me. I walked along battle lines where great-great-grandfathers fought each other. I stood in the green quiet, arms spread, reaching out to both of them."

At first I investigated spending thirteen days in Tasmania, roaming the island with a company called Tasmanian Expedition. Seven days of riding bicycles and rafting followed six days hiking. The tour was listed "on an international list of the 100 great trips for the 21st century." Eager to find something to fill the children's hours, I struggled to book the trip. For the four of us the Expedition reduced the price 20 percent. For five days all flights to Tasmania were full. Then the morning seats became available, Vicki refused to go on the trip. "I have not ridden a bicycle since I was eight, and I have never carried a backpack," she said. "You and the children go without me." I jettisoned the trip. The next day I contacted Bogong Horseback Adventures in Victoria and booked a week's riding the high country, "the highest horseback riding available in Australia," a brochure stated. Next I booked five nights in Melbourne, three before the ride and two after. I gasped at the price, almost three hundred dollars a night. Happily a roundtrip flight from Perth to Melbourne only cost $429. "Do you think we are up to riding?" Vicki said. "Yes," I said, "afterward the mountains will tower in memory." Although I regretted not going to Tasmania, I wondered if I could have stood bicycling. In Connecticut I ride a bicycle to the English department. The bike has twenty-one gears, but I always pedal in the same gear. Moreover my handlebars do not curve like rams' horns but stick straight back, and I suspect that bending to shift gears would have loosened the spokes of my spine.

Two hours after I purchased flights and confirmed the riding, Vicki's brother Geoff telephoned from New Jersey. "Mother died last night," he said. Even an expected death brings disorder. Vicki knew she had to clean her mother's house in New Jersey. "Only the dates are indefinite," Vicki said. On January 18 we were scheduled to fly to Melbourne. On the twenty-ninth we returned to Perth. Vicki decided to fly to the United States early in February, once school started. "I will probably stay in Princeton until you return to

Connecticut in August," she said. "Life won't be easy for you." "I'll manage," I said. The next night we walked to Manners Hill Park in Peppermint Grove for Carols by Candlelight. People spread blankets and ate picnic dinners. Packs of children scurried about, and friends gathered in familial groups. I felt out of place, and good cheer seeped away. We sat on the ground. Almost immediately I noticed two mounds of dog droppings. The carols were my favorites: "Hark! The Herald Angels Sing," "Away in a Manger," "The First Noel," and "Joy to the World," among others. Usually I belt carols. On this night isolation surrounded me in a fog, and I whispered words. I did not recognize anyone in the park, and after the raffle we walked home. In hopes of awakening feelings of belonging, I bought eight raffle tickets. Five prizes were given away: a boogie board, a pearl necklace, an acoustic guitar, two bottles of wine, and a $250 gift certificate from the Boatshed Grocery. "We did not win," Eliza said, pausing then adding, "again."

The next morning Edward turned the television on during breakfast. "I don't think I can endure summer," Vicki said. An hour later I arranged a three-night stay at Bolganup Homestead, a 520-acre farm abutting the Porongurup National Park, 385 kilometers south of Perth. Seven years ago we spent two nights in Burnley Cottage at Bolganup. This time we were next door in Fernbrook. We left Mosman Park at 9:45 the next day and arrived at Bolganup at 3:30 in the afternoon. Once past the Darling Range the Albany Highway ran like a pallet past open fields, sheep grazing and looking like stubble, and cattle, lumpy remnants of figurines. Salt pans gleamed leprous. "The sheep," Eliza said, "chew the soil dry." In the south timber plantations destroyed land. To plant blue gum, a pulp wood, property owners shredded bush. Blue gum stretched in vacuous rows across squares of land. Between lines of trees the ground was barren. No shrubs grew, and the plantations were sterile, the soil bleached by spray and fertilizer. Animals could not live amid the trees, and birds didn't forage through them. Trees could be harvested three times. Afterward the land was a garbage tip of stump and salt. "Spraying," a man told me, "poisons water and people, but no one cares." "The blue gums," he continued, "suck aquifers from the ground in the process draining fields on neighboring farms and ruining the land."

Greed and money determine land use in Western Australia. Environmental policy is the stuff of words not deeds. In Australia corporations celebrated the election of George Bush. "He does not care about the environment," a man told me, "and won't criticize business here." "The blue gums are an ecological disaster," Vicki said. "Don't people realize that?" "Yes," I said, "but ways of corporations are the ways of the world—during my time, money; after me, the desert."

On the way to Bolganup we ate lunch at a concrete picnic table near the Beaufort River. We sat under marri trees. Bush flies swarmed around us while a horde of black ants pillaged a refuse barrel. From the table paths radiated in spokes, each collapsing in wads of toilet paper. "Not the Ritz," Eliza said, "but the company is good." Christmas trees bloomed beside the highway, their limbs opening into orange baskets. The door of Fernbrook swung into a sitting room shaped like an *L*, kitchen and dining cove forming the base. Beyond the sitting room lay a bathroom and three bedrooms, windows in two of the bedrooms facing a meadow and Bolganup Creek. From the living room one stepped onto a covered porch. Behind the cottage, away from the creek, marri and jarrah grew in rough scrub. Amid them hunkered farm buildings: a shearing shed and several nondescript outhouses, their roofs tilted to pour rain into cisterns. Beyond the buildings were sheep paddocks. One evening twenty-seven western gray kangaroos grazed a paddock. In the morning kangaroos foraged next to our porch. Along a wall of the cottage grew statice, daisy bushes, and hollyhocks so red they were almost black. Fruit fell from a plum, and in a pasture oranges glowed like lamps. South of the cottage the Porongurup Mountains rose in green mounds. At the top of the range bare domes loomed like skulls.

Furnishings were rustic. Cheesecloth covered table tops; the bottoms of chairs sagged into deep dishes, and old books leaned akimbo on mantles. I thumb books, ever hopeful that treasure will slip loose. On December 19, 1890, O. Branner, a teacher at Lyndach School presented George MacDonald's *The Wise Woman* to Ida Kauffman "for Excellent Work & Conduct." Days were cool, and drizzles stitched lines across fields. I spent much time on the porch. On my left grew the shrubby remnant of an orchard. A small pond shined like a mirror, and gums rose tall along the bank of the creek, trunks bare and tinged with green. Beyond the creek fields pitched up toward woods. To my right a vineyard spread across lowland in green ringlets. I rose early in the morning and sat on the porch, dreaming in solitude of solitude. Furniture on the porch was iron and smacked of a slower time when people didn't shift chairs about. "A good place for writing a novel," Edward said. I didn't write; instead I watched and listened. Roosters crowed, and ravens ground song into gravel. Across the valley magpies fluted, distance making the music pale as wind. Kookaburras held jamborees, and black and white cockatoos perched like ornaments in karri tree. A cat twitched through brambles; nearby a rabbit hunched in couch grass, its ears semaphores.

About the house birds fluttered like illuminations decorating a holy book. A splendid fairy wren clung to barbed wire, its feathers diamonds, facets of black and blue. Eight wood ducks filed across the field while a pair of white-faced herons fished the pond. Tree martins swept joyfully through the air, and grey-breasted white-eyes skipped into the plum. A pair of yellow-rumped thornbills hopped through a barren peach. A golden whistler called from a jarrah, its chest a harp tingling with song, "wheat-wheat-seto-wheat." Behind the shearing shed a red-capped parrot dozed in a marri, and a grey fantail hawked insects, looping over a woodpile. Two pairs of scarlet robins bustled through shrubs near the house, breasts of the males blood oranges.

Henry Thoreau ended *Walden* by describing an insect gnawing its way out of a table. The insect represented modern man deadened by getting and spending, smothered and imprisoned by wooden duty. "Who knows what beautiful and winged life, whose egg has been buried for ages under many concentric layers of woodenness in the dead dry life of society," Thoreau wrote, "may unexpectedly come forth amidst society's most trivial and hand-selled furniture, to enjoy its perfect summer at last." For a moment at Bolganup I bored through the varnish of responsibility and let eyes and ears follow the vagaries of birds: a wedge-tailed eagle floating sculpted through the air, a black-faced cuckoo shrike beating over the ground, and in a woodland damp with marri and jarrah, a red-winged fairy wren pinching through bushes, shards of bluebell creeper hanging over twigs in ribbons.

At the end of the dirt road leading to Fernbrook stood the Porongurup Shop and Tearoom. Seven years ago we ate in the Tearoom. Owners were the same, their lives altered, however, by three children. The first night we ate dinner in the Tearoom. In a side yard grapes and passion fruit tinseled an arbor. Apricots dangled from a tree, and chickens raked the ground. Inside the tearoom a pine branch stood in a barrel filled with sand. The branch served as a Christmas tree. Gold braids wound between twigs, and white balloons hung in clusters. On the walls of the tearoom were paintings by Ron Taylor, an artist living in Albany. The paintings were for sale. One painting appealed to Vicki, a sixteen- by twelve-inch depiction of kingia growing in a karri forest. Light floated pale blue through the undergrowth, creating a quiet otherworldly mood. The morning we left Bolganup I bought the painting for $145.

At dinner the first night Liquorice, a black cat, rubbed mazes between our legs. During dessert Vicki fed Liquorice, scooping heavy cream onto the little finger of her right hand then hanging her hand below the table. After dinner Vicki and I roamed a paddock. A kangaroo hopped a fence surrounding three thick lines of rolled hay. One line consisted of nineteen rolls. When we returned to Fernbrook, Edward and Eliza were playing checkers. They hadn't played checkers in Perth. Later I sat in the living room and read the guest book. "A home away from home. Makes me want to sell up in the city and move here," a man wrote in 1992. "No one ever sells up," Vicki said. "If there were a Nobel Prize for architecture, our vote would go to your veranda," a woman wrote. "Porch," Vicki said. "Porch is a better word." In 1991 a guest introduced herself as Clanette Jordan—Perth—Single." "Back again," she wrote. "Still Single. This is such a beautiful place—I can't wait to come down with my man, when I find him, so if you are 175cm, dark hair, medium build and have a great personality—call me!!!—and Single!" At the end of her note the writer drew a smiling face, eyelashes shooting up like beams of sunlight.

In 1996 a member of the Faulkner family, the original settlers of the homestead, visited Fernbrook. "I first slept here 83 years ago and stayed for 24 years," she wrote. "I see many changes since then. The faithful old mangle in the back garden brings back memories both good and bad. It would be interesting to know just how many sheets have been pressed through over the years." The mangle was no longer in the garden but on the porch. A pyramid of nine iron bands pressured rollers, a screw with a butterfly handle on top rising above the bands. The rollers looked like small logs and were four and a half inches in diameter. While the iron had rusted, its smooth surface now pocked, worms bored into the rollers and loosened strips of wood.

Vicki packed cereal in the car before we left Perth, and we bought milk in the tearoom. Early the next morning we ate breakfast in Fernbrook. Afterward we set out for the Stirling Range, thirty-five kilometers north on the Chester Pass Road. One hundred million years old, the Stirlings are relatively new mountains in comparison to the Porongurups, which are eleven hundred million years old. Time had rounded the Porongurups, and peaks slumped into foreheads. In contrast the Stirlings fell into sharp seams, and slabs of granite broke and sank into slopes like the remnants of teeth. Land between the Porongurups and the Stirlings stretched like a table. In the Stirlings gray currawongs and black and white cockatoos broke cover and dashed across the pavement. We planned to climb Bluff Knoll, at 1,095 meters the highest peak in the south. The face of Bluff Knoll was a brow jutting out against the sky, and the trail wrinkled upward behind chins of rock. Seven years ago we climbed Bluff Knoll, Francis, Eliza, and I reaching the top, Vicki stopping halfway to comfort Edward who broke into tears near a ledge. Time had changed us.

To me Time brought fifteen pounds and two notches on my belt; to Edward, a lack of fear. Time also changed the mountain.

At the turnoff for Bluff Knoll, lapels of black swept over the road. Recently a bush fire seared the area, flames drafting through the gullies like chimneys. I asked three people when the fire occurred. One said four months ago; another said four weeks, and the third, two weeks. Only wind and flies made sounds, the former stealthy as it thrummed through tree and valley, frets broken. In a pool created by a slow-dripping stream, three fledgling white-breasted robins tossed water over their feathers. The robins were the only birds I saw. On the ground lay the body of a feral cat, the skin crisp, seared black and gold. The fire baked termite mounds into brick. Grasshoppers flew loose over the black earth looking like fluffy seeds. Able to burrow beneath the flames, skinks survived. A heath goanna waggled off the trail, and at the edge of the burn, a Rosenberg's monitor shimmied into bush high on its legs. Gray ash blanketed slopes and in pockets gathered in pillows. The ground itself seemed pudding stone, baked, then shingled with loose rock. Tree trunks were charred, and the air was dry and smelled like a fireplace. Nuts hung from marri like handfuls of chocolate bon-bons. Seeds on hakea resembled the skulls of small animals, mouths open and gasping.

From the trunks of a few trees, tufts of leaves erupted in cowlicks. The only large green plant was kingia, brooms of leaves bursting from black trunks and glowing silver in the sun. In some places fire melted kingia, the sap cooked into spoon-sized clumps. The fire shaved away low scrub exposing folds of rock, turning slopes into stubbles of blackened mallee. Sometimes the mountain shined black and polished; other times, blue. "Enjoy the walk," I told Edward and Eliza. "You won't see a landscape like this again." Edward and Eliza bounded up the trail. The ascent was steep. Still Vicki and I reached the top in two hours. Seven years ago caravans of people walked the trail. On this day only six other people were on the mountain, a Scotsman, two Germans, and three Norwegians. The Scotsman raced past, saying, "Born in the Highlands." Fire hadn't touched the south face of the mountain, and as we circled overhangs to reach the peak, plants appeared: gravel bottle-brush, red with blossoms; Southern Cross, creamy and damp over the ground; hakea; drumsticks; Witters mountain bell; and dampiera, centers yellow and petals so dark blue that shadows seemed to float through them.

For twenty minutes we roamed the summit, taking pictures and trying to snap views into memory. Returning to the car park took two more hours. On the way downhill Vicki's calves cramped, and my left hip splintered into pain. We ate lunch at the Bluff Knoll Café on the Chester Pass Road. I had my usual road sandwich, egg and bacon, topped with salad—onions, beets, lettuce, and tomato. While eating I watched a splendid fairy wren hunt insects. After-ward I drove the Woogenellup Road to Mr. Barker, and Vicki bought groceries at SupaValu. While Vicki was in the grocery, I crossed Lowood Road and at Heath 'n' Herbs bought quince cheese and rhubarb and ginger jam, each jar costing $2.50. During the next two days we spent much time in Mt. Barker. We ate lunch at the Boronia Café and at Fifteen Streets Berry Farm munched apple and blueberry pie, topped off with raspberries buried beneath whipped cream. Both the Berry Farm and Café were for sale, the café for $70,000 plus stock evaluation. All Mt. Barker seemed for sale, Lockwoods Bread Shoppe where I bought the worst raisin bun I have ever eaten, then the bank building that once housed Indulgences, a café advertised in the local tourist guide.

The Berry Farm perched on a hillside. Below the farm vineyards rippled in green waves. In the distance the Stirling Range faced the sky. Bud vases of baby's breath sat on tables, and splendid fairy wrens frisked along a porch railing. The owner and her husband had put the farm up for sale in hopes of slipping free and joining their children in Mandurah. "Why don't you buy our place?" the owner said. "What a change it would be for you." Like many people who have aged into immobility, I dream of movement. "You spent the past three months helping Edward with college applications," Vicki said. "Where he goes and where we live don't matter." Still dutiful habit cannot be shed easily, and dreams of pitching pencil and convention will remain hankerings.

On the road food interrupts driving and walking. One afternoon in Mt. Barker we stopped on Martin Street and for eight dollars bought a kilo of white cherries, the girl who sold them still in pajamas. On leaving Bolganup to return to Perth, we drove to Mt. Barker and took Werburgh's Road, a gravel road that passed two wineries and a tree farm. Until the farm made the landscape monotonous, the drive was scenic. I stopped at St. Werburgh's Chapel, a church atop a shady hill. The chapel was built in 1873. The roof was tin and painted red. Walls were made from clay then white-washed, and a small bell tower stood above the church. On each side of the aisle in the church stood seven pews. Daisies blossomed in six stained glass windows, the centers of the flowers red. Five yellow petals spun around each center while a pair of green leaves opened below, welcoming and friendly. Wrought iron grape vines twisted through the altar rail. Outside the church was a small graveyard. Wooden markers stood at the tops of twenty graves, numbers not names pressed into the wood. The graves were in two rows. The first row consisted of thirteen graves, the numbers running left to right. Along the second row numbers ran from right to left. Over a barbed wire fence someone had dumped last Sunday's flowers: jasmine, hydrangea, and coils of trumpet vine. Country churches relax me, and instead of hurrying back to the highway, we lingered on the hill, watching a Hereford drift across a paddock.

The third day at Bolganup Eliza, Edward, and I roamed the Porongurups. Vicki stayed at Fernbrook, saying climbing Bluff Knoll had reduced her calves to veal. We started in the Karri Grove at Tree-in-the-Rock picnic ground and climbed Nancy and Hayward Peaks then Devil's Slide, at 670 meters the highest point in the Porongurups. We returned to the picnic area along Wansborough Walk. The ramble was seven kilometers long and lasted three and a half hours. Because the Porongurups are soft, they suit the aged walker. Moreover range and park are small, the range stretching only twelve kilometers and the park consisting of only 2,511 hectares. In contrast the Stirling Range is 65 kilometers long and eighteen wide, and the park is 116,000 hectares. Instead of challenging and appealing to youth as does the Stirling Range, sight of the Porongurups soothes. Slopes are lush and comfortable, and walkers cannot get lost.

When I parked at Tree-in-the-Rock, magpies rushed the car and gleaned insects from bumpers and undercarriage. The Porongurups receive more rain than the Stirlings, and ferns swirled through undergrowth. Karri trees towered above the forest, their leaves so high that they looked like lids floating on mist. In the damp under domes at the top of the range, daisies patched the ground. Froths of white lichens swept rocks. Between peaks the trail bored through tunnels of acacia and sweet-smelling hakea. The path up Devil's Slide was stony and steep. On shelves beside the path mountain villarria bloomed, spikes of yellow flowers potted in pods of glossy leaves. Along the pass between Morgan's View and the Wansborough Walk, dead karri trees stood in white columns, their limbs broken against the blue sky looking like spider webs. Climbing Devil's Slide tired me; and the big toe on my right foot began to ache. "Mountain toe," Vicki called it. Driving back to Fernbrook, I stopped at Jingalla Wines and bought a Shiraz. The wine cost twenty-three dollars, ten dollars more than I usually pay for a bottle. "This full-bodied pepper Shiraz," the label stated, "is enhanced by soft tannins from French oak maturation." That night Vicki and I drank the wine at Maleeya's Thai Café, a restaurant in a field on the road to Mt. Barker. The café was listed among Australia's top six hundred restaurants, and food was good. Vicki ate Penang Curry prawns while I had red curry chicken with bamboo. "When are you going to say, 'I wonder what brought the owners here?'" Edward said. "Soon," I replied. The owner was an American who had spent most of his life in Switzerland and spoke English with a German accent. Although I went to the Porongurups to purge the fret of family and city from mind, traveling awakens the inquisitive instinct. I had long wanted a jarrah box. Before leaving Bolganup I visited Unique Jarrah Products on Spring Road. There lay the perfect box, grain rippling the top like curly maple. Unfortunately the home of Vicki's mother in Princeton came to mind, and the box, I decided, would become just another knick-knack cluttering the children's lives after my death. Once back in Perth, I regretted not buying the box.

Leaving Bolganup I drove the Mt. Barker–Denmark road to Denmark, an empty back road that made the south appealing. At Nornalup I drove through the Valley of the Giants. Red tingle trees grew in the forest. Near the ground the trees slumped into huge butts. Fire had scraped the heartwood out of many trees, so that trunks opened into dark huts. Inside trees spider webs draped from the wood like napkins. One of the most publicized attractions in the south is the Tree Top Walk, a six-hundred-meter loop through the tops of tingles. Sixty-meter steel trusses held in place by pylons stretched through trees. The highest point of the walk was forty meters above the ground. Trusses swayed, making Vicki nervous. While I ambled crowns of trees, wrens chattered beneath me. A thrush shrike shrieked from a branch. Below grew wattles, yellow tingle, tassel flowers, and karri oak. Bark peeled from the trunk of a fallen tingle, and its roots shrank into brown stubs, leaving the tree bare except for a comforter of red dust. On the walk we saw numbers of tourists for the first time during the trip. Many arrived on buses. From Walpole I took the South Western Highway and taking the cut off to Northcliffe approached Pemberton from the south.

At Pemberton we stayed in the Karri Forest Motel. Old habit rarely vanishes. Once in our room Edward switched on the television. That night Vicki and the children watched *Alien III*, a movie about space monsters. The next day, however, was electric with doing. Early in the morning Vicki bought a newspaper for the children. A small boy sat outside the newsagent's playing Christmas carols on a trumpet, "Joy to the World" and "Hark, the Herald Angels Sing" while Vicki was in the shop. Before we left, Vicki gave the boy a dollar. Next we explored Fine Woodcut Gallery. Furniture in the gallery was best I saw in Western Australia. I coveted a jarrah and banksia coffee table. Vicki urged me to buy it, but I resisted temptation. Instead I bought Eliza a pewter bracelet decorated with pearls and pink and purple crystals. From a vendor parked across Dickinson Street, Vicki bought a dozen peaches. From the gallery we hurried to the railway station and took the tourist train from Pemberton to Warren Bridge, a ten-kilometer trip lasting two hours. The small red cars rolled slowly through the bush. At the edge of Pemberton stood a mill, beside it paddocks of giant karri logs, cut and pared, beached and blistering far from the wave of leaf and life. Near the tracks logging roads burned scars through the forest. Along the right of way bull banksia bloomed. Purple splotched holly-leaf grevillea, and blossoms curdled in yellow clumps on native willow. Low along the banks of Lefroy Brook, blackberry bloomed. Weeping peppermint leaned over the rails and as the train passed switched through open windows. Near Warren River land was for sale. On properties wooden buildings leaned awkwardly. "If we lived here," Vicki said, "what would you do?" "Nothing," I said. "I'd slump bone and flesh into the ground." After the train ride we picnicked under peppermints in the small park commemorating the Pemberton Historical District. A steam engine and tender stood in the park. I climbed into the engine and slammed levers back and forth. I urged the rest of the family to join me. They didn't. "Too many flies for so short a trip," Eliza said.

From Pemberton I drove the Vasse Highway to Nannup. Beyond Pemberton the karri forest ended. Marri and jarrah woodlands appeared, and air dried. The road peeled through Nannup, one-story shops pinching both shoulders. The town attracted me. "A perfect place for hippies," I said to a man. "We had plenty in the seventies," he said. "But they settled and turned conservative. Ferals have replaced them." At Crafty Creations Vicki bought a pair of candleholders carved from banksia nuts. At the Good Food Shop next door, I drank a banana smoothie. Behind the shop was a terrace, jasmine and clock vine blooming on trellises. Tacked to the wall of the lavatory were poems. "A poem," a note attached to one paper explained, "by an author found fastened to a tree in a Portuguese forest." "Was the author or the poem fastened to the tree?" Eliza asked. Both Creations and the Shop were for sale. "We'd have more fun here than at the Berry Farm," Vicki said.

"And the children could visit once every six or so years," I answered. "Only if you paid for the flight," Edward said, meandering shops not being to his taste.

Even less to his taste was Blythe Gardens, an advertisement for which I noticed while strolling Main Street. Admission cost a dollar, and a collection box was attached to the front gate. Under a trellis above the gate were the words, "Take A Walk On The Quiet Side." The garden was private, the owner's house sitting in the middle. Once in the garden Edward and Eliza parked themselves on a bench. Vicki and I, however, roamed the yard. According to the 1988 and 1990 editions of *The Guinness Book of Records,* the tallest dahlia in the world grew in the garden. "Now blown over," the son of the owner said. Jacaranda, duranta, and tree fuchsia blossomed. Green fruit hung from tree tomato, and Chilean willows stood in pencils. For several minutes Vicki and I hunted cicadas. The insects were less than an inch long, and we searched by ear not eye, listening for their quick snaps.

We explored the garden for forty-six minutes. From Nannup I hurried to Busselton. The jetty at water's edge extended a mile and a quarter into the sea. We walked it in order to loosen kinks in the children. From Busselton I drove to Bunbury where we ate dinner in the Friendship Chinese restaurant. Seven years earlier we had eaten in the same restaurant. Later Eliza bought an ice cream cone, chocolate in honor of Francis, she said. I suggested spending the night in the Rose Hotel in Bunbury, the wrought iron decorations magnets pulling me like a filing. "No," Eliza said, "I want to run tomorrow morning." I drove through the dark back to Perth, and we arrived home at 10:38. The trip covered 1,419 kilometers, excluding those by foot. "Here we are," Vicki said as I unlocked the door. "Maybe we never left." "We left," I said, "and now we are back."

Christmas

I didn't want to return from the Porongurups. On a trip days fold anonymously into each another, and calendar vanishes. In Perth the temperature rose into the nineties, and Christmas was so far out of Connecticut season that celebration seemed unnatural. Moreover because the holiday was less commercial than in the United States and the children had grown beyond being delighted by stocking stuffers, Vicki and I hadn't purchased presents. On the road the day would have drifted past like asphalt under the thrum of tires. Unfortunately Eliza and Edward urged us home on the twenty-third. Two cards met us, the first from AMSouth Bank in Tennessee, the second from Kathryn, Father's first cousin. Kathryn was eighty-four. Recently the partner of her daughter Anne died. He and Anne had started a florist business. Kathryn wrote that she missed our laughter. "I never knew how I could miss anybody so much," she began. "I think of you every day and wish you were not so far away. Do hope you are enjoying your stay. Nothing is going on around here. Anne lost her business partner and friend in October. That makes for a very sad Christmas for her and without Dick [Kathryn's husband who died three years ago] it's just another day for me. I'll be glad when it is over." "Only youth should go abroad," I said to Vicki, putting down Kathryn's card. "People my age should not leave home."

The next afternoon the temperature hovered at ninety-eight. That morning I drove Eliza and Edward to the university so they could check email. Thirty emails accumulated in my box during the trip. I deleted twenty-eight unread. The only two I looked at concerned the estate of Vicki's mother. Edward received no mail. Eliza got several emails, most with cards or videos attached, none of which my computer could open. On the way home I stopped at Martineau's and bought a blueberry coffee cake, the only cake left in the bakery. "For Christmas," I explained to Edward and Eliza. Once home Edward shut his door and read *The Brothers Karamazov*. At Coles Vicki bought a leg of lamb and at Mosman Heights, a bottle of Tasmanian champagne.

That afternoon Eliza made decorations for the window in the dining room. From green construction paper she cut a tree with five pairs of branches. The tree was twenty-six inches tall and at its widest point nineteen inches. On each limb she glued swatches of sprinkles and small stars, these last, blue, yellow, silver, and red. To the top of the tree, she attached a star, eleven inches tall with five points, the lower two legs of the star long and thin, the side arms pudgy. She cut the star from yellow construction paper after which she wrapped it in translucent yellow paper. She attached the star to a white plastic spoon that she also covered in yellow paper. She glued the handle of the spoon to the back of the tree, the bowl behind the star. After hanging the tree in the left pane of the window, she covered the right pane with a chain made from red crêpe paper. The chain was four feet long. From the middle of the crêpe paper, she cut hearts, covering the gaps with the yellow translucent paper. In the center of the chain, she glued letters spelling MERRY CHRISTMAS. Two and a half inches tall, the letters were cut from wrapping paper decorated with green wreaths.

At five o'clock on Christmas Eve, I decided to attend the Festival of Lessons and Carols at St. George's Cathedral in downtown Perth. Eliza and Vicki reluctantly accompanied me. Edward stayed in his room reading. Eliza's presence pleased me. Most of her friends in Connecticut are Jewish, and she has spent more time in synagogues than in churches. In fact the last time she was in a church was Christmas seven years ago in Perth. St. George's is lovely. Rails of red jarrah support the roof, and walls are orange brick. I think religions separate people. Doctrines raise barriers that force believers to view neighbors as others, abstractions easy to criticize. Still while trying to shield the children from the abuses of faith, I have stripped richness from their lives. When we entered St. George's, heat billowed tidal. But once the service began, I forgot temperature. Words unfurled, and thought grew wings, blown aloft on a breeze of song. "I loved it," Eliza said later. "I am so glad we went. The service makes the season Christmas." "Sing choirs of angels," I thought. "Sing in exultation."

On Christmas Vicki cooked the lamb, surrounding it with onions, potatoes, peas, and carrots. For dessert she sliced peaches and spread them over vanilla ice cream. For my part I cut the coffee cake. After champagne and wine I strolled the yard. Across Kalgoorlie Street sunflowers bloomed at the edge of a yard, a Christmas bouquet of forty-six blossoms. The hibiscus in the back yard had burst into pink flowers, the petals wide as hands, emblems, it seemed, of good will. At six o'clock we went to Cottesloe and swam for an hour. Afterward we walked the beach. Lorikeets scudded into Norfolk pines. For a time I watched the birds turning through branches like ornaments, colors dangling, purple and orange, green and red. "Merry Christmas," Vicki said. "I brought your present with me." Opening her purse she handed me a Nestle "Club" candy bar, two hundred grams of "Rich Dark Chocolate." "Want some?" I said to the children. "Sure," they said.

New Year

"What is the most martial day of the year?" Nigel asked, adding, "the day that urges people to press ahead." "What?" I said. "March fourth," Nigel answered, right hand slapping his thigh. Rarely does a holiday prompt me to attention. I slouch through the year, a field pack of errands on my shoulders. Early on New Year's Eve I drove to the university to check email. Eliza accompanied me. In hopes of seeing the old year out with a semblance of order, we charted the journey, sketching the terrain: one stop sign, two roundabouts, and eleven traffic lights, the distance from Kalgoorlie to Hackett No. 1 parking lot remaining 9.2 kilometers. Eleven emails awaited me, eight of which were advertisements. On the way home I stopped at Martineau's and bought three sultana rolls. To fortify myself for the hours ahead, I ate two of the rolls.

At one o'clock I drove to City Beach and swam for forty-five minutes. At four-thirty, Vicki, Eliza, and I walked four kilometers through Bold Park. Two weeks earlier a bush fire swept the Coast Highway, charring a sixth of the park, blackening and souring the air. Still kookaburras posed motionless on limbs, and shingle-back lizards twitched through ashes. At six I drove to Broadway Pizza and for New Year's picked up two family pizzas at the special price of $21.60, one garlic cheese and the other Broadway, the top a salad of cheese, tomato, ham, bacon, pepperoni, olives, mushrooms, and capsicums. That night we ate on a picnic table above the bluff in Mosman Park. Below us a crowd of men in dinner jackets and women in long dresses milled about a long table, champagne glasses glittering like icicles. At eight-thirty Vicki, Eliza, and I took the train to Fremantle, hoping to buy New Year's dessert at a café. Edward stayed home and read. Teenagers turned cars on the train into chicken coops, cackling and peering this way and that, looking, so far as I could tell, at nothing. Crowds rumbled through streets, and diners crowded restaurants. Not able to snatch a table, we drifted to the foreshore and bought ice cream cones at Baskin-Robbins—Eliza, chocolate peanut butter, and Vicki and I, swirls of black and white chocolate. By ten-thirty we were home. "The teenagers frightened me," Vicki said. "I felt uncomfortable." "As well you should have," I said. "You are civilized."

At eleven-fifteen I walked up Glyde to the bluff overlooking Mosman Bay. Music blared from the parking lot. At midnight fireworks punctuated the horizon, colors dangling like participles, explosions banging like periods. On the ground behind me a young couple bumped against each other. A crowd gathered on a dock sticking out into the water. For a moment or two they laughed. Then they jumped into the bay. Children ran across the grass waving sparklers. On a porch across Bay View Terrace, the plastic horn section of a party stood and welcomed the New Year. "How about a glass of champagne?" I said to Vicki later. "We still have a heeltap or two left from Christmas." "I'm too tired," she said; "besides the champagne must be vinegar by now."

Early next morning we went to Ascot, our second day at the tracks. The Perth Cup was the featured race, and more than thirty-two thousand spectators crowded the track. Admission for adults was twenty-two dollars a head, so I lied and said Edward was sixteen, enabling him to get in free along with Eliza. Scrums of people caught us and pushed us about. Once I found seats in the grandstand, we moved only to bet or buy food, this last just nachos and French fries. The crowd was young, composed mostly of people in their twenties and thirties. Instead of the primitive cacophony with which teenagers in Fremantle announced their presences, people wore costumes. Hats perched on heads like nests. Crêpe tails swayed, and black feathers swam downy through the air. Men donned loose dresses, and women wore tights that clung like plaster to croup and gaskin. Cowgirls pranced about in orange and black, and a herd of men disguised themselves as Holsteins, donning black and white and for hats wearing horns. A small man wore lavender and sequins. Between races six skydivers plunged onto the track, one breaking an arm and a leg. In the Perth Cup, Heed the Toll broke down and was destroyed. Five days earlier the horse finished last in a thirteen-horse field. "Why did the trainer run him?" Vicki asked. By afternoon's end Vicki was tired, so I picked horses for her in the last two races, Lottila Bay and Rebate. Both won. As usual each of us bet two dollars on a race, either to win or place, for total of eight dollars a race. At the end of the day, we were $7.80 ahead, runs of horses named High Revs, Southern King, Liquid Honey, Finito, Thurston, Fred Who, and Hide the Halo earning us three to five dollars. That night we ate leftover pizza. Again I suggested drinking the dregs of champagne, but Vicki said she was too tired for anything other than beer.

The next morning I roamed Peppermint Grove. White kurrajongs bloomed in the corner of a yard. As I leaned on a wall gazing at a tree, a woman asked, "Are you all right?" The woman wore running shorts. Strapped to her shoulders was a blue backpack. "Look at that kurrajong blooming in a fanfare of pink," I said. "The tree is lovely," the woman said. "Where does it originate?" she asked, then said quizzically, "South America?" "No," I said, "the white kurrajong comes from New South Wales and Queensland." That night I drank the champagne, and the family watched Mel Gibson in *The Patriot*. New Year's had passed almost unnoticed.

I wore drab clothes to Ascot: sandals, thick gray running socks, a short-sleeved shirt with a soft blue collar, and blue shorts with four side pockets, all sealed with Velcro. Occasionally I imagine tarting up, but before I purchase rouge, an errand scrubs hankering from the mind. New Jersey requires that heirs settle an estate within nine months of a death. Vicki and her brothers put the family home in Princeton up for sale. Built in the 1830s, the house

SAM PICKERING

consisted of fourteen rooms, a three-room attic, and a huge basement, all the rooms, the attic, and the basement crammed with things. So the house wouldn't sink out of the market, moored to possessions, Vicki planned to spend two months in Princeton, her first inclination having been to leave Australia for good in February. On January 3 I bought Vicki a return trip ticket to Hartford. Because flights from Perth to Sydney were booked, Vicki had to fly Air Malaysia, leaving Perth on January 30 and arriving in Hartford at midnight on the first of February, her journey consisting of twenty-nine hours and seventeen minutes in the air and sixteen hours and forty-two minutes on the ground, including a night in Kuala Lumpur. "Holy cow," Vicki said.

The next morning life brightened. The English department at the university opened, and I collected my mail. Frank, a friend in Ohio, sent a column written by the president of his university. "Earlier this academic year, on September 20," the man wrote, "I addressed the university community and presented my thoughts and intentions in fulfillment of the common task that all of us have undertaken—to shape others and teach them to think with their hearts and minds and to foster and nurture scholarship and creativity in all its forms." "Clay can be shaped," Frank commented, "not adolescents. I say nothing about the anatomical reference to thinking with the heart." The president believed research important. In the column he stressed his support for research. "At least I think that is what he said," Frank wrote. "There are many facets of research support but the most important of these is financial—money," the president continued. "Allocation of research monies will be predicated on a varietal of the principle of the greater good. Monies will be allocated to those research endeavors whose outcomes will be positive for all concerned, be they society, the University, the researcher, students, corporate partners, or government." "We will continue," the president wrote, "to look at service centers—such as animal care—and institutes, and the procedures under which they function, to assure that the field upon which they play is a level one; that their relationship, one to the other, is the same. We will not put service centers or institutes at risk, because we all know and concur that multi- and interdisciplinary research is the wave we must necessarily ride into the future."

That morning Eliza finished Henry James's novel *Portrait of a Lady.* "James is often opaque," she said, "but this column is impossible to read. What does it mean?" "It means the New Year is old," I said. Among other mail was a letter from Carthage. In September, Turlow Gutheridge recounted, Zouch Townley spent a wet evening at Enos Mayfield's Inn in South Carthage. While returning to Carthage over the Cordell Hull Bridge, Zouch met a little boy dressed in a white robe, "a halo of light above him clear as mid-day." In the cradle of his left arm, the boy held a large green cat. The boy raised his right arm in front of Zouch and said, "A miracle will occur in December." "Sure enough," Turlow wrote, "two weeks ago Narcissus Luttrell's cow Button gave birth to a heifer. Instead of being inside the rib cage, the calf's heart was outside, hanging below her chest like a goiter." Every time the heart beat veins outlined the United States. Between beats the word *Sugg* became apparent, sprawling from Nevada to North Carolina, the tail of the second *G* running like a highway straight into downtown Charlotte.

No matter the season Carthage and my essays are ripe with death. Measor Grindle spent Christmas Eve sitting with the corpse of his cousin Spoor. Loppie Groat had just finished reading a tract damning Catholicism, and later when he met Measor in Ankerrow's Café, he asked, "Was it a wake?" "Awake?" Measor said; "Hell, no! Spoor was deader than a doornail. He died from the putrid fever, and all night long he gurgled something fierce. At first I thought Cousin Mary had left water running in the bathtub upstairs. Toward morning Spoor started swelling, and I tied a rope around his left ankle, so he wouldn't float up to the ceiling and maybe explode like the *Hindenburg* and burn the house down. The evening sort of took my appetite away, and I could hardly stomach Christmas lunch. Just looking at Cousin Mary's giblets made me queasy."

Vicki, the children, and I spent part of last Sunday at the Fremantle Arts Centre, once a lunatic asylum. Three exhibitions ran:

"About Face," portraits selected from collections at Bunbury and at Edith Cowan University; "Cape to Cape," landscape photographs; and finally "Gatherings," composed of "fragments of urbanalia," as a catalogue writer put matters. "A strange conjunction" exists, the writer explained, "between construction and deconstruction which informs a myriad of ambiguities about the inhabited urban landscape more commonly known in Australia as 'back yard.'" On the floor of a room sat a flowerpot, false teeth falling out of it in an overbite. Scores of ballpoint pins bristled out of a brass bowl. I am always short of pens, and for a moment I considered pocketing a handful. Not cream cheese and Jell-O, but safety pins clumped together in an aspic mold. A crow's nest of plastic twine filled a flat basket while high heels pried from women's shoes spilled out of a reed basket. A wicker basket contained 111 toothbrushes, but, Eliza said, "No toothpaste or floss."

After roaming the exhibitions I went to the courtyard and sitting in a white plastic chair in the shade of a plane tree listened to a quartet play jazz. Light shifted through the trees like music from a xylophone, and while Vicki and the children ate lunch in a restaurant across Finnerty Street, I dozed. After forty minutes I shook myself and went to join them. At the entrance to the Arts Centre, a man handed me a broadside. Printed at the top of the broadside between illustrations depicting two holly leaves and three berries was the title "The Humble Donkey." I read the broadside. "Familiar with the statement, 'You are a bloody ass-hole'? I still don't know what is the connection between 'the ass' and 'the hole'!! May be I am innocent. But Christmas is a time for us to talk about merrier things. Unfortunately, in a society where the rich enjoy the most and the poor suffer the most, the terms like 'Christmas,' 'Religion' make me look like a 'bloody ass-hole.'" The second paragraph was as strange as the first. "In a 'throw-away' and 'recycle' society like ours, we tend to throw away and recycle terms like 'God,' 'Christmas' and 'religion.' We tend to feel at home with terms like, 'AFL,' 'Olympics,' 'lap-top,' and 'digital.' We like to cling to things that give us pleasure and excitement the most. Yes, perhaps terms like 'God,' 'Christmas' or 'Religion' may not give us pleasure or excitement. For that matter, sex is not a pleasurable thing either (except for the 'fakies'!)."

"An alumnus of the asylum," I thought, "a collector of toothbrushes and high heels knocked loony by education." "What's that?" Eliza asked leaving the restaurant and seeing the broadside in my hand. "Nothing," I said, stuffing the paper into my right hip pocket. "Did I tell you that Turlow Gutheridge's neighbor Fetiplace got married in December?" Fetiplace was five feet tall. Before the ceremony he talked to Slubey Garts. "Can short people," he asked, "enter the Temple of Hymen legally?" "Good Lord," Vicki said walking down the street toward Ord. "My New Year's resolution," I said hurrying after her, "is to spend more time in Carthage. Hours there are charmed."

SAM PICKERING

January

Along with hot summer January brought a second blooming to Mosman Park. Plumbago hung from walls thick as macramé. Flowers on the lemon tree sweetened the back yard, and grevillea burst into a string section of red violins. Nubs of frangipani clawed upward then opened, blossoms whirling clockwise, petals curling, white rolling over yellow. In front of Iona Presentation College, figs fermented and spilled seeds on the sidewalk. In January I, too, enjoyed a second blooming and saw things I hadn't seen before. On the bluff overlooking Mosman Bay, wattle grew in scouring thickets. In January tips of branches dried into cindered spirals. Earlier insects bored into the wattle, transforming ends of branches into hospitable galls and spreading fungus. I opened several galls. Fluid oozed yellow and brown from them, resembling humic acid. Clusters of minute eggs floated on the liquid. On dry twigs small beetles hurried about, and cocoons and frass lurked in elbows of wood. In Fremantle I noticed that six swans decorated the roof of the railway station. Three birds clustered above the right of the entrance and three, the left. In each group the middle bird was white, the other two black. The black swans craned their necks up while the white bent their necks into intimidating loops, heads low as feet. At home I looked at Eliza's room for the first time, this despite having spent hours sitting on her bed. Four stuffed animals leaned against her pillowcase: Pogo flat on his belly, a small hound five and a half inches in length; Fuzzy, a panda five inches tall, his head three and a half inches thick, ears pouches, body slender, almost an afterthought; and Nanny, a large panda, ten inches tall and eight inches wide at the hips, into whose arms Fuzzy had originally been sewn.

Pogo had belonged to Vicki's father, Eliza appropriating him for memory's sake when her grandfather died. "I'll take good care of him like Grandpa Dudley did," she said. The fourth animal was Kitty, a small gray kitten, Eliza's companion even when she was too young to recognize animals as animals. Kitty's nose had vanished and been replaced by stitches. Her blue plastic eyes were so scratched they seemed cloudy with glaucoma. Affection had rubbed off Kitty's fur and flattened her to one and three-quarter inches, thin as a pad of paper. Around Kitty's waist Eliza sewed brown shorts. Someday somebody will wander into an attic and find Kitty in a trunk. For a moment the person will wonder what child loved Kitty. Wonder will be brief, however, and Kitty will become garbage—a thought that makes me unspeakably sad. Kitty has traveled with us to Nova Scotia. She has gone to camp in Maine. She has been lost and found in three countries. She has endured sand and salt water on beaches. Clothes dryers have tumbled her, and stormy nights have pounded her. Seven years ago she came to Australia with us. I associate Kitty with the early days of childhood, that long-ago time when the children didn't judge but loved unconditionally, when they wanted to accompany Vicki and me on our little doings, when ice cream cones made their days, and mine, sparkle—before they grew into certainty, before they realized they would be superior to their parents, in short those years when we were a family bound to each other by need and affection.

In a well built into the wall in Eliza's room stands a wood stove. Eliza transformed the stove into an altar, celebrating being fifteen years old. From the back of the stove rises a gray pipe. Taped to the pipe were two postcards Francis sent Eliza from Germany. On one card appeared cartoon characters from *South Park,* a television show. While Death sliced Kenny in half with a chainsaw, Carmen stood to the side, bemused indifference marking his face, a green cap on his head, ear flaps purses. Pasted to the wall bracketing the pipe were two eight- by six-inch pictures of animals. Both were advertisements for Optus Telephone. To the left of the pipe, a thorny devil perched on hot laterite, legs extended and toes stilts, the caption below reading, "I Want To Surf." On the right a raccoon ate a watermelon, the melon sliced, and the caption declaring, "I Choose to Have My Cake and Eat It." On the wall above the stove hung a poster, twenty-seven by nineteen inches and a mosaic of parrots, ten birds, two each of five varieties: cockatiel, ringneck, rainbow lorikeets, and crimson and eastern rosellas. To the left below the birds, Eliza hung a cereal box. The box once contained 450 grams of Uncle Toby's Honey Grinners, the cereal itself round faces half an inch in diameter. "Nutritious" with wheat, corn, and oats, the faces were "High in Fibre" and resembled carvings on pumpkins, eyes and noses triangles and mouths smiling, the lower halves of circles. Now twigs sprouted from the lid of the cartoon: hibiscus, lemon, and leggy grevillea.

A blue Snugli clung to the handle of the firebox. Sewed onto the Snugli was a small, white kitten. The kitten was two and a half inches tall and had black eyes and a yellow nose. She wore a pink dress, at the neck of which was a pink bowtie. Eliza found the Snugli on the sidewalk behind Nedlands Public Library. When a child leaves home and the familiar appointments of room, found objects fill days. Lying atop the stove were a blue star Eliza plucked from the ground outside Coles and a small plastic orange horse she discovered amid grass in the Great Court at the university. The horse had only three legs. "If the horse rests, he may recover," Eliza said, dropping it into her pocket. A stew of objects brewed atop the stove: seven Baxters Soup cans, washed, their tops removed. Imported from Scotland, the cans had each contained 425 grams of soup: red lentil and lemon, carrot with crème fraîche, mushroom, chicken with mild korma spice, asparagus with fromage frais, Italian tomato with basil, and salmon, tomato, and basil. Inside a plastic container that once held 500 grams of Casa yogurt with nectarines, a pink plastic rose and single blue marble rested on four scallop shells. In order to eat the scallops, snails had drilled holes in the shells, making the shells easy to string. From the mouth of a clear plastic bottle six and a half inches high and once brimming with Glenrowan ginger waved a fan of blue tissue paper. In front of the fan stood a length of white wire around which Eliza twisted claret paper and to which she glued pods of silver paper, resembling pussy willow buds. Next to a box that had held fifty Bushnells Blue Label tea bags rested the plastic container for two liters of Cadbury lamington flavored ice cream with chocolate coconut sauce. "May contain Traces of Gluten and Nuts," the label warned. The gluten and nuts had vanished, their places taken by three fruits of firewood banksia, two of the fruits containing nine valves, the other seven, all the valves grinning clownishly.

Hanging off the front of the stove and held in place by the ice cream carton was a pale yellow tablecloth a foot square. Printed on the cloth was a map of Western Australia. In the middle of the map paddled a black swan, the names of thirty-one towns bobbing about it: Kununura, Wyndham, Derby, Manjimup, Coolgardie, Narrogin, and Meekathara, among others. Standing upright and resembling doors swinging from frames were five wrappers from bars of Cadbury milk chocolate, the wrappers depicting "Furry Friends." Eliza's friends included a grey-headed fruit bat, a bilby, a brown Antechinus, a feather-tail glider, and a mountain pigmy possum. At the end of the breeding season, male Antechinuses die, as at the end of childhood stuffed creatures are entombed in attics. Next to the friends lay three betting cards from Ascot, two-dollar bets wagered on Inveritas, Decoder, and Awesome Annie to place. None of the bets paid.

On a spongy pink packing pad Eliza found in a waste can at St. Hilda's lay a yellow residential parking permit. "Valid for Kalgoorlie Street," the permit was number 180 and had been laminated. Print on the permit was black. The seal of Mosman Park appeared in the top right-hand corner of the permit. In the upper part of the seal, a castle turret curved like a crown. Below the crenellations three windows stood open. Through the left window sailed a wooden ship. A grass tree flourished in the middle window while on the right rolled a mill wheel. Next to the permit stood a small book, three by three and half inches, *The Golden Age of Australian Art*. Ninety-five pages long, the book contained minute reproductions of well-known pictures by painters like Tom Roberts, Arthur Streeton, and Frederick McCubbin. In front of the book lay an enameled lapel pin, the insignia of Eliza's house at St. Hilda's depicted on it. The pin was shaped like a shield, and gold letters scrolled across a black background spelling DE GREY.

Leaning against the wall on each side of the recess were books and magazines. To the left stood fourteen Latin books, including *Latin Metre* by D. S. Raven, *Vocabulary of Caesar's Gallic War*, *Ritchie's Fabulae Faciles*, J. F. G. Potter's *Gradium*, *The New College Latin and English Dictionary*, and *New Latin Grammar* by Charles E. Bennett, this last a 1925 reprint of the 1918 edition. Inside the front cover of the book, Eliza's grandfather had written his name, Dudley Johnson. Propped against the right wall was a rack of magazines, the sort which would appeal to a fifteen-year-old, three issues of *Cosmopolitan;* the January 2001 number of *Vogue Australia;* two issues of *Harper's Bazaar,* and *Marie Claire,* the number for October 2000 costing $6.80. Headlines on the cover of *Marie Claire* advertised articles: "Festival of Fun," "Sun and Sex: The World's Wildest Party," "Can You Tell Who's Had Plastic Surgery," "Where Women Are Married for Money," "I Slept with Three Men a Week without My Husband Knowing," and "Why India's Rich Kids Are Getting Away with Murder."

"Why would readers care about decorations surrounding the stove in Eliza's room?" Vicki asked later. I didn't answer. What matters in my life, and, I suspect, what matters in the lives of most people are the small appointments of days, the details of which one wishes he could remember as he ages but which he cannot. Achievement does not make a life. Doings that slide quickly past, almost unnoticed, compose the texture of days. A cereal box scruffy with twigs, a half circle of soup cans—such things make one weep. When these objects vanish from memory, cloud smothers joy.

I spent only part of January genuflecting before the altar of youth. Instead of decorating our room with oddments, Vicki and I wandered the familiar. On weekends we bought fruit and vegetables in Fremantle. At the docks I recognized ships, the *Zebu Livestock Express,* for example, bound for Arabia, and the *Astral Ace,* an automobile carrier. Twice I ate lunch at the Boatshed, buying four wontons for a dollar, a vegetable pakora for a dollar and ten cents, then a spring roll for sixty cents. I washed the food down with mango smoothies costing four dollars each. When Vicki and I spent afternoons in Fremantle, we had coffee and cake at the Mill Bakehouse. One afternoon Vicki bought a slice of chocolate honey lace cake, and I, a lemon and lime brûlée. On the thirteenth we attended a reception aboard the USS *Bunker Hill,* a cruiser-destroyer, one of five ships in Abraham Lincoln battle group. Returning to the United States from the Persian Gulf, the ships docked in Fremantle for five days. At the reception we ate egg rolls, shrimp, and kangaroo satay. Afterward a sailor escorted us through the ship. The sailor had only two months left to serve, and time had dulled enthusiasm. "I have spent my tour of duty cleaning and painting, painting and cleaning," he said. "Everything is political," he continued. "The navy encourages sailors to spy. People report others in hopes of being promoted." "Once," the man said, "an operator cut me off three times while I was talking to my parents in New York. After the third time I slammed the receiver into the cradle. A supervisor heard the bang and ordered me to attend Anger Management." Once out of the navy the sailor hoped to become a policeman. He apologized for sounding tired, saying he only slept three hours the night before, explaining that he and two friends rented a hotel room in downtown Perth. Weariness may have loosened his grasp of fact. On beginning our tour he said 350 people served on the *Bunker Hill.* Later he said 180. Corridors in the ship were gray and narrow. Pipes twisted through them like arteries. Three days earlier the sailor fell sideways against a fitting and cut a question mark into skin in front of his left ear. A soft drink machine stood in one corridor. Only Coca-Cola was sold, and I wondered if the company had purchased a soft drink monopoly from the navy.

As books determine what people notice, so movies structure sight. In the control room the ordered jumble of charts, screens, and swivel chairs seemed the familiar furnishings of film. On the forward rear deck was a series of raised rectangles looking like the ends of larval cells in a wasp nest. Under the rectangles lurked missiles. I stood atop a rectangle and felt uneasy. At the conclusion of the tour, we walked through a hanger that housed two helicopters. Suspended on hooks from a beam was a mountain bike. After exploring the *Bunker Hill* I chatted with officers. All were pleasant, but in white uniforms, they seemed pressed out of angular, thoughtful individuality, making me long for dark mood and cacophony.

Four days later I drove the family downtown. Early in December I arranged a week's riding in the Alpine National Park in Victoria, the High Country or the Australian Alps, as the area is known. We planned to cross Mr. Bogong, at 6,400 feet the highest horseback riding in Australia. In anticipation trips seem adventuresome. In accomplishment they are onerous. In part I travel in order to adorn passive life with tags, paragraphs that from the distorting perspective of years will wave colorfully. When I was young, I acted thoughtlessly, exuberant hormonal innocence thrusting me into the presence of the new. Age dissociates one from contemporary life. Now misgiving pinches my stride, and the unknown makes me timorous. To park in Perth a driver does not pay an attendant. Instead he pays a square white machine. After estimating the time he will be parked, the driver drops coins into a slot. Afterward he receives a ticket that he puts inside his car on the dashboard. Several variations of this method exist. On entering some lots the driver receives a ticket. Before leaving he inserts the ticket into a machine. After he pays what the machine tells him, he takes his ticket back. At the entrance to the lot, he inserts the ticket into another machine. If the amount paid is correct, a barrier lifts, and he drives away. For a fortnight after we arrived in Perth, I avoided driving downtown for fear of not being able to master parking. At the airport parking is more complicated and involves tokens. At the end of January Vicki flew back to Connecticut. Because I worried that tokens would prove too complex for me, I pondered bundling Vicki off in a taxi.

Unlike Edward who could ride in his R. M. Williams boots, Vicki, Eliza, and I needed boots. At Wellington Surplus we bought Blundstone 500s, useful and cheap at ninety-eight dollars a pair, at least in comparison to boots at R. M. Williams that sold for two to three hundred dollars. In the first boot I tried on, a tack of silicon jabbed my big toe. The clerk tried to snip the tack off with finger-nail clippers. Next he attempted to file it into a nub. He was not successful. "I guess I will have to return the boot," he said. Buskers flourished on Murray and Hay streets. A bearded boy juggled dull knives. A one-man band played tunes by Stephen Foster, while I listened, "Old Black Joe" and "My Old Kentucky Home." On a sidewalk a boy drew pastels; in one a girl with a mane of blonde hair rode a unicorn. Outside the entrance to the Piccadilly Arcade, a man stood on a box. He dressed like an eighteenth-century burgher, square-toe shoes with buckles the size of bars of soap, knickers, and a coat that flared like a hoop. He had stained the clothes and himself bronze so that he looked like a statue. Often passersby didn't notice him, and his movements startled. When someone dropped a coin into a red box at his feet, he bowed slowly. In my family shoppers never confine visits to a single store. Because Vicki would soon return to the United States, she brought presents, among other things, a closet full of T-shirts with emus and kangaroos on the chests. For her Aunt Sallie stored in a nursing home in New Jersey, she purchased a stuffed kangaroo, its arms wrapping a joey. At home she snipped off the tag stating, "Made in Taiwan." She also bought boxes of chocolate macadamia nuts, the candy coming from Gympie in Queensland.

Two days later at 7:30 in the morning, we took the "Express" from Fremantle to Rottnest, an island nineteen kilometers from the quay. Eleven kilometers long and four and a half kilometers wide at its broadest point, Rottnest was once a penal settlement for Aborigines. During the world wars it was an internment camp. Now, an advertisement declared it to be "one of Western Australia's most popular holiday resorts," offering relaxation "from the pressures of city life." We landed on the island at eight o'clock. At eight-thirty the bicycle shop opened, and we rented bicycles. The bicycles were terrible, and Vicki called the people renting them "bandits." All treads had worn off the rear tire of the first bike I was handed. In places rubber had vanished, exposing slashes of fabric. "The last time I went to Rottnest," a woman said to me later in the Lane Bookstore in Claremont, "my rear tire exploded at the west end of the island, and I wasted most of the day walking back to the bicycle shed." "My husband and I rented a bicycle built for two," another woman interrupted, "and it snapped in half as we were going up a hill. Think what would have happened if we had been riding down a hill." "Outlaws," she continued, "the store should be called Outlaw Bike Rental." Despite bald tires and palsied frames, our bicycles lasted the day. We spent the morning circling the island, a twenty-four-and-a-half-kilometer trek, stopping at Parker Point, Little Salmon Bay, Nancy Cove, Fish Hook Bay, and Crayfish Rock, among other spots.

Near Government House we smelled then saw quokkas. The fragrance smacked of hay black with mold. Small wallabies, quokkas have leathery quirts for tails and ears like those of Teddy bears. During our circuit of the island, I saw scores of quokkas, nine of them on the roadside, sun-dried, their bodies, forks of bones, tablemats of hair collapsing over them. Near Porpoise Bay a dugite rolled out of the bush and loosened into a line in order to cross the road. On seeing me, however, the snake knotted itself back into the scrub. At Little Salmon Bay bridled terns straddled the wind. A shawl of Caspian terns blew around Cape Vlamingh. Ruddy turnstones foraged Porpoise Point while banded and black-winged stilts hunted the shoreline of Lake Baghdad, their legs bracketing movement. Stands of moonah billowed over the ground in green fogs, and cypress and tuart grew in curves before the road straightened into forearms. Coast sword-sedge diced light and shadow into orange and green, brown and black. Sweaters of prickle lily grew in unruly bundles. Off shore under water color blossomed bacterial, green, blue, and orange splotches round as petri dishes. At the west end of the island, I stared at limestone. One moment the shoreline seemed sharp as a grater, the next soft as margarine.

At times I pedaled hard. From the Crossroads to Cape Vlaming, four and half kilometers, I raced, and water gathered in salty pools on the backs of my hands. After completing the circuit of the island, we ate at the Settlement. Both food and service were the worst I'd experienced in Australia. "Yes," a woman agreed. "There is no worse food on the continent. But just think how tourists would swamp Rottnest if the food were decent." After lunch Vicki roamed the Settlement while Eliza, Edward, and I cycled to Little Parakeet Bay and swam. I changed into my bathing suit on the beach. "Now we will have a treat," a large woman said to a friend sitting next to her. I shuffled in and out of towels easily, and the women were disappointed. We left Rottnest at 4:30 on the Express. That night Vicki's legs tingled. The muscle above my right knee rolled into a bun and ached. My left hip throbbed, the pain hollow and echoing like sound deep in a well. "If a little cycling makes us this sore," Vicki said, "how will we cope with horses?"

Packing preceded endurance. Vicki is slender; yet she stuffs suitcases. Although I am rotund, I force bags onto no-fat regiments of clothes, or at least attempt to do so. Rarely are our bags light. Because we spent five nights in Melbourne then six nights in the high country, Vicki packed for heat and cold. Each of us lugged a duffel, a foot wide, a foot tall, and two and a half feet long. With two wheels at one end, a handle at the other, and sundry zippered pockets, the duffels accommodated last-minute additions: gloves, extra underpants, and work shirts. Each duffel contained three pairs of shoes: the Blundstone boots, sandals, and in my case, a pair of Saucony jogging shoes bought twelve years ago for fourteen dollars. I didn't wear the jogging shoes and many of the clothes: sweat pants, a gray sweatshirt, khaki trousers, and most pairs of underwear. Hours in a saddle knead underwear into grainy loaves. Riding did not chafe me, however. Before leaving Perth I bought a 250-gram canister of *Baby,* a blend of zinc oxide and castor oil, "wonderful," the girl who waited on me at the chemist's said, "for treating nappy rash." To help keep streams

SAM PICKERING

clean, I didn't bath in the Alpine forest. Neither did I shave or wash my hands. As a result slag collected under my fingernails. I brushed my teeth at least once a day, however. Chafng aside, riding corrugated my bottom, grinding dirt into crevices and creating a rich environment for fungus. On returning to Perth I discovered a rash of the sort I thought I'd abandoned when I hung up my helmet and shoulder pads and left high school forty years ago.

In the saddle I wore two long-sleeved shirts, one for the first three days, the other for the last two. I wore long sleeves in order to protect my arms from sunburn. During the trip I wore a single pair of blue jeans, even sleeping in them, only taking them off one night when the sleeping bag became an oven. Over my shirt I wore an orange vest, purchased sixteen years ago from Forestry Suppliers in Jackson, Mississippi. The vest resembled gear worn by highway workers. Across the front stretched three pockets. In them I stored pads and pens, eyeglasses, and hand lenses. High on the left side of the jacket were five small pockets, each wide enough to hold a twenty-gauge shotgun shell. Into these I crammed oddments, leaves, for example, which I snatched from branches. On the shoulders of the vest was a backpack in which I kept binoculars. Not once while in the saddle did I use binoculars. Neither did I take notes on horseback. Ascents and descents were steep, and instead of holding a pencil, I clutched the saddle horn. Only after they end do adventures become the nouns and verbs of paragraphs.

In addition to the duffels Vicki took a large handbag crammed with toiletries to Melbourne. For my part I carried an ancient black backpack. In it I stored pens, notebooks, wallet, and glasses, two pairs of these last, one for reading, the other for distance. Even when I wander downtown Perth, I carry my wallet in the backpack. To steal the wallet, a thief would have to tear the pack from my back, ripping my shoulders off then unzip two pockets, in the process negotiating four zippers, two of which have been frozen for eleven years. In Melbourne I carried a small library in the backpack, three guidebooks, the *Blue Guide* and *Frommer's* and *Fodor's* 2000. Eliza and I studied the books in order to plan days. Vicki and

Edward refused to look at them, their ignorance freeing them from responsibility. "Where shall eat?" Vicki said one night. "You've read the books. You should know a good place."

On the eighteenth we were scheduled to leave Perth at 5:15 in the afternoon and arrive in Melbourne at 11:40 that night, the difference in time zones accounting for three hours. On the morning of the eighteenth, I called Ansett. Our flight had been cancelled, and we were shifted to another plane, this one departing at 6:50. The new flight got under way late, and we arrived in Melbourne at 2:35. I do not sleep well on planes. Alas, watching a movie is impossible, my hearing having deteriorated beyond distinguishing static from syllable on earphones. We stayed in All Seasons Premier Grand Hotel at the corner of Flinders and Spencer streets, a useful location since the train for Albury and the high country left from the Spencer Street Station two hundred yards away. Once the home of railway administration, the hotel had a grand facade. Inside flanges had broken, making the running rough. The elevator in the lobby rarely worked, and usually we climbed stairs to our room on the fourth floor or took the freight elevator, the door of which faced a pantry, shelves boxy with cereals, corn flakes, Crispix, Special K, and Uncle Toby's Shredded Wheat. Unlike the elevator our room was convenient, the downstairs consisting of a dining alcove, kitchen, and combination sitting area and bedroom where the children slept. Vicki and I slept in a loft above the sitting area. Next to the loft was the bathroom. We arrived at the hotel at 3:44. Once I sorted out the reservation downstairs, got additional towels, and changed the reading on our clock, the time was 4:50. We slept five hours until ten, the sleep costing each of us $17.50 an hour. Actually I got up at eight-thirty and walked to the Spencer Street Station in order to book travel to Albury. I worried that trains would not run on Sunday, the day Bogong Horseback was to meet us in Albury. For years I have carried the burden of family travel, not simply deciding where to go and what to see but also making bookings, thus becoming liable for bumps in the road. Holidays exhaust me; relaxing is difficult, and I sleep less than at home. If I am not charting a path to a zoo or calling a taxi to take

SAM PICKERING

us to the airport, I worry about the next meal. At the station I bought tickets for a train leaving Melbourne at 9:20, and reaching Albury at one in the afternoon. On the twenty-seventh we left Albury at 4:15 in the afternoon and got back to Melbourne at 8:10. From the station I walked along Little Collins Street in search of a restaurant where the family could eat breakfast. That night at a Seven-Eleven store, Vicki purchased cereal, milk, juice, and bananas. For the next two mornings we ate in our room. After returning from the high country, I purchased milk and cereal at another Seven-Eleven, one I noticed during our wanderings around Melbourne.

No matter where one goes, much travel is ordinary. Routine domesticates the unfamiliar. We roamed downtown Melbourne, following the grid of streets: Flinders and Flinders Lane, Collins, Little Collins, Bourke, Little Bourke, Lonsdale, William, Queen, Elizabeth, Swanson, Russell, and Exhibition. When we returned from riding, we spent two nights on Exhibition at Saville Park Suites. Our rooms were on the seventeenth floor, and at night light floated upward between tall buildings then drifted east across the distance. London plane trees lined Melbourne's streets, and English sparrows plucked meals out of gutters. We spent time in arcades, Collins Place rising like a cloud, the Royal, silvery to the touch, and Melbourne Central, ledges of shops. Occasionally a building pasted itself to sight, on Collins, Portland House, once a townhouse; on the same street a Baptist church, portico scrubbed white and sinless. For the most part, though, buildings hung over us indistinct as bluffs, casting shadows, rarely allowing us perspective. Much sight, I suspect, depends upon association. Green and yellow trolleys clattered along streets, rumblings and clangs making me nostalgic for childhood and Centennial Park in Nashville where a red trolley had jumped the rails and run into a playground, furnishing the imaginations of decades of children.

"Melbourne is grittier than Perth," Vicki said. "Here buying and selling has a gray pallor." Below the All Seasons, rail and dockyards sprawled across a metallic wasteland. North of Melbourne the train to Albury passed through Moonee Ponds, Oak Park, and

Broadmeadow, suburbs in which houses were coupled in rows and in which flatcars of warehouses had been parked, the ponds, oaks, and meadow no longer visible. At Glenroy an old man watched the train pass. Holding his grandson's hand, he stood amid a knot of ties, weeds growing through the wood as if they were planters.

When I stood on the banks of the Yarra, I escaped catchments of buildings, and attention spread. The river itself flowed red and viscous, and from the shore came the yelps of horns advertising tourist barges. Red and yellow along the north bank, the Flinders Railway Station brought Kipling to mind, the station's luster fogged by pollution. Beyond the station the spire of St. Paul's Cathedral sliced upwards, its majesty anonymous amid a background of skyscrapers. On the south bank glassy buildings stood shelved: windows murky with color, those of Colonial green and blue and Phillip Morris turquoise.

The first day we walked to the Royal Botanic Gardens on St. Kilda. As I ambled Hopetoun Lawn, the city disappeared behind a curtain of trees: bunya bunya pine, its branches, rakes; Captain Cook's pine; and sugar gum, fugues of blue and yellow marking the white bark. Borers drilled finger-sized holes through a gully peppermint, and beetles chewed leaves of an English elm into lace, turning the foliage into an ivory fan. Yellow trickled from tecoma; shottia blossoms dried into red beans, and on saw banksia, fruits looked like pickle jars. Plaques stood at the bases of many trees. On May 12, 1901, the duke of Cornwall and York, later George V, planted an Indian cedar. On March 26, 1895, the younger son of the governor of Victoria planted an Algerian oak. While the child has long been compost, the tree had risen into its own halo, branches turning up green then curtseying and sweeping the ground.

I longed to linger in the garden, but Eliza's and Edward's passions are not green. Moreover temperature had climbed into the nineties, and I neglected to carry water bottles in my backpack. Consequently we trekked in straight lines over lawns: Oak, Princess, Eastern, and Tennyson. Occasionally flowers broke my

SAM PICKERING

stride, kahili ginger, for example, the flowers yellow spiders, the stamens fangs. In Fern Tree Gully flying foxes hung from trees like brown sacks. At the Terrace next to Ornamental Lake, I purchased fruit juice, and we sat on the grass and watched water birds: coots, swans, black ducks, and moor hens.

We walked back to Southgate and ate lunch in the food court. At Eliza's insistence we visited the aquarium. The building stood on the bank of the Yarra; to reach the aquarium we forded roads awash in cars. The best aquarium I've seen is in Chattanooga, Tennessee. In comparison, the Melbourne aquarium was second-class, not something I mentioned to Eliza. Rarely do I criticize during a trip. Instead I praise, hoping that enthusiasm becomes infectious. In the aquarium I learned that ten milliliters of box jelly poison could kill 50 adult males. While ten milliliters of venom from an inland taipan could knock off 250 men, the same amount of toxin from poison arrow frogs could erase a city of 50,000 people. For a long time I watched moon jellyfish pump ghostly through a tank. Brown sea nettles looked like golden umbrellas. Their innards were white as cottage cheese, wispy red strings trailing from them in snags.

That night we ate at the Supper Inn in Chinatown, an upstairs room at the end of Celestial Street, a dark cobbled way. I ordered quail cooked in spring onions and ginger, mud crab, a pot of satay seafood, lo-han vegetables, and pork sweetened with lotus. The meal was the best Chinese food I've eaten. Around my plate shells collected in heaps, spilling onto my shirt and shorts. We were the only tourists in the restaurant. "How did you discover the Inn?" a woman said as we walked down the street after the meal. The following night we ate at Pellegrini's on Bourke Street, topping spaghetti and cannelloni off with chocolate plum cake. So long as I followed suggestions in my library, we ate well. Sometimes, however, the family balked at hiking around Melbourne, and we ate conveniently, and poorly, making ourselves bilious with syrupy Thai curry or Greek sweets baked before the Battle of Marathon.

When traveling alone I chat with strangers. Such conversations embarrass Edward, and once I begin to talk, he strides off, only stopping when he is thirty yards away. In the Grand when I asked the concierge if a Rolls had arrived to fetch the family, saying that if the car were late we would hoof it, Edward fled the lobby. One night on Little Collins Street a man spoke to us. Edward wore a shirt with "Sewanee," my old college, emblazoned on the front. The man had visited Sewanee and was in Melbourne, he said, to referee the Australian Open, a tennis tournament. He earned a good living, he told me, traveling the world and refereeing tennis. On my asking the man questions about his life, Edward walked away and crossed Elizabeth to the next block. In truth Vicki and I do embarrass the children. We have aged beyond thinking that strangers think about us. From Perth Vicki brought a handful of yellow Poo-ch Pouches, plastic bags in which dog owners are supposed to stuff droppings. In the pouches Vicki crammed snacks, usually fruit, and I carried them in my backpack.

Often people who speak to tourists do so because they want money. "We've just come from Cairns. I left my wallet on the bus," a boy said to me and Eliza, his friend silent beside him, eyes gray, drugs grinding thought to frass. "Could you give us money for dinner? I will mail it back to you." "Bullshit," I said, pulling Eliza away. "Daddy," Eliza implored. "Be quiet," I commanded. "This is for you," a girl said, handing me a broadside. Entitled "To You!—With Love!" the broadside was published by "The Family." "Dear One," it began, "You are MY child and I love you. It's just that simple. No matter what you've done or what you haven't done, I love you! You have an eternal spirit living within you, and I know your spirit intimately, and I love you." "There is a comma blunder in the first sentence," I said to Eliza. "Isn't that petty?" Eliza said. "Yes," I said, "petty and commonsensical." That night on Flinders a man unloaded a van and handed sandwiches, doughnuts, and coffee to the down and out. The broadside said "The Key to My Vault" was Jesus. "Good works," I said to Eliza, "open vaults. Doughnuts and coffee matter more than words." "Maybe," Eliza said, "but look in the window." In the window was a display of toilet seats. For $295 I could purchase a "Loo with a View." The top of the seat was clear plastic. Beneath it frolicked a reef of sea creatures: star fish, periwinkles, scallop shells, lips of coral, and sea horses.

On holiday busyness is all. At home when hours gape, association evokes the familiar. A snapshot brings loss to mind, and like a collar, story wraps a Staffordshire dog. Hotel furnishings are generic, evoking not the rich design of life but cloudy recollections of other hotel rooms. A child switches on the television. Programs are the same as they are at home, and parents wonder why they left their living rooms. Keeping busy fosters the illusion of accomplishment and thus satisfies. Tourists cajole themselves into believing frenetic activity educates. In Melbourne we rode the elevator up fifty-five floors to Rialto Towers Observation Deck. About us the city circled like hands pressed wrist to wrist, fingers of growth digging across the distance. For ninety minutes we wandered the Old Melbourne Gaol. During its early years warders ran the jail on the silent system, and when prisoners left cells, they wore calico hoods. Cells were small and dark, and the interior of the building resembled a cave, grim testimonial to inhumanity. Displayed in cells were death masks of executed criminals, some of whom were evil, others simply poor people broken by bad luck. Stories of prisoners sucked sunlight out of moments, not something that enervated, however, but perversely invigorated as brutality often does. In the shop Vicki bought me a T-shirt. Reproduced on the chest was a lithograph that originally appeared on the front page of the *Australian Sketches* on July 3, 1880. Under the illustration ran the headline, NED KELLY AT BAY. A bushranger, Kelly is the stuff of folklore, in part because he wore armor. In the lithograph he is firing a pistol, iron plate bulging beneath his coat, on his head an iron bucket. The jail contained a leather imitation of Kelly's armor. Children stood in line to put the armor on and have their pictures taken.

Melbourne is an ethnic stew, streets crowded with all peoples except Aborigines. "I did not see one Aborigine in Melbourne," Edward said. "Neither did I," Eliza added. "I doubt Reconciliation [a vague policy of the government blending good will with legislation in hopes of bettering the lives of Aborigines] means much to

people here, except guilt-ridden descendants of the British."
"Right, people who aren't happy unless they are melancholy,"
Edward said. "Not only are recent immigrants imprisoned by
parochial ethnicity, but in struggling to better their lives, they
don't have the leisure to worry about strangers." At the zoo Vicki
and I heard a United Nations of languages, the range of Arabic
dialects startling. We went to the zoo on Sunday after returning
from Albury. Strollers clogged walkways. For a while I counted
people on whose calves tattoos clung like leeches. I stopped at
twenty-six. I thought about counting tattoos on shoulders but
didn't, the number being defeating. Zoos do not nurture brother-
hood. Two boys threw stones at baboons, and a mob of children
chased pelicans down a walk shrieking in an unknown tongue.
Despite the crowd we spent three hours at the zoo. We watched
meerkats eat mealy worms. A keeper fed wombats. A red panda
dozed in a tree, and a leopard paced a tight knot. In the Reptile
House an eastern diamondback rattlesnake unwound and flicked
its tongue. "The snake should be in the Everglades under a pal-
metto," Vicki said. Eliza said she wished we could buy an elephant
and free it.

Before taking a trolley to the zoo, we roamed Queen Victoria
Markets, a switching yard of indoor and outdoor shops. Strewn
through the shops were heaps of sweatshirts, shoes, and leather
jackets. For seven dollars Vicki bought a new watchband. Across
the aisle from the watches, posters were for sale, all depicting bare-
breasted women, athletic jerseys painted on their bosoms. For the
Swans the paint was red and white; for the Tigers black and yellow.
For a while I watched a Weazel Ball, a mound of fur glued to a red
and yellow ball that waggled, creating the impression that an animal was trying to swallow it. A busker in a top hat played blues on
a battered schoolroom piano. A Pakistani sang country and western music, and children rode a camel in a circle. From a rafter
hung a Boyds Bear rug. On the fabric a mother bear sat in a comfortable arm chair reading the *Book of Love,* her feet atop a foot
rest, toes splayed and claws soft curls. She wore a thick cable
sweater in the center of which throbbed a red heart. To her left a

lamp stood on a table, the shade blue but patched with pink. On the wall hung a paraphrase of Elizabeth Barrett Browning's poem, "How do I love thee? Let me count the ways," the *thee* emended to *you*. The rug sold for $165. I asked the owner of the stall if he sold many rugs. "Lots," he said. I assumed the rug was made in Asia. "No," the man said, "North Carolina." "Good God," I said.

Whenever we travel, we visit art museums. The National Gallery of Victoria was in the process of moving to a new building. In the State Library on Russell Street, a sample of the gallery's holdings was on exhibit. We spent a morning wandering a floor, smallness pleasing by concentrating attention. George Le Fefebvre's nude *Chloe* once decorated a bar. In the painting Chloe stood by a stream. Unlike the water Chloe's skin glistened, her body a necklace of natural pearls bumpy at hips and elbows. Over Arthur Streeton's *Hawkesbury River* heat rose thick and purple. Wearing overcoats battalions of people marched across John Brack's *Collins St. 5 P.M.*, faces liverish and sharp, pressed out of individuality. In Frederick McCubbin's *Lost* a little girl wearing a straw hat and blue dress, an apron over the front, stood amid mallee and gum. "She is not as lost as that crowd on Collins Street," Eliza said, "even though they know where they are."

On display was *Wow*, seventy-two garments designed by Versace from 1982–1997. We wandered the wardrobe. Icons studded leather jackets. Printed on a silk robe were the faces of Marilyn Monroe and James Dean. Gold and silver safety pins clamped the right sleeve of a jacket to a coat. On a placard a critic described Versace's influence. "Women's fashions were empowered with a defiant approach directed against mainstream dressing with the use of leather, denim, brash prints, bondage references." "Ho, hum," I thought. Albeit tarty the exhibition entertained. Eliza selected her favorite dress, a silk chiffon, gray, white, and black, decorated with imitations of Calder mobiles resembling serving spoons. "Women who wear that kind of dress only eat celery," Vicki said, adding, "Enough fashion. Where are we going to eat lunch?"

Because we left Melbourne the next morning, I slept poorly. At 2:36 that night I inhaled a banana and a bowl of corn flakes. At 6:33

the alarm jangled, and I roused the family. We were on the platform eighteen minutes before the train left for Albury. While we waited for the conductor to open Car C, the honey wagon passed, a yellow tank on a flatbed. "Getting the train ready for us," I said. For the first part of the trip, an afflicted man asked me questions about the presidential election. Two rows forward a man wearing a green and yellow shirt drank beer, seven cans by the time we reached Albury. On the return to Melbourne every seat in the train had been sold, and people sitting opposite alternated knees with us. To pass time I read the names of towns through which the train passed. They sounded poetic: Wodonga, Chiltern, Springhurst, and Wangaratta, Benalla, Violet Town, Euroa, Avenel, and Seymore. As the train slid eastward, small flocks of sulfur-crested cockatoos wheeled across paddocks. White-necked herons fished pools. In fields bulbous tires of hay sagged deflated. Trusses supported weathered sheds, and under eaves cisterns hunkered beneath appliqués of dust. Just beyond the right of way, stumps bristled, the trees having been sawed into poles and firewood. After Chiltern the land thickened in green wrinkles, fattening Herefords so that red seemed to burst through their ribs.

Bogong Horseback sat north of Mt. Beauty in Tawonga in the Kiewa River Valley. Steve Baird had run the business for sixteen years. Earlier he had been a builder. Now he and his wife Kathy owned fifty-three horses. Being able to construct something other than paragraphs was necessary to the business. Not simply horses, but gear of sundry sorts, packs, stables, and four-wheeled drives, required tinkering. Mick, the Bairds' only paid employee, fetched us from Albury. Like Steve, Mick had been a builder. Out of trekking season he rode bulls. "A good rider," he said, "can make thirty thousand dollars a year." The Bairds bartered room, board, and close contact with horses for work. During vacations children of former clients appeared at their door. Kathy was motherly, and children who wilted in cities sometimes bloomed in the country. Because we were the only clients who booked the trip scheduled for the twenty-first, the Bairds opened the ride to people helping at Bogong. Riding with us were Steve, his son Clay a secondary school student, Mick, Joyce a teenager who worked at Bogong during vacations, Lisa who had helped Kathy for a year, and Sabena, a Dutch girl who traded a fortnight's work at Tawonga for half the price of the ride. All were capable, pleasant, and responsible. But having known each other before the ride, they constituted an insiders' club. While they slept together under a tarpaulin, we slept elsewhere. A greater number of customers would have diluted the Bogong group. Instead of conversation's turning toward topics familiar to group, words might have ranged, making campfires spark. Instead as soon as dinner ended, Vicki, the children, and I bedded down, something we might have done no matter the number of customers, the hours of riding having made bones ache for sleep.

We spent the night before the ride in a cabin near Bogong Homestead. The cabin looked down on a lush valley. Beyond the valley the Alpine National Forest rumpled high and hazy. Beside the cabin grew a blue gum. Six feet above ground the trunk of the tree shattered into a web of branches, leaves thick at the ends and sharp as steel wool. Flails of bark dangled from limbs. Pieces broke and sifting to the ground, skittered across fallen leaves in a dry patter. A Lewin's honeyeater darted into the tree. White-winged choughs flew along a windbreak of silver trees, and a crimson rosella settled into a gum, its red head and black chest bright against the blue sky.

For an hour I sat in front of the cabin. A white horse stood in a paddock, and Herefords grazed high grass. An airplane towed a pale glider into the mountains. A black-faced cuckoo shrike sat on a fence post. A pair of nankeen kestrels treaded the air. The kestrels hunted an arm of pasture between a telephone pole and a skeletal blue gum, the tips of its branches bony perches. When a person is still, life collects around him shaping place. In contrast movement forces place outward, and to see particulars the eye hurries, soon tiring the observer. Superb blue wrens skipped through a thicket at my feet, most brown females or males in eclipse, that is, dull brown after the breeding season.

At seven the next morning we ate breakfast with the Bairds.

Two hours later, seventeen horses left the stable, six of them pack-horses, ten carrying people, and one spare. Vicki rode Swindler; Eliza, Eric; and Edward, Mac. My horse was a twelve-year-old chestnut named Lawson. At sixteen hands he was strong enough to carry a frame sprung by five months of cake and cappuccino. Height made him difficult to mount. I stuffed my left leg into the stirrup and pushed my toes through with my right hand after which I bounced four times on my right foot in hopes spring would elevate me. Attached to the back of the saddle were two bags. Into each I crammed a black bag with a drawstring at the top. The bags carried three pairs of socks; a pair of underwear; and two clean T-shirts, on the front of one a yellow and black garden spider, on the other, twenty-five insects, including a stink bug, a spotted cucumber beetle, a velvet ant, and a Jerusalem cricket. Also in the bags were toothpaste, brush, floss, and a water bottle. I filled the bottle at mountain streams, Steve having assured us the water was pure, something I wondered about when we rode through cattle grazing the high country. Still I avoided sickness, and days were so hot and humid, I would have drunk directly from streams, no matter the manure.

Strapped across the saddlebags and behind the saddle was a bedroll, consisting of sleeping bag, pillow, a black plastic garbage bag sliced open to form a six-foot strip, and a semi-waterproof canvas cover, Velcro straps running its length. Holidays are work. Pressing the bag into a tight roll while sealing in it both the plastic bag and the cover exhausted me. First I stretched the cover open on the ground. On it I laid the garbage bag. In the garbage bag I placed sleeping bag and pillow. At each end of the cover were pockets. Into the pockets I forced the head and foot of the sleeping bag, the garbage bag underneath forming a protective raincoat. Once the sleeping bag was secure in the pockets, I turned the cover over it, kneeling on it, my knuckles white from the effort of kneading it into a roll small enough for me to seal by pressing the Velcro strips together. Once the bedroll was sealed, I tied it to the back of the saddle with leather thongs. At night I placed a swag beneath my sleeping bag, the swag being a water-repellant canvas. The swag consisted of two flaps, a bottom and a deep pocket into which I pushed the lower two-thirds of my sleeping bag. Once on the ground I could pull the flaps over me like shutters and shield body and head from rain. In the morning I beat the swag into a square bundle after which it became part of packhorse's load.

My arms trembled when I hoisted my saddle off the ground. More often than not riding seemed ordeal not vacation. "By the time you have been in Perth for a week," Vicki said, "you will remember this trip fondly." Vicki was right. However, riding was sweat-intensive. After each day's ride I stacked blankets and saddle against a tree. In mornings after mincing my bedroll into a sausage, I saddled Lawson, recognizing him because a constellation of three white stars flickered across his flank. Getting Lawson to take the bit was tiring. I swung my right arm around his head and pushed his head down. Next I pulled the bridle over his ears and buckled the straps. Afterward I smoothed Lawson's mane, combing it with my fingers. Straps and buckles seemed fertile, not only dangling mysteriously, but during nights producing foundlings. Once the bridle was buckled, I put two blankets on Lawson's back, making sure to form an upside down *V* over his withers. In the humid weather blankets didn't dry. Early in the morning they were heavy, and I had trouble positioning them. Once the blankets were in place, I picked up my saddle and using both arms threw it atop Lawson, making sure saddlebags, stirrups, and sundry straps, especially the girth, did not catch underneath the seat. Afterward I rested, slumping against the saddle, my forehead damp on the leather. Eventually I lifted Lawson's tail and pushed it through the tail strap. Next I buckled the chest strap and slipping the girth through a loop buckled the girth. Because of my weight, a second girth strap cinched under Lawson's belly, this being inserted through a buckle after a puzzle of twists and turns. Lastly I adjusted the stirrups and tied Lawson's reins to a low branch.

Once Lawson was saddled, I ate breakfast, always muesli soaked in fruit cocktail. I drank two cups of tea then a cup of coffee. In the heat liquid ran from me in faucets, and never was I forced to dismount and trot behind a bush. Lunch was a respite from the saddle, providing opportunity to straighten legs, sit under a tree, and drink water. Lunch consisted of ham stuffed into a yellow bun round as a dinner plate. Along with the ham one could squeeze in beets, mustard, cucumbers, in fact a delicatessen of edibles. After the first lunch I never ate more than a quarter of a sandwich. At night Steve and Clay cooked. Both were first-rate chefs, and we ate spaghetti, lamb, steak, and pasta. During dinner I drank a bottle of beer and two bottles of creek water.

Twice during the trip Lawson stepped on my left foot, initially when I saddled him at Bogong then at the end of the trip when I removed the saddle for the final time. In Perth the nail on my second toe turned black but instead of falling out clung to my foot like a loose horseshoe. Every morning Lawson led me around paddocks, the reins I tossed at him swishing the air. Nevertheless, he was an easy horse, translating my muddy riding into a steady pace. I wore a riding helmet the entire trip. I was the only person to do so. "My brains aren't special," I told Vicki. "But until Eliza finishes college, I need wit enough to earn tuition." As horses climbed and descended rocky paths, shoes clacking and slipping, I wondered what would happen if Lawson fell. My ability to spring from chairs, porches, diving boards, and stirrups had gone the way of all muscles. I imagined one of my legs exploding like a firecracker. Age has made me faint-hearted, if not faint-talking. At the end of the trek, I longed to ride more. Yet, completion of the ride also relieved me. Accident had not bucked any of us into broken bones. I enjoyed riding: the smooth saddle, the mulled fragrance of horse, and the pitch and pull of muscle. By trip's end I was a better horseman, not a good or decent rider, but someone more alert in the saddle. Awareness breeds melancholy. When I dismounted in the barn, Time reared and flashed its hooves. I knew I would never ride again.

The first day we rode fifteen kilometers. Near the park entrance dogwood bloomed, flowers hanging from twigs like loose white gloves. Flax lilies lined the trail in a blue curb. In spots springy with damp necklace ferns hung over rocks; water ferns clustered together metallic, and beneath tree ferns shadows bunched dark in thick plush carpets. That evening we camped at Bogong Creek Huts, a soiled apron of cleared land clinging to a slope. Vicki and I cooled off in Bogong Creek. Beside the creek a black snake lay braided between rocks. Although Edward and Eliza saw several black and tiger snakes, I saw only one other snake. Near Holland's Knob a juvenile brown snake combed through grass to avoid Lawson's hooves. We spent the night under a eucalyptus tree on a pan above the creek. Snakes coiled in my imagination, and I did not sleep well. Humidity was thick as batter, and by morning I'd removed my trousers and underpants. A *discophlebia,* probably a *catocalina,* fell on Vicki's arm during the night, the hairs on the caterpillar irritating Vicki's skin. By morning small lumps were grainy across her arms and upper chest. During the following days the lumps reddened, filled with pus, and burst. At the camp native bees worked the ground, so many that the grass seemed strings the bees sawed into music. Swarms of March flies, heavy green-eyed horseflies, plagued the camp. Once I counted fourteen on my right ankle. March flies are slow and easy to swat. My record for swatting and not missing was eleven. The flies were sturdy, however. Only crushing killed them. After being knocked to ground, flies rolled onto their backs and feigned death. After a few moments they flipped over and throbbed back into irritating flight. When I rode, bush flies patched my sleeves, at times so many that my orange jacket seemed brown, only mottled with orange.

At the huts I sat on the ground and leaned backwards, my left hand a strut. The strut quickly collapsed as a needle ran hot into my fourth finger. I'd put my hand on a bull ant. Above tree line holes pocked the ground. Inside the holes lurked spiders the size of fifty-cent pieces, short thick legs supporting bodies that looked like miniature half-tracks. In Linda's Meadow, Clay said the spiders were alpine funnel webs, "more dangerous than the Sydney funnel web." I think the spiders were alpine wolf spiders, creatures capable of spoiling an afternoon but not ending life. Insects vary more than verbs and nouns, and if I could start school again, I'd be an entomologist. Pale orange lady bugs the size of thumb-nails clung like galls to eucalyptus leaves. A walking stick jutted out from a ghost gum. In wet grass near the paddock at Tawonga Creek, shield-backed katydids resembled yellow and green lattices. A female mountain katydid humped dark amid the grass, its body one and a quarter inches long, three-fourths of an inch tall, and two-thirds wide. The katydid's tegmina folded over its back, veined like leaded Tiffany glass. Blue and green speckled the insect's body, and its legs seemed black and white brackets. As the horses climbed through blue gums, small azure butterflies flipped about the trail like coins. Australian admirals lounged in sunlight that dappled the forest, forewings black at the tips, amid the black two pools white as salt. Higher in the mountains xenicas swarmed orange and nervous.

Set against the hillside at Bogong Creek was an outhouse. Raised on tales of black widow spiders napping under outhouse seats and of black snakes twirled around rafters, I avoid outhouses. At other stops Steve dug a hole and after draping a quilt between trees set Jimmy's Thunder Box over the hole. The box was a wooden cube with a circle cut out of the top and the bottom open. The box collapsed, making packing it easy. Although I studied the box, noting that it was made in Koonbrook, Victoria, I did not use it.

Bogong Creek Huts lacked a paddock. Because we were near Tawonga, Steve shut a gate along the trail and hobbled the horses. At dusk two mountain bikers slid down the trail, nearing the end of a fifty-kilometer ride. Twenty minutes later they returned. Their sudden appearance frightened the horses grazing beside the trail. Despite the hobbles the horses bolted, bashing the gate to the ground. Clay, Mick, Joyce, and Lisa grabbed four of the remaining horses and pursued the bolters. Two and a half hours later they returned, driving the other horses before them. One horse went lame, the hobble having worn the hide away beneath the fetlock. Flies swarmed over the raw flesh, lifting momentarily when Lisa sprayed the wound with an iodine solution. The breakaway altered the trip. "Bogong Crossing," Steve noted later, "dumped in favor of Fainter Crossing for the sake of sore horses." Fainter was easier and not so high as Bogong. The decision to cross Fainter disappointed me. I wanted to cross Bogong and boast that I had done the highest riding possible in Australia. I booked Bogong on purpose, avoiding a trip over Fainter that left a week earlier.

Plans had not changed when we broke camp the next morning. I wanted to help pack the horses. Sixteen years of trips had hardened procedures, and my presence, despite being well-intentioned, would have irritated. Each packhorse carried between 100 and 120 kilos, the load for a horse changing each day in order to lessen the chance of saddle sores. Much gear fitted into back leather boxes shaped like deep drawers in a file cabinet. Across the back of each horse lay a saddle shaped like a yoke. Iron hooks curved out from the sides of the yoke. From the hooks hung bags. Lashed atop the bags was a tarpaulin that served as a tent, and sundry containers, for example, a "vet set" shaped like a log.

The second day was the most difficult and consequently the best of the trip. We rode between seven and eight hours, climbing through eucalyptus forests, following spurs atop mountains, and then camping in Frost Hollow, tucked into a corner of Wildhorse Creek. Wind-beaten ghost gums gnarled about the campground, sawfly larvae wrapping leaves in bracelets, branches torn apart by cockatoos digging for beetle grubs. From Bogong Creek we had climbed through blackwood; blue and gray gum, the trunk of the latter smooth, its leaves small fingers; and alpine ash, this last heavily lumbered beyond the park. To prevent erosion loggers clear-cut small patches of forest in which new growth soon sprouted bushy. Nevertheless, lumbered portions were pedestrian. Trees were the same age and height and did not attract a diversity of life. A forest in which trees are different ages furnishes habitats for sundry creatures. Moreover variety awakens the eye and stimulates the mind. Because variety first intrigues then makes passersby appreciate place, it shapes environmentalists. In contrast uniformity dulls people into indifference.

In the eucalyptus forest gardens grew beside the trail: yellow speedwell; Victorian mint bush, purple stippling lower petals; hop bush; blanket leaf; and penny royal. The medicinal fragrances of penny royal, mint bush, and eucalyptus drifted through the thick air almost as if sprayed from atomizers. The calls of whipbirds diced the heat, and songs of lyrebirds bounced saucy with mimicry. When seams opened through trees and light shone on the trail, Billy buttons bloomed. Cups of earth between rocks became planters, rich with sunrays and everlastings. Clumps of snow daisies blossomed, their pale leaves seeping up leached from the ground. Under the lips of gullies grass trigger plant and royal bluebell flourished. As we climbed higher, alpine mint bush, cattleman's lettuce, and heath myrtle appeared. A pair of brown falcons hovered off Fainter. We cantered, and a herd of Herefords scattered tumbling like barrels.

We spent the third night at Tawonga Creek Huts. A rail fence surrounded a paddock, and we didn't hobble the horses. Three streams trickled past the huts and emptied into a creek that rolled through rocky pools. The sky was yeasty with thunderclaps when I spread our swags near a small hut. Over the swags I laid the plastic garbage bags. After dinner rain galloped through the camp, chopping the ground until after midnight. I rolled the children's sleeping bags and put them in the hut where Steve cooked dinner. The Bogong group raised a tarpaulin over their bags and guttered the area with a trench. After arranging the children's bags, I pulled Vicki's and my bags into another cabin, one rarely used and mothy with spider webs. I worked alone in the heavy rain and got soaked. Although my sleeping bag was wet and the floor of the cabin hard and flat, I slept well, the rain playing the tin roof of the cabin like an accordion. By the paddock stood an old ghost gum. The trunk was massive and bulbous. After the rain the wood looked pickled, green, blue, orange, and cream. Limbs rose thick then swung out in massive pipes. Weather had shattered many small gums along the train. From rootstock new limbs grew weedy. The tree beside the paddock was so big, it seemed thoughtful. Ravens squatted in its branches, their calls shredded and grinding.

We spent the last night of the ride in a paddock, tacked to the edge of a ridge. Supposedly Bogong Jack, a rustler, had built a paddock in the same place. Gang-gang cockatoos rushed across the paddock and perched in the crown of a eucalyptus, looking like pink jewels set in green. Flame robins flickered above the ground. The day was gray, and the orange breasts of the birds lit the grass. That night rain fell in a thin curtain. Vicki and the children squeezed under the tarpaulin, but I pulled the swag over my head and slept.

The next day we returned to Tawonga. That evening Steve and Kathy cooked dinner for us. The following afternoon we rode the V-Line back to Melbourne. Two days later we were back in Perth, and I checked email at the university. Forty-two letters awaited me. I deleted thirty-seven unread. A student wrote me from the University of Connecticut. "I am sorry I will not be in class Wednesday the 31st for our quiz. my girlfriend was flown into the hospital, near her school in Virginia Tech after a car accident. I drove through the night to see her ont he 29th. I wil be back for class on the 2nd of febuary though. If you need documentation of her accident, I will not be offended, and would gladly provide it so that i could make up the quiz. thank you very much. She will be fine if you are wondering. Email me back with a response to this request. Thank you so much!!" The spelling and grammar appalled me, and for a moment I thought about correcting my correspondent's letter and mailing it back to him. I resisted the urge. "I am glad your girlfriend is better," I wrote. "I regret, how-ever, that I will not be able to reschedule the test. Changing the date from Australia would be difficult, especially since I am not your teacher." I ended by reminding the student that the road from Blacksburg, Virginia, to Storrs was long, and I urged him to drive carefully. "Oh, but you are a sweetie," Vicki said. "Yes," I said, "I'm a sweet one."

Man about the House

The last day in January Vicki left Perth for Hartford and weeks of
cleaning her mother's house in New Jersey. The trip was long, over
forty-six hours. Vicki's ordeal dropped from mind, however, as
soon as her plane pushed into the clouds above Perth. Two
decades ago Vicki banished me from the kitchen, my rattling ways
with pots and pans jarring her. Similarly she jerked the vacuum
from my hand, saying I banged the legs of chairs and sofas into
scabs. The death of Vicki's mother, though, forced me back into
the kitchen, thrusting soup, salad, and scrub brushes into my
hands. Driving back from the airport, I wondered what sort of
man about the house I'd be. I was fifty-nine, and vigor no longer
rolled my eyelids up like shades every morning. For twenty years I
had been true to pad and pencil. Now I would philander days,
shopping, cooking, cleaning, and currying children's moods out
of hot into mild.

Eight weeks have passed, and I am wondrously content. Boxed
domesticity is as exciting as the outback. Of course Vicki's absence
has caused changes. No one irons the children's school clothes.
The sun presses shirts, and when I remove trousers from the line,
they hang like stovepipes. Without Vicki meals are smaller but just
as nourishing. Never do I cook more than one vegetable. Still
more meals are vegetarian, consisting of salad and pasta. Not once
during the past eight weeks have I snacked on anything other than
fruit. A month and a half of sane eating cannot atone for five

intemperate months. Nevertheless I have dropped two notches on my belt. Every night Vicki drank beer or wine with dinner. To be social I accompanied her. Wine has vanished from the table, and now I drink only orange or mango juice at dinner. Vicki's and my conversation often nagged shortcoming into rancor. As a result hours seemed raw and chaffed. Since no one is near with whom I can rub words into blisters, slights drain from mind. Consequently, days are sunnier, and the children are better companions, not just selfish teenagers.

At Cottesloe once or twice I've noticed women sunning themselves, their bare breasts slowing me as if I were approaching a traffic light. Never do I stop. Chores hurry me on beyond yellow and red to the green aisle of a grocery. In truth instead of hankering for fleshly moments, I pine for shops. I shop every day, driving along Kalgoorlie to Glyde then along Harvey to Mosman Park Shopping Center, the distance six-tenths of a kilometer. I drive in order to carry groceries home, somewhere between forty-five and seventy dollars' worth, all in white plastic bags. At the Center I sometimes buy meat at Pronto Cuisine, a butcher, and fruit and salad makings at Mosman Fresh. Many afternoons I walk to the Grove, a shopping center on Stirling Highway. If I go the short way, the entrance to the Grove is 1,334 steps from the front door of my house. Often I cross Stirling and go to Nature's Harvest on Napoleon Street, 218 steps from the Grove. Afterward I walk home the long way, along Leake to View then Johnston then Palmerston and Swan to my back door, 1,786 steps from Nature's Harvest. This last walk winds through Peppermint Grove. Edward never accompanies me. Sometimes Eliza comes with me. "Amble," I tell her. "Look like we live here. Only people who belong would dress as poorly as I do." Eliza is not old enough to understand that a T-shirt, butterflies ragged across the chest; baggy green shorts; sandals and athletic socks, tops rolled down ankles into sausages, constitute the dress of someone at ease in the world. "Someone so at home," I said last week, "that he can ignore fashion and wear what he wants." "And dress conversation in embarrassing adjectives and adverbs," Eliza said. "Babe, you know it," I said.

Sometimes in the Grove I buy an item or two at Woolworths, but usually I shop only at the Grove Market, a green grocer, or purchase meat from Grove Meats. Recently I have bought almost all my fruit from the Market. Four weeks ago I tried to purchase a container of strawberries. The owner is meticulously honest. "Don't buy those berries," the man said. "They are going off." He tried to find a good box but failed. I follow season. Right now grape, melon, and pineapple are in season. Every day the grocer at the Grove selects one or two rock melons for me, and the children and I eat them at breakfast and dinner. Every two days I cut up a pineapple. I whack off both ends, including the topknot of leaves. Then I slice the pineapple into halves. These I quarter then cut into eighths. Next I cut away the thick middle and horny hide. During the day I munch hunks, and Eliza takes pieces to school. At breakfast she eats other bits in a bowl stuffed with fruits, these including bananas, rock melon, and until recently peaches and nectarines. "Stone fruits are almost gone," the green grocer told me. Earlier in the year, peaches were lush. Now they are woody. "If you buy peaches," the grocer advised, "you must eat them when they are hard."

Vicki force-fed the children fruit, and resentment gagged them. I say little, and they eat orchards every day, Edward taking nectarines and now apples and bananas to school. The fruits balance cakes from Nature's Harvest. The cakes are small and come in aluminum dishes. "All natural," each cake is four inches wide and seven and a half long. Stacked in the refrigerator are five varieties: Decadent Chocolate Mud, Orange, Carrot and Pineapple, Passion Fruit and Banana, and Chocolate Beetroot, this last being Eliza's and my favorite. Eliza shovels ice cream over the beetroot, Connoisseur's "All-Natural Chocolate Obsession" being her favorite. For my part I eat Sara Lee chocolate ice cream. Also in the refrigerator are Sara Lee's French vanilla and Connoisseur's Café Grande, a chocolate and Grand Marnier blend; cookies and cream; and blueberry cheesecake, this last "bought by Mom," Edward said before commanding, "Throw it away." To prepare for ice cream Edward and Eliza exercise rigorously. Eliza gets up at

5:45 in the morning and runs for an hour. Edward plays basketball at Christ Church, and throughout the day both children tie themselves into muscle-stretching knots on the living room floor. To keep fit Eliza went on a Monday, Wednesday, Friday dessert regimen, banning desserts from the other four nights. The schedule lasted one evening, a container of Chocolate Obsession derailing the plan.

Sometimes I shop in Claremont, opposite Edward's school, 4.2 kilometers from the house. On the way home from the university I stop in Claremont at Coles. Bigger than the Coles in Mosman Park, the store is more upscale and is fatty with thin women. On my excursions I see few men, and they appear grim. Although I smile, I rarely talk to people other than cashiers. Yesterday I helped two elderly women buy yogurt, print on containers being too small for them to read. "How nice of the store to station you here to help old women," one of them said, thanking me. Inside the Grove or outside Coles in Mosman Park, people sell tickets for charity raffles, two dollars for a chance on a Toyota or Holden, the proceeds going to fight dyslexia or arthritis. If we planned to stay in Australia, I'd purchase chances. "Somebody has to win," Eliza said. Behind Napoleon on Jarred Street sits Boatshed Grocery. Prices are high at Boatshed. One day pineapples that sold for $2.95 at Coles and Woolworths were $5.99 at Boatshed. Despite the prices sometimes I buy baguettes at Boatshed. The day after Vicki left Perth, I purchased a date book for $9.95 at the university. Six inches wide and eight and half long, the book is bound in leather and colored claret. Stamped across the front in gold is "The University of Western Australia—2001." Each page contains thirty-six lines, perfect for grocery lists. On February 21 I left the book in a cart at Boatshed. On the twenty-third I fetched it when I bought a baguette. For the most part I buy bread at Barrett's on Fairway near the university, pan bread, the loaf crusty and moldy with flour. At Coles in Claremont I buy bagels, no other grocery I patronize selling them.

For a fortnight after Vicki left, I purchased prepared meat: mango chicken burgers and lamb kebabs marinated in rosemary and garlic from Pronto; at Peters in Claremont, quiches and, my favorite, beef and mushroom pie. Because the children refuse to eat beef, we ate the pie only once. "The age of industrial agriculture is slowing," Eliza said. "BSE is spreading like acid rain, and no country can avoid the fallout." Breakfasts are easy, fruit bowls or fruit over cereal, Grinners for Eliza, for Edward, Uncle Toby's Shredded Wheat. The children drink Tone, a milk containing no fat. For my part I sip green tea and eat bananas sliced over "natural muesli," a grainy blend of cereals containing nuts and dried fruit. Aside from chopping fruit and quartering cantaloupe, I let the children prepare their own breakfasts. I simply fill orders at the grocery. Vicki always prepared breakfast, a kindness that irritated. She also prepared lunch, another irritant. I let the children fix their own lunches, too. They eat well and seem happier. Into a bag Edward stuffs sliced carrots; a nectarine or apple; a bagel thick with bean sprouts, cheese, and turkey; and lastly a container of Yoplait Lite, 99.7 percent fat-free yogurt. Eliza's lunch is similar except she packs her bagel with hot dogs made from soybean sausages.

I cram the refrigerator, and the children graze afternoons, harvesting bread and cheese, watermelon, and hummocks of cereal. Occasionally I buy muffins. Instead of putting them on the table, I place them on the counter. When the children come home from school, they discover the muffins and more often than not eat them before dinner. Old enough to be their grandfather or grandmother, if the apron fits, I like seeing the children eat. For dinner I prepare salads heavy with roughage: celery, spring onion, radish, broccoli, spinach, bock choy, cauliflower, purple and Chinese cabbage, and sundry lettuces, grocers labeling many of these "fancy." Once I made Waldorf salad, one of my childhood favorites. Because I greased ingredients with mayonnaise, the children refused it. Only in pizza or pasta sauce do they eat tomatoes. When avocados came into season, five for two dollars, I added them to my salad. Avocados were rare in my childhood. Mother called them alligator pears and served them only on formal occasions. Beside the Waldorf salad another dish that failed was

SAM PICKERING

chicken tacos. I bought five at Lenard's in the Grove. The young woman who waited on me instructed me to cook them for twenty minutes at 190 degrees, adding, "I think." She thought incorrectly. While the pastry wrapping the chicken turned black, the chicken remained raw. Never again have I shopped at Lenard's. As a general rule the younger the person waiting on me, the more suspect the information.

Actually not eating Waldorf salad served the children well. The nuts and raisins I used were wormy. Two days later gray moths swirled through the cupboard like ashes. Vicki so overstocked the larder that foods ran to green worms. Not only did I throw out raisins and nuts, but also flour, rolled oats, two bags of dried fruit, Ritz crackers, and a bin of breakfast cereals, among others, Nut Feast, Fruity Bites, corn flakes, Mini-Wheats, puffed wheat, and All-Bran, in the boxes of which worms had woven cocoons. Squads of worms humped across the ceiling and attached cocoons to the molding. In addition to cereals I threw out packets of spices and then cookies, chocolate chip and Tim Tam among a bakery of others. The children were glad the cookies vanished. "We don't want them," Edward said. "I told Mother not to buy them, but she didn't listen." I tossed the food into the back yard. All-Bran was popular with doves, and corn flakes, with magpies. For their part ravens proved to be eclectic gourmands, eating cereals and raisins, but preferring fists of stale bread, cramming their beaks until they spread into scissors.

Since the kitchen and dining area face the back yard, I spend much time watching birds, learning, for example, that doves won't eat meat, at least lamb cooked and seasoned with basil, oregano, and rosemary. Four times a day Urn Bird and Bird of My Bird land in the yard, trot to the terrace, and warble for food. One morning I left the back door open when I walked to the Corner Deli to buy the *West Australian*. On my return I found Eliza rushing about, trying to shoo the magpies out of the house. Down flew from the birds like stuffing as they pounded windows. I grabbed a towel off a rack in the children's bathroom and quickly caught the birds, wrapping each so it couldn't batter wings into fractures. "We won't see them for a while," Eliza said after I freed the birds in the back yard. At eleven that morning they were warbling on the porch. I have grown accustomed to the magpies and can recognize their songs two houses away. Moreover I can distinguish some calls, the wavering warble that summons me and the high fluting that Bird of My Bird uses to communicate her whereabouts to Urn Bird.

Not all worms are nuisances. When a worm fell from an ear of corn I was shucking, I felt reassured, deluding myself into thinking that industrial insecticide did not coat all the vegetables and fruit I served. The worm was the only worm I have found on dozens of ears of corn, and I have concluded it must have crawled out of the cupboard and wandering across the counter burrowed under the shucks. Worms infested the corn I ate as a boy. Shucking an ear always disturbed two or three. The corn was sweet, and never did I worry about swallowing poison along with kernels. During one lunch at my grandmother's house in Virginia, I ate thirteen ears, all from the garden. Nowadays I balance meals, hoping that blends of fruits and vegetables will lessen the virulence of agricultural venom.

Along with corn I serve potatoes sliced and cooked in wedges. I try to mirror season, cooking broccoli as a side dish when the price of a head falls below two dollars. Sometimes we eat frozen vegetables, peas, green beans, or Brussels sprouts. Eliza is fond of sprouts, but Edward won't eat them. Consequently whenever Eliza and I eat sprouts, I cook another dish for Edward. Three times a week I serve meat, lamb chops, chicken satay, and lean pork. At least twice a week I cook pasta: bowties, curls, spirals, corkscrews, twists, wagon wheels, and large, small, and frilled shells. Over the pasta I dump a twenty-six-ounce bottle of ready-made sauce, usually the Five Brothers brand: Summer Tomato Basil, Olive and Mushroom, or Romano and Garlic. Often I stir meat through the sauce, tuna packed in water, chicken, pork, or lamb that I've diced and seasoned. I enjoy seasoning, dusting meats with fennel, sage, bay, rosemary, oregano, whatever comes to hand until fragrance rises cloudy above the stove. Vicki is a fine, meticulous cook. She reads recipes closely and can taste dishes before she prepares them. For my part I like the feeling of spices between my fingers, shavings of thyme, dry and crisp; shreds of tarragon like bits of sawdust. After marriage I accepted banishment from the kitchen. Vicki's and my culinary ways would have clashed. Spontaneity can, of course, disrupt a meal as well as life. To a Thai red curry I added so much curry paste that a can of coconut milk could not prevent the brew from broiling tongue and throat.

I like cooking. If Vicki had not swept me from the stove, I suspect I would not have seasoned days with trees and flowers. In part I roam Connecticut in order to escape the domestic whiskbroom. That aside, however, the excitement of the new spills into imagination and makes change attractive. During Vicki's absence I often ponder retirement. I dream of vanishing, unbuckling schedule and duty and slipping into a looser life, one in which spilled milk doesn't matter. Responsibility, however, always mops up dreams. By eight-thirty every night I'm in bed. Vicki usually serves dinner at eight or eight-thirty. By six I have food on the table, an alteration popular with the children. Besides meals I changed the way the children receive money. Not long after Vicki left I set a plastic dish on the dining room table and into it dumped coins and bills—five-, ten-, twenty-, and fifty-dollar bills. I instructed the children to take money whenever they needed it. "Don't bother to ask me," I said, adding that I would keep the box topped off. In contrast Vicki put the children on allowances. Slights, however, led more often than not to withholding the money, making small financial dealings unpleasant. Moreover she demanded exact accountings from the children. In contrast I believe coins should be banished from familial conversation. In Connecticut Vicki and I live modestly. We have two cars. One is eleven years old, the other eight. Never do we dine away from home or go to a movie. Only in Australia do we travel, using the savings from seven lean years. What large moneys I spend have been spent in hopes of giving the children bright childhoods. Francis is in Europe. For Christmas Vicki instructed me to send him three hundred dollars. I did so. However, I didn't tell her that the previous week I had mailed him $2,250. "Travel," I wrote. "Use the money to enrich days." "But do not," I warned, "mention this gift in an email or letter." I could be accused of buying the affection of my offspring. If that's the case, I haven't succeeded. I could also be accused of teaching financial irresponsibility. The truth is I just want my son to have fun before he becomes corporate.

In one's fifties life constricts. Vision becomes watery. Sharp sounds become muffled, and instead of standing, a man sits to pull up his trousers. Shopping and cooking have expanded my life. Moreover instead of sensing the deterioration of skills, I have mastered things new. Chores that have long bored Vicki invigorate me. Almost as if I have changed the furnishings of a house to fit season, details of domestic life appoint days, bringing green tufts of pleasure. I like sitting in the living room and compiling a grocery list, across the room the television flickering, canned talk tumbling from politicians. "The man is a boob," I thought one night, hearing the American secretary of defense damn China, North Korea, and Iraq, "a dumbbell who doesn't know the difference between Massaman and Panaeng style Thai curry." Another evening while I wrote "Cling Wrap," "Spree," and "Multix Alfoil" on a pad, a panel discussed trimming taxes in the United States. "At this point in time," a man began, defending the cut. "What flabby English," Eliza said. "The windbag suffers from intellectual palsy. Saying *now* instead of *at this point in time* would save four words, reducing the phrase by 80 percent, sharpening meaning." "Yes," Edward agreed, "three letters instead of seventeen, reducing the fat by 567 percent."

At six-thirty every morning I walk down Swan to Harvey and at the Corner Deli buy a copy of the *West Australian,* the distance from my front gate to the Deli being 318 steps. While the children eat, they read the paper, Eliza returning from her run around six-forty-five, often after I have started a load of laundry. Three days a week I do laundry, usually two big loads. First I dump the contents of the hamper into the bucket of the machine, the line between white and dark clothes too gray to make any difference. After switching the power on and filling a small plastic drawer with detergent, I program the wash, first setting "On Sensing" to "Speedy." Then moving from left to right across the front of the machine, I set water temperature at warm, water level at large, wash for nine minutes, rinse for one revolution, and spin for five minutes. Lastly I press "Start." By seven-thirty clothes are on the line. Hanging clothes relaxes me. I've noticed that Edward who dislikes showering changes clothes every day while Eliza who bathes every day changes clothes no more than once every three days.

By late morning the clothes are dry, and I remove them from the line, placing them on the children's beds. After the children finish breakfast and pack lunches, I wash dishes in the kitchen sink. Although a dishwasher is built into a cabinet beside the sink, neither Vicki nor I have used it. Washing dishes and utensils, like pinning clothes on the line, occupies the mind, freeing it from worry. After I finish the dishes, I sweep and wet-mop the kitchen and dining room floors, whisking dust into a plastic scoop. I also sweep after dinner. Next I remove glasses, dishes, knives, forks, and cutting boards from the mesh strainer beside the sink and put them into drawers or in the cupboard. I wash three times a day, the other two times after dinner and then in the afternoon at school's end when the children snack. At night pots and pans increase the work. Next I scrub the kitchen counter, usually scrubbing the outside of the stove for good measure. This I also do three times a day. At night chopping vegetables for salad transforms the counter into a garden, so I clean the top twice, once after I finish the salad and then again after dinner. Twice daily I empty the garbage pail, a small blue bucket that stands by the stove. I line the bucket with plastic bags from grocery stores. Once a bag bulges, I tie the handles on the top together then dump the bag in the garbage can by the back fence near the door to the garage. Once a day I carry glass, plastic, and newsprint to the recycle can next to the garbage. Once the kitchen is clean, I make my bed and see if the children have made their beds. Edward's room is always neat. Eliza's is messy.

After I have made beds, the magpies reappear. I toss them scraps I've minced from dinner. I've tried to teach them to say hello, but acquiring a second language does not come easily to birds. At nine I shop. At the Coles in Mosman Park, I pay at the register manned by Marjorie. Marjorie is my age and is unfailingly pleasant. If I buy vegetables at Mosman Fresh or meat at Pronto Cuisine, I add them to a cart from Coles and roll the cart to the car and load the purchases in the trunk. I always return the cart to Coles, parking it inside the front door. At the Center I run other errands. At Australia Post I mail letters; at the chemist, I buy face wash for Eliza, and at the stationers, school supplies, pens, and rubber bands. At the muffin shop I purchase muffins for $1.90 apiece.

Three days a week I go to the university after shopping. I visit, check mail, roam the library, and buy bread at Barrett's. Often at Barrett's I drink a cappuccino and read the *Australian*. I sit on a stool. If the person next to me is a woman my age, I chat. Errands punctuate days. Three times I have driven to Woolridges, a bookstore on Scarborough Road that stocks texts for Eliza's classes. The first time I exchanged a book, a clerk having mistakenly given Eliza *Reading Fictions* instead of *Reading Stories*. The second time was occasioned by Eliza's dropping art and in its place taking history, forcing me to return art supplies and to buy a history book. The third time I purchased an edition of Henrik Ibsen's *A Doll's House,* Eliza's English teacher having rearranged the schedule, shifting Ibsen's play from the third term when Eliza would have been back in the United States to the second term.

I begin dinner shortly after five, first fetching ingredients for salad from the refrigerator in the garage. Although dinners go smoothly, they are messy. Tonight we are eating salad, corn on the cob, and lamb chops. Grease will turn the top of the stove measly. One night a gas burner on the stove broke, and flames flared toward the ceiling. I turned the gas off at the switch outdoors. By the next evening water in the hot water tank had cooled. At noon the following day a repairman fixed the burner. Another night the burglar alarm system began peeping, a sign the battery was low. For a while the house sounded like a hatchery. Throughout days I clean house. Cleaning imposes discipline on life. I wash window sills and scrub the outside of the refrigerator and the microwave, places Vicki didn't touch. I sweep porches and dust pictures and mirrors.

Saturday is the major cleaning day. First I vacuum the entire house, both rugs and floors. When she cleaned, Vicki refused to disturb spiders. The week after she left I brushed a spider web from behind a curtain in the living room. A red-back inhabited the web, a particularly venomous spider. When the red-back shuffled across the rug, I scooped her up in the vacuum. Later I put on rubber gloves and emptied the bag of the vacuum outside, the only time I have put on rubber gloves. Vicki wears rubber gloves when she washes dishes. Because I have lost feeling in my fingers, hot water doesn't bother me. Shortly after ridding the living room of the red-back, I scoured the back porch and removed webs of black house spiders, bites of which cause necrosis. After vacuuming I mop the hall and floors in the bedrooms and bathrooms. Next I clean the lavatories, scrubbing toilets and tubs with Ajax. I also spray the outside of toilets with antibacterial Pine Clean. I empty waste cans and polish knobs and handles. I clean the telephone and doors to rooms. I take the two small rugs in the dining room outside and beat them. I spray Windex on windows, mirrors, and the glass walls of showers. The children do not help. Most Saturdays Edward plays basketball for Christ Church. For her part Eliza hibernates in her room studying mathematics or chemistry. "Eighty is an A here," she told me. "The registrar at E. O. Smith won't understand that, so I have to make above 90 in my courses."

I don't spend all Saturday working. In the afternoon I usually drive us to Scarborough, and we ride waves. At night we watch a movie. Generally the movies are terrible, the worst being *The Idiot Box*, an Australian film. "Hilarious," the clerk at Rewind said. "A fast corrosive comedy," *Variety* testified. "Crackles with original-ity and humour," a critic wrote in the *Sydney Morning Herald*. Edward and Eliza walked out of *The Idiot Box*, Edward to read Edgar Allen Poe's short stories and Eliza to finish Henry Fielding's novel *Tom Jones*. I clung to the celluloid. Not once did I smile.

For the man about house, season is a matter of foods not

flowers. Rarely do I roam the out-of-doors. Marri and paperbark bloomed and were taken for granted like old wallpaper. Strings of bees vibrated around fiddlewood in a courtyard by the Arts Building at the university. If the blossoms hadn't been sweeter than ambrosia, I wouldn't have noticed the bees. One afternoon while Eliza ran at Perry Lakes, I walked through Bold Park. A flock of rainbow bee-eaters sallied through the scrub. "Tomorrow," I thought, "I will spend the whole afternoon here." Instead I remained at home, dicing chicken and slicing vegetables for stir fry.

Occasionally mail transforms the high seriousness of home life into guffaws. From Ohio a ninety-six-year-old friend wrote that his seventy-two-year-old son had visited and tried to straighten his affairs. "Instead," my friend wrote, "the boy messed everything about. He is too damn old to think clearly." The title of my new collection of essays is *The Last Book*. From Atlanta, Nowell wrote, "Tell me you are working on another book, and this will not be the final one. Hell, just because you are sixty is no reason for stopping. You have plenty more to write about. Why think of old age, ailments, having your children look after you and Vicki, all the medicines you will wind up taking for nearly everything." Colleges also wrote. Early in March Tulane admitted Edward, awarding him a scholarship. The letter arrived by Federal Express. The same day I received a letter from Kentucky. My correspondent was familiar, a librarian who shortened nights by thumbing nineteenth-century periodicals. "Enclosed is a dandy," the man wrote. "I would I were a cassowary / On the plains of Timbuctoo; / I'd catch and eat a missionary, / Legs and arms and hymn book, too."

Contentment is to the mind, as the old saying puts it, as moss is to a tree. Moss smothers growth. Routines of shop and table had seduced me. Afternoons vanished in marinades of rosemary and coconut milk, tamarind and ginger. The smell of ink clung to the letters, however, making me long for ingredients robust beyond the kitchen. Consequently I decided to take a vacation from Coles and the Grove and visit Carthage. I went on March 16, six weeks and two days after Vicki left Perth, and, according to the calendar attached to the Geneva Bible throughout the 1570s, the day on which Christ raised Lazarus from the dead. During the trip I discovered Hollis Hunnewell had brought a new show to town, advertising it as "The Wonder of All the Wonders That Tennesseans Ever Wondered At." Perhaps because I had spent the past weeks cooking, the wonders seemed almost bland, lacking spices that made previous shows tickle the esophagus. Among exhibits were two sheets of papyrus, remnants of the card catalogue of "The Great Library at Canaan." "The only pages," Hollis claimed, that survived the flood. Noah used them to plug a hole in the hull when the ark slammed into the body of a unicorn. The unicorn, Hollis said, overslept after a night at the trough and after missing the boat had drowned. Because salt water scrubbed the writing away, little was visible on the papyrus except for a barn owl, three black birds resembling buzzards, and the lower half of a brindled cat, its tail curved into an *S*, standing, Hollis said, for "Savior."

Also in the show was Zadkiel's Crystal Ball, in which observant patrons could see the nine Muses and the baby Apollo, a naked "bundle of joy" clutching a lyre in his left hand. Next to the crystal ball stood the petrified hog, rollers attached to its hooves. A guano digger discovered the hog buried on an island west of Peru. "Sugar-cured by phosphate." Confined in a bamboo cage were two Aztec pygmies, Massoudi and Maharaja. Aside from smoking cigarettes and shaking their fists, the pygmies didn't do much, and Carthaginians dubbed them Dildrum and Doldrum. Arousing more interest was the coffin of a giant. At death the giant was seven feet, two inches tall and weighed one thousand and one-quarter pounds. His waist was six feet, one inch in circumference, and stuffing him into the coffin took fourteen men. "But what happened to the giant," Cincinnatus Rigshaw asked, leaning into the coffin and looking first one way then the other. Rarely was Hollis at a loss for words. "Coffins are Christian Breadbaskets, and the bread has risen," Hollis said, rolling his eyes. "When I bought the basket at a going-out-of-business sale at Mt. Olivet Cemetery in Nashville, only a few crumbs of the giant remained behind, not enough to feed a possum for two days." For ten cents a person or fifteen cents for a couple, these last "being married or almost married," people could stretch out in the coffin. The coffin was not the only money-maker at the show. Dr. Toe, so named because he was lame, sold patent medicines, Pills of Goof and the Oil of Talcum Distilled, a wash of the latter turning skin white for a month, the former a panacea for everything from eczema to horseshoe head, a condition in which plates of the skull didn't join before birth. Perhaps the most interesting object at the show was an ancient Koran. Bookworms had chewed through the text, their holes forming the words *Not True* in cursive.

The Church of the Chastening Rod sponsored the other show in town. Anaxagoras Bellford preached in the church for two nights, *Anaxagoras* and *Bellford* being names assumed for the tabernacle. Anaxagoras was christened Hammerton Snagg and was the son of Belial Snagg who hawked Bibles and life insurance in Cheatham Country. Hammerton inherited his father's oratorical skills. "One saves your loved ones; the other saves you," Belial told prospective customers. Anaxagoras called himself an Apostolic Halleluiahist. His sermons were entitled "A Sure Guide through Hell with a Stop at the Tar Pits" and "A Swift Kick Launched at the Behinds of Big-Buttocked Christians." In introducing Anaxagoras, Malachi Ramus called him "a true Nathaniel and Christian Israelite," saying "our church service has many fine passages, and when we sing our hymns, they abound in beauty, but standing before us now is a man who has outdistanced us all." Anaxagoras was a histrionic preacher, falling to his knees whenever he quoted Scripture. He began sermons with poetry. "Will o' the wisp skips in the dell, / The owl hoots on the tree. / They hold their nightly vigil well / And so the while will we." Whenever inspiration flagged, he tossed verse into paragraphs, saying, for example, "Old Satan is a liar and a conjurer, too, / And if you don't mind, he'll conjure you" or "Much in sorrow, oft in woe, / Onward Christians, onward go; / Fight the fight, and worn with strife, / Steep with tears the bread of life."

Phrases, not paragraphs, formed the fabric of Anaxagoras's sermons. "A man might as well eat the Devil as sip the broth in which he was boiled," and "I'd rather lick milk off a toad's back than listen to a priest." Anaxagoras condemned identifiable denominations, calling Episcopalians "mushroom Christians, ripe today, rotten tomorrow." Anaxagoras mined pockets of folk wisdom, occasionally unearthing a nugget. "To deny that God made the tapeworm leads to denying God made man." Sometimes Anaxagoras was oddly humble. "I know," he said, "that the word *and* occurs 35,543 times in the Old Testament and 10,684 in the New, but I can't tell you the name of King David's mother. I know that God used Indian hemp as an anesthetic when he removed Adam's rib in order to make the Mother of Mankind, but I don't know if Paul ever married." Anaxagoras bounded from mood to mood, one moment spreading his arms wide as a tub, shouting, "Come to the green savannah, to the wild wood Indian bower," the next smacking himself in the forehead with the palm of his right hand and moaning, "That miracles are ceased / Some confidently tell. / But I do know it is not so / Whilst I am out of Hell." Homespun conceits peppered the sermons. "There ain't no briars in Abraham's bosom," he declared, "only sweet blackberries; no sweat, just milk and honeydew melons." "The only snake in paradise is the King Jesus snake, the bands around his body rings solemnizing the divine nuptials. The Lord is my shepherd, no want shall be mine; / In pastures of verdure, he makes me recline." "Many people," he warned, "are ambulators, roaming around and about, up and down, here and there until they tumble into sin. Instead of ambulators they should follow the Lord's guidance and become decambulators"—*decambulator* being, as Turlow Gutheridge later explained, a portmanteau word combining ambulator with Decalogue (the Ten Commandments). "Follow the Law, not law books," Anaxagoras advised. "Trust the Lord. He pays high interest. Put your money in the collection plate not in the hands of Dryall and Skinboots, Esquire." Sometimes Anaxagoras strayed from good taste. "As knights of old buckled the keys to chastity belts to their scabbards and denied sinners access to hidden treasures, so St. Peter holds the key to God's Kingdom, barring the way to those who leave the Lamb at the altar and spend life scoffing at holy matrimony."

"Too great a familiarity with God," Turlow Gutheridge said later in Ankerrow's Café, "corrupts good manners." "Christ came, but then he went away for our good." Not in a dozen books have I heard Turlow say much about religion. The death of Bean, his dog, must have focused Turlow's mind on high matters. A fixture in Carthage, Bean was thirty-six when he died. A short-haired, spotted fice, Bean was born in Turlow's barn. He wasn't a traveler and spent his life catching rats. After his ratting days ended, Bean dozed in the sun, lying on a mat on Turlow's side porch. He remained spunky, however, and snapped at flies. Although expected, his death was sudden, a cardiovascular storm brought on by sight of a fox creeping toward Turlow's henhouse. Because Turlow was a popular bachelor and Bean lived longer than any other four-legged canine in the history of Smith County, the crowd at Ankerrow's bought a tombstone and set it over Bean's grave. By the time Isom Legg carved the stone, Turlow was back on his haunches and for the inscription supplied a quatrain. "Go where the water glideth gentle ever, / Glideth by the meadows that greenest be, / Go by our own beloved river, / And bark once or twice for me."

Eloquence in the service of absurdity is bacterial. On my return from Carthage I wrote the manufacturer of Jimmy's Thunder Box, a collapsible wooden privy seat. I'd studied the box in January while riding in Victoria. In the letter I suggested improvements in design, adding railings, for example. In hopes of elevating a low subject, I addressed Jimmy as James. My study of the box verged on the scientific, and several people contributed to the letter. "A brown-haired woman," I wrote, "urged fitting boxes with seat belts. 'To keep folks who dined on onions and beans from being blasted off the commode and rising like rockets toward the blessed Southern Star.' In the all too common event that sitters disturbed snakes coiled in the shade under the box; belts should have quick-release latches. If the engineering proved too complex, the woman thought wheels attached to corners of the box would be effective. 'One push and a gal would zoom down a slope, snakes and shit left

SAM PICKERING

behind.'" "James," I then interjected, "I apologize for the crudity of this language. All I can say is that the woman is an Anglican."

"An antique dealer," I continued, "wanted to know if you made a box with a softer, fluffier seat, one decorated with pink unicorns or pudgy naked boys, fountains sprocketing out of their little pinkies, anything to divert the mind from flies. He was also curious about the wood used in making the seat, reckoning that jarrah would appeal to the cappuccino trade, society folks temporarily bereft of indoor plumbing. Moreover jarrah wouldn't splinter easily, an important consideration if a big female slammed her buttocks down on the box. Years ago a wooden pot shattered under a cousin of mine, jabbing a splinter so far into her backside that a dentist had to extract it. She framed the splinter, and today it hangs over the mantle in her living room just above a needlepoint reading, 'Home, Sweet Home.' She did that needlepoint when recuperating from the wound. 'It won't easy to do,' she told me, 'what with me being on my stomach and my ass high up behind, a bandage hanging down it like snow. Obadiah [that's her better and skinnier half] said I looked like one of those Everest mountains.'"

"Ours is a medicinal age. A doctor, a proctologist by study and by inclination, asked me to advise you to elevate the box. People, he said, who spent a long time at the stool, in medical terminology suffering from slow movement of the bowels, were liable to succumb to deep vein thrombosis. They would sue, and not even a gold digger could save Jimmy's from bankruptcy. The good doctor said he'd treated a score of people with DVT brought on by spending too much time on the crapper. To guard against DVT, the doctor suggested attaching pedals to the front of the box. That way folks could exercise while sitting, thus not only preventing DVT but also facilitating excretion." I concluded the letter with "Too-dle-Loo" and my address. "Daddy," Eliza said after reading the letter, "you didn't mail this?" "You bet I did," I answered. "Well," Eliza said, "meals are good, and the house is clean, but the time has come for Mommy to return."

Dixie

For the first hundred years of his life, Methuselah, Bocotian story relates, slept on the ground, sand for a blanket and a rock for a pillow. At dawn on the first day of Methuselah's 101st year, the angel Gabriel woke him up. "Arise Methuselah," Gabriel said, pointing a sword toward the yellowing horizon, "arise and build thee a house for thou shalt live yet five hundred years longer." "Great God, it's early!" Methuselah exclaimed then lifted himself on his elbows and looked around, combing wool out of his thoughts. "Gabe," he eventually said, digging his toes under a rumpus of sand, "if I'm going to live only five hundred more years, building a house ain't worthwhile. I just think I'll keep sleeping in the dirt as I've always done." Refusing to let pebbles gnaw his hide and disrupt rest, Methuselah appeals to me. As I drift into old age, I've grown comfortable in my bed. I wouldn't change house or wife if Gabriel appeared in Connecticut with a chariot loaded with heavenly plumbers, carpenters, and electricians and promised to build me a designer home in earth's plushest suburb, not even a house with seraphim and cherubim for neighbors, a rakeless place where leaves vanished in a golden zephyr, where the winds of blight never blew, where children said, "Thank you," and where wives percolated with affection all the year round, spring, summer, fall, and white winter.

Last Wednesday as I drove through Claremont, a radio station played "Dixie." As I listened, I tapped my fingertips on the steering wheel, and the switching yard of cars around me disappeared. The music made me sentimental. At the end of the song I mouthed the old rhyme: "My ancestors are Southern, a Southerner am I, / And 'tis my boast that I was born beneath a Southern sky." Three kilometers later near Red Rooster where I turned off Stirling on to Johnston, thoughts of the South lay slack like a flag on a still day. For two decades I pondered leaving Connecticut and returning to Tennessee. Years, however, have turned me into a New Englander.

Time, as the proverb puts it, softens intelligence into wisdom. Maybe Time just softens, making a person so malleable that the present, no matter its knobs, rarely seems so uncomfortable that one shifts bedding. In younger days events pinched, and words burst from me like bricks. Now I rarely speak out, having learned that the man who dogs the heels of truth too closely is liable to be kicked in the teeth. Of course occasionally spontaneity yanks the bridle from my jaws, and I bray. On Friday Eliza and I went to the Nedlands Library. Tacked to a board was a flyer advertising a lecture entitled, "How to Prevent Aging." "There is only one sure way to prevent aging," I said to the librarian. "What's that?" she said, stamping books and lending a single ear to my words. "Death," I said. "What?" She said, looking up and pushing back from her desk. "Death," I repeated, stepping closer. "Death is the only certain cure for aging. Only fools will attend the lecture." "Daddy," Eliza said later, "you frightened that nice woman." "Truth disturbs," I said. "Then eschew truth," Eliza answered. "All right," I said; "I won't say that it's more important to protect freedom from its friends than its enemies." "Good," Eliza said. "You'll feel better. Truth depresses, and lies invigorate."

Although doings in Washington provoke colitis, my interest in politics has waned. The best qualification for a prophet is a good memory, and most of the commentariat on television haven't lived long enough to have memories. Among the youthful or the haphazardly learned, hunch migrates through opinion into zeal. In the fourteenth century nuns in a convent in southern France sliced off their noses in order to protect their virginity, believing that homeliness would vaccinate them against lust. The prophylactic didn't work, not only failing to isolate them from the bacteria of desire but instead damning them to the never-ending corruption of sinusitis.

Passions fail when cacography loosens. In Carthage exceptions exist. If-Jesus-Had-Not-Died-For-Thee-Thou-Had-Been- Damned Brown was an unrepentant miser. In January he suffered apoplexy on Main Street near the entrance to the Walton Hotel. Bystanders failed to revive him. "Their medical knowledge was slight," Turlow Gutheridge said later in Ankerrow's Café. "If they had thrust a coin purse into IJH's hand, then tried to remove it, our departed brother would have leapt from the concrete and hightailed it to the bank." Although I am a corporal in the Cold Water Brigade and have forsworn intoxicating political matters, abuses of the environment elevate my spirits. Instead of splashing high-octane words about, under Eliza's tutelage I mutter soothing quatrains. "Bricks and mortar!" Eliza taught me last night, "Bricks and mortar! / Give green fields a little quarter. / As sworn foes to Nature's beauty, / You've already done your duty."

Inconvenience and embarrassment result when passion outlives grammar. Unlike IJH, Eusebia Cotgreave was not parsimonious and throughout life distributed her charms widely, tossing herself into the laps of the impecunious as well as the wealthy. Eusebia's democratic nature so discommoded Rundle, her relic, that during his last illness he instructed Slubey Garts to chain his coffin to that of his wife. If Rundle's fervor had cooled after Eusebia's death, he would have enjoyed the end of life more. For my part not even Pretty Polly Oliver could lure me from the easy chair. Along with passion my curiosity has declined. "During the Deluge rain fell for forty days and forty nights," Nigel said recently, bursting into my office. "The Israelites wandered the wilderness for forty years. Goliath defied the armies of Israel in the desert for forty days, thus Lent is forty days long. What do you think forty represents?" "A great deal," I said picking up *The Girl on the Boat*, a novel by P. G. Wodehouse that I shut when Nigel appeared. Nowadays I read entertainments, books that neither preach nor inspire. For appearance I occasionally grunt and groan. Never do I lift, however. "It was," I read to Nigel, "a glorious morning. The sample which he [Sam Marlowe the hero of the book] had had through the porthole had not prepared him for the magic of it. The ship swam in a vast bowl of the purest blue on an azure carpet flecked with silver. It was a morning which impelled a man to great deeds, a morning which shouted to him to chuck his chest out and be romantic. The sight of Billie Bennett, trim and gleaming in pale-green sweater and white skirt, had the effect of causing Marlowe to alter the program which he had sketched out. Proposing to this girl was not a thing to be put off till after lunch. It was a thing to be done now and at once. The finest efforts of the finest cooks in the world could not put him in better form than he felt at the present." "Sam," Nigel said," you're no better than a Freemason." "Right," I said, "now leave and let me bootless trod the azure carpet, romance for a chorister and honeyed whisperings for hymns."

When I am up and doing, I sit. Sometimes I write. Rarely do I explore the faraway in hopes of flushing excitement. Now stories come to me. None are adventuresome, but most are pleasing. For six years Basker Gummidge has eaten dinner in Tattle's Boarding House in Maggart. At six every evening Tittle Tattle rings the dinner bell. Basker always arrives at Tattle's at five-fifty. He roosts in a green chair in the parlor, hands on knees, shoulders flexing in anticipation of flight. I had long known Basker was a hardy trencherman, wielding spoon and fork like a shovel and pickax. Not until last Friday, however, did I know that as soon as the dinner bell rings Basker springs from the chair and swooping down the hall toward the dining room, shouts, "Off we goes."

Doings in Carthage appear in back paragraphs of my books, never on the front pages of newspapers. Usually, however, I read papers and magazines back to front. Far from the rail of headline, grazing is rich. In February Zonus Pedrinus, a migrant portrait painter, stayed in Carthage for six weeks. Pedrinus advertised himself as "One of the Seven Marvels of Tennessee." "The only thing marvelous about him," Turlow Gutheridge said, "is his name. If a restorer scraped the varnish off Pedrinus, he'd discover Gorsuch, Snosswell, or Puckle." Zonus specialized in visual pedigrees, family portraits into which he inserted distant relatives. The most popular cousins in Nashville were George Washington and Robert E. Lee, both men always visiting in battle regalia, usually sharing Sunday dinner with their newly discovered kinfolk. In Carthage Jesus was more popular than either Lee or Washington. For Hink Ruunt Zonus painted Jesus standing in Hink's new tobacco barn, His arms full of Burley. Hink himself leaned against the door of the barn, a twist of chewing tobacco in his left hand, in his right a Bible. In the portrait for Juno Feathers, Jesus sat at one end of the dining room table, Juno at the other, between them a silver centerpiece modeled on Phryne, Juno's prize sow. Phryne sat upright in a basket, bulrushes waving above her snout, tongues of water lapping the bottom of the basket. In her right hoof Phryne held a banner that said, "Among the Bulrushes." For His part Jesus held a fork in His right hand. Skewered on the tines was a hunk of pure white pork. Jesus wore blue overalls and a long-sleeved red shirt. He was laughing. In fact in all portraits in which Jesus appeared, He laughed. In contrast Lee and Washington were dour despite sitting behind platters heaped with corn, greens, and sweet potatoes. "Jesus looked neighborly," Turlow said after viewing Juno's painting, "the sort of fellow who would invite you to heaven to sit a spell and who'd introduce you to His entire Holy Family, the kind of guy who would talk about butter bean poles and high school baseball and who wouldn't stand on doctrine, but who'd serve forgiveness along with homemade pound cake."

A few portraits avoided the fervor of barn and silver service. That of Turlow Gutheridge contained a portrait within a portrait. A likeness of John Hampden, the seventeenth-century English patriot, hung on the wall behind Turlow, who sat at his desk, three volumes of Blackstone's commentary on the law piled to his left, to his right a coffee cup made from country china, a bouquet of buttercups and violets decorating the bowl. In their portrait Eustace and Naomi Bludgell posed in front of a fence. Facing sideways, they gazed into their garden. On the other side of the fence stood Eve, extending her right hand toward Adam. She held a Winesap apple, around the stem a gold wedding band. Fifteen years earlier the Bludgells immigrated to Carthage from New Jersey. Eustace had attended the Presbyterian Seminary in Princeton, and he and his wife called themselves Elijah Christians. Behind a privet hedge in the backyard, they planted "Eden," stocking it with thornless plants. On warm summer evenings they cavorted in the garden, dressed in the attire, they said, "of our first parents." Antics in the garden lasted until Eustace got frostbitten during a cold snap in September and Naomi caught two colds in one day. Carthaginians are tolerant. After a peeping session Proverbs Goforth reported to Ankerrow's that the "bobbing for apples" wasn't special, particularly when compared "to what some of the offbrand religions hereabouts get up to during Revival Week." Contributing to Proverbs's reticence was the knowledge that Naomi was the best third-grade teacher ever hired by the local school. "The sowing and planting Naomi and Eustace do in the garden ain't none of my business," Hink Ruunt said, "especially since she's taught my little boy Peppercorn the multiplication tables out to nine times nine. Before she took him in hand, Peppercorn couldn't add nine and nine."

In portraits of children Zonus often inserted Joseph dressed in his coat of many colors. "And Jacob made for his son Josey / A little coat to keep him cozy," Zonus told parents. The coat was so resplendent that Malachi Ramus said it smacked of Fifth Avenue. "A Christian portrait would depict these fragile lumps of clay in their coffins," Malachi Ramus declared in disgust, then quoted Charles Wesley, "Ah, lovely appearance of death! / What sight upon earth is so fair? / Not all the gay pageants that breathe / Can with a dead body compare." Zonus's most elaborate portrait was of Miss Mabel Crabtree, the town librarian. In her youth Miss Mabel was known as "The Sweet Singer of Carthage" and had published a book of sentimental verse entitled "Country Garlands." "Sweet chickens," one poem began, "that kitchen winging / From endless corn thy feathered way, / Now hither fryest thee, bringing, / Drumstick and bosom to my lips today." Miss Mabel's poetic fit was not fatal. In later life she published occasional verse in the *Courier,* much of which puzzled subscribers. One Armistice Day she wrote, "Whatever's good or great in men, / May be traced to hydrogen. / Much that is sublime in men / May be traced to nitrogen."

For Miss Mabel Zonus painted a poetic supper. Seated around a picnic table under a chestnut tree were Miss Mabel and twelve poets. Miss Mabel sat at one end of the table, the poets gathered about her in a horseshoe, the Brownings side by side, Robert's hand heavy atop Elizabeth's and as spotted as a bunch of bananas. Beside Robert sat John Milton, the lenses of his eyeglasses black. Beside him Longfellow leaned backwards staring upward into the foliage. Tennyson faced Shelley, the former cradling a lapwing to his chest, the other tossing a skylark aloft. Across from the Brownings sat "The Three Muses," Felicia Hemans, Lydia Sigourney, and Adelaide Anne Proctor, all wearing white robes, laurel wreaths in their hair. At the far end of the table, opposite Miss Mabel, William Cullen Bryant read "Thanatopsis." While Bryant held the poem in his right hand, his left fumbled with a watch fob. Bryant was portly. In contrast Reginald Heber was thin and ascetic. Heber's head tilted left, his right ear a scoop open to the heavens, as if he were trying to catch notes falling from angelic harps. Next to Miss Mabel sat George Gordon, Lord Byron, dressed like a brigand, head bound in red and black cloth, a silver dagger at his waist, in his right hand a crystal goblet. Byron's presence startled Hilkiah Cruttenden, secretary of the local chapter of the Woman's Christian Temperance Union. Turlow was not surprised. "Age may have frosted Miss Mabel's locks," Turlow said. "But when she was young, she grew Diana grapes and on holidays wore red heels and took the express train to Nashville."

Doings in Carthage can be strenuous, even when I don't leave my chair. To keep my pencil jogging, I follow routine and conserve energy. This past Sunday, though, Edward and I drove to Perth. Government House and the surrounding garden were open to the public. In the garden the "Band of Angels" sang "Roll Jordan Roll." Parked beside Government House were antique cars, a

Reo, a Flint, and four Rolls-Royces. At the edge of the lot, Morris Men danced jigs, knocking sticks together and wearing white trousers and shirts, bells around ankles, red and yellow suspenders, and straw hats decorated with graveyards of plastic flowers. In the ballroom inside the house, members of Humphrey's Dance Studio performed, children pliable and weedy, adults hot-housed and sequined. The jazz band from St. Hilda's played. The band was so good an old man left his seat and soft-shoed around the room. I roamed the house. On a side table in the dining room sat a centerpiece that at auction would have drawn bidders from Carthage. A silver swan swam though reeds and lotuses thick as peas. Ceilings in the house were high, fifteen feet said a docent; sixteen, another; eighteen, a third, and nineteen, a fourth. "What happened to seventeen?" Edward asked. "Who knows," I said, blowing air through my teeth, unconsciously piping "Dixie." "It's a tic, Daddy," Eliza said that night at dinner; "you do it all the time."

Sweeping Days

Vicki spent seventy-three days in the United States, most of the time in New Jersey cleaning her mother's house. Getting rid of possessions was hard, and she carted mounds of furniture and bric-a-brac to Connecticut, piling them into a storage cubicle in Willington. In Perth life was neater. In the university library I thumbed books. "My tastes are with the aristocrats, my principles with the mob," the Reverend F. W. Robertson wrote in the nineteenth century. "I know how the recoil from vulgarity and mobocracy, with thin-skinned and over fastidious sensitiveness, has stood in the way of my doing the good I might do. My own sympathies and principles in this matter are in constant antagonism, and until these can be harmonized, true Christianity is impossible." "Exactly," I thought, closing Robertson's *Life and Letters*, saving the book for Connecticut, for nights following afternoons spent sorting in Willington.

On March 4 Edward, Eliza, and I spent an afternoon at Perry Lakes watching a track meet sponsored by a telephone company. Members of the Australian Olympic team participated. When I was a boy in Nashville, Father took me to track meets at Vanderbilt. In Perth proximity to the past, not celebrity, created enjoyment. Sitting between Eliza and Edward, I imagined myself my father. When I said I looked forward to the 800- and 400-meter races, I spoke more to a younger me than to Edward or Eliza. For a decade I ran road races in Connecticut. One year I ran nineteen races. My goal was to finish in the lower 50 percent of runners. I was successful seventeen times. In 1985 my neck grew painful with bone spurs, and I stopped racing and began swimming. Because Kalgoorlie Street wasn't close to a pool, I started jogging in Perth. Twice a week I shuffled through Mosman Park and Peppermint Grove. When I noticed gardens, I stopped, not to catch breath but beauty. After the track meet I increased the jogs to three times a week, each run covering 5.37 kilometers. On April 8 I ran my first race in sixteen years, the twenty-fifth Bridges Fun Run, ten kilometers beginning at Langley Park, going west along Riverside Drive then crossing the Swan River at the Narrows Bridge. The course circled Perth Water. After crossing the Narrows, runners turned east along the South Perth Esplanade. At the Causeway Bridge the course crossed back over the Swan and turning west again returned to Langley Park. I wore a baggy blue bathing suit, high gray socks, and a white T-shirt, printed on the front of which was a husky dog, the mascot of the University of Connecticut. Beneath the dog I pinned my number, 1833. Six years old, the shirt was ready for first grade. My shoes were old enough for middle school. I plucked them off the reduced rack at Nassiff's Sports Store in Willimantic twelve years ago. Because I wore them when I mowed grass in Connecticut, they were green. Eliza stood by me at the start. Once the race was underway, I didn't see her until the finish where she sat on the ground and cheered me across the line. The race took sixty-two minutes and fourteen seconds. I started at the rear of the pack and during the race passed several barrel-shaped people. I also chatted with runners who trotted beside me. Few wanted to talk. People who ran my pace were either aged or unfit and had to concentrate energies in order to finish. After five kilometers my left hip began to hurt, and I worried that the bone might warp into shards, a thought that helped me ignore the tick of distance.

For me the run was the high point of Vicki's absence. For Eliza the race was so flat that it didn't smack of event. At home Edward waited to hear from colleges. In November Edward behaved willfully. Instead of taking three Scholastic Achievement Tests, as most colleges required, he took two, saying, "I'm tired of tests." At Christ Church he quarreled with an art teacher and received a C. "Not my first," he said. Still he made an 800 on the SAT II in writing. Vicki and I didn't know what to expect. "He'll get in somewhere," she said before leaving Perth. "If worrying about him gives you pleasure, do so, but otherwise don't." I shouldn't have been concerned. Half a dozen schools admitted Edward. I was surprised and reread his applications. Writing helped. In response to a question asking what was important in life, he wrote, "'The most important thing is not life, but the good life,' Socrates said in *Crito*, adding, 'the good life, the beautiful life, and the just life are the same.' In his dialogues Socrates did not define terms clearly. Essentially, however, Socrates's good and just life forbade hypocrisy. To link my seventeen-year old self to Socrates is presumptuous. Yet, I believe that honesty is the foundation of character. A 'good character' must avoid convenient hypocrisy and act honestly and straightforwardly. Even so, because our understandings are limited, we are bound to cause pain to others, no matter the decency of our purposes. If one is not a hypocrite, though, atoning for bruises brought about by good intentions may come easier, and instead of hiding under corrupting excuse, one might be able to live justly and honestly."

Students had until May 1 to accept a college's offer of admission. Most colleges mailed acceptances near the end of March. Because we were leaving Perth on April 18 and not returning for a fortnight, I fretted that Edward would not hear from all the schools to which he had applied. My concern was real. On such things as the mail hang the fragile doings of lives. Only after we returned to Perth in May did Edward receive an acceptance from Bowdoin. At the airport on the eighteenth, Edward mailed a letter to Middlebury College in Vermont, saying he would enroll. He'd spent the previous week in the library roaming the Internet comparing Middlebury and Duke, another school that had taken him. For once I kept my mouth shut. Big and booming with an international reputation, Duke smacked of the future. "Atlanta and corporate," Vicki said, "the Stanford of the East." With only twenty-three hundred students Middlebury accepted a smaller percentage of applicants than Duke, among liberal arts colleges the fourth lowest percentage. "Middlebury offers the best that a liberal arts college can give," my friend Jay Parini wrote. "Edward won't get lost here. I'll watch him." "I chose Middlebury because of writing and language programs," Edward said later, adding, "and I don't want to take math. Duke requires two math courses." "After finishing Duke," Edward continued, "I'd have gone to law school and lived in Dallas. Now I will live in a small New England town, teach English, own two golden retrievers, and be concerned about the environment." "Jesus," Vicki said, "is he serious?" "No," I said, "he's writing a story. While you were in New Jersey, Edward started a novel. The prose is good." "Will he finish?" Vicki asked. "No," I said. "Teenagers don't finish novels." Talk about schooling was in the air, and while Edward waited to hear from schools, Eliza and I chatted about colleges. "Odd, that you worry where you will spend thirty-five thousand dollars a year," Eliza said. "Seventy thousand when Francis returns to Princeton," I said. By the time Eliza graduates from college, I will have depleted my savings. "You have aged beyond pleasure," my friend Josh wrote from Connecticut. "Your money can go either to schools for diplomas or to nursing homes for johnnies. Both institutions are ravenous."

Vicki missed Eliza's and Edward's birthdays. For each I ordered chocolate cakes from Martineau's, Edward's layered with strawberries, Eliza's with Cointreau. The cakes were so good that we celebrated Vicki's return with a Sacher torte. Rarely do I let days drift by unsweetened. Even though Francis was in Germany, we celebrated his birthday with another chocolate cake from Martineau's, "Happy Birthday Francis," written in cursive atop a medallion. On June 1 Edward will leave Perth, bound for Connecticut and a summer spent working as a counselor at a boys' camp in Maine. For Edward's farewell I have ordered a Black Forest cake from Martineau's. Appearing on the medallion is "Have Fun, Edward." Since Edward will study English at Middlebury, I made certain that a comma followed *Fun.* I fetch the cake on May 30, providing Edward with two nights of dessert.

The day after Vicki returned she, the children, and I drove to Fremantle for the annual Buskers Festival, the title not including an apostrophe. In Australia apostrophes are endangered. That aside, performing at the festival were buskers calling themselves Rumplestiltskin, Mr. Spin, Larrikin, Dado, Happy Harry, and Cell-Out, among others. Near the E-Sheds, Fabulous Brendan did handstands on top of four chairs. A slinky of hula-hoops spun in a coil around a girl. Docked beyond the sheds, the *Al-Khalee* loaded sheep for Saudi Arabia. "That tarnishes the day," Vicki said. My favorite busker was Lucky Rich, the "Exterior Decorator." Tattoos stenciled "99%" of Rich's body, and stainless steel caps transformed his teeth into fangs. Over his navel the word NOMAD formed a halo, the letters green and gothic. Rich swallowed a sword, rode a unicycle, and told jokes. Despite his appearance Vicki said, "He seems good-natured and almost normal." Rich's jokes were corny, not smutty. Instead of performing tricks or acting, many buskers talked, leaning so heavily on off-color humor that performances bored. To invigorate a sleepy show, Madame Chou-Chou adorned her assistants with epaulettes, sticking sanitary napkins, the "light days" variety, on the men's shoulders. Escaping smut in Australia is impossible. Low humor cloys hours, ultimately making sexual matters so tedious that I suspect the Australian population will collapse in the next decade. On television repartee gropes rather than lances. Yesterday on Stirling Highway I passed a moveable crane. Painted in black on the door of the cab was "Great Erections."

On the back page of the latest number of *X Press Magazine,* Samsung Electronics advertised a cell phone. The ad was mostly photograph. Wearing a tattered straw hat and chewing the remnant of a wooden match, a young Australian posed in jockey shorts. The boy's stomach muscles ripped like a whelk. Below his navel hair flowed like seaweed, the roots out of sight below the underwear's elastic band. Printed in white letters across the boy's nipples was "JOYSTICK." Protruding from the opening of the jockey shorts, aerial erect and pointing toward the boy's right shoulder, was a portable phone, casing red, dial luridly yellow,

"JOYSTICK" printed on it. On the third page of today's *West Australian,* Bayswater Car Rental advertised Toyota Corollas. In the lower third of the ad appeared a white box in which rates were listed, fourteen dollars a day for a Corolla Hatchback, for example. In the upper two-thirds of the ad appeared a woman's bare bottom. A small car the size of a tumblebug climbed a ham. "Raw and not cured," Vicki said. "What do you suppose," she asked, "will be the long-term effect of humor and advertisement based solely on tits, bums, and pricks?"

"Imbecility," I said, opening a letter from Nowell, a friend in Atlanta. In the letter Nowell described patrons of Horace's Fine Foods, a restaurant where he ate breakfast. "One old fellow arrives here at 6:30 every day. What his real name is I don't know, but everyone calls him Red, even though he is bald. Red's wife died a year ago, and he cannot bear to stay home. He starts breakfast by reading the newspaper, but then he remembers his wife and begins to cry, leaving eggs and bacon congealing on the plate. Now who in his right mind wants to come to a restaurant and sit next to someone squalling like there is no tomorrow! A customer might wonder if the man was crying because the food was horrible or the service even worse or if one of the waitresses came on to him or no telling. After he has his cry, then he begins to eat his breakfast and leaves soon after."

Although Nowell described Dead Dan and Lumbering Linda, I did not read carefully. I surfed the wave of tears to Carthage. Last month Genova Breeks died. Genova was married to Fisher Breeks, a farmer in Big Isle. A large woman, Genova had a chin like "a cow's bag." When she was angry, which was often, her chin shook like a "calf was sucking on it." Fisher Breeks was recording secretary of the Tennessee Cauliflower Society and an Eagle, the Feathered Bektashgee of the Carthage Roost. Years with Genova battered him, but at her "passing," he was generous. "Grace," he told Turlow Gutheridge, "is often better than dinner. Vamping Genwa whetted appetite, but marriage brought indigestion." "Still," he continued, "she's walking the Boulevard to Paradise now. In her right hand she holds a silver ball peen hammer which she'll use to rap on the Gate of Heaven; in her left, a gold dollar, the price of admittance to Glory." "Genova will have a fine house on a leafy street," Fisher concluded; "I just pray that through the kindness of the Lord she and I will live in different suburbs." Despite his prayers for bachelor digs Fisher had a conventional epitaph engraved on Genova's tombstone. "Tho' lost to sight, to memory dear / Thou ever wilt remain. / One only hope my heart can cheer, / The hope to meet again."

Fisher loved words, and the crowd at Ankerrow's Café concluded that fondness for poetry determined the epitaph more than devotion to mate. For twenty years Fisher had sent letters to the *Carthage Courier.* In April he urged right-spirited Protestants to put title pages and prefaces at the backs of publications in order to separate "themselves from the degenerate Roman practice of placing prefatory matter at the fronts of books." In February he argued that personality could be detected by examining human ears. "The heads on which ears grow determine development," he wrote. "Like cauliflowers in a garden ears absorb nutrients from the dirt in which they are planted. If soil is poor, ears will be thin and weak. In contrast a head black with morality produces fat, healthy ears." Fisher compared schooling to manure, saying that education enriched heads and contributed to virtuous ears. "Too much nitrogen," he warned, however, "could stunt development and make minds indecisive, causing ears to blight, the tops withering and curling over in dieback." On reading ears for personality Fisher was ambivalent, noting that the National Institute of Mental Health had underwritten a study of such auditory matters conducted by specialists from "the Harvard University." "For my part," he concluded, "I reckon that ears which spread like fans above the hole indicate powerful cranial potential. On the other side of the head, a small ear circling the hole like a ribbon may indicate a predisposition to imbecility." With regard to lobes Fisher thought little lobes indicated "stunted animal propensities," noting that a person with such lobes probably would not make a fruitful mate. Big lobes, though, indicated hearty appetites, and the best of all possible mates "for bed and children" would have "large ears, lobes and uppers, blooming like petals and pistils." Words influence behavior. For a fortnight following the publication of Fisher's letter, some of the local female gentry concealed their endowments beneath hats and scarves. In contrast a few ladies exposed their blessings and pulling hair back from the sides of their faces, bound it behind their heads. Because hair stuck out from his ears like asparagus, Loppie Groat had his ears waxed.

After Genova's death Fisher wrote a letter to the *Courier* that swept ears from mind. A marbled liver killed Genova. Not even a case of Puckle's Blue Tonic could strip the suet from her lights. "A silent perambulator, a liver encourager, and a kidney persuader, Puckle's," a drummer told Fisher, was "as mild as Mary's lamb and as searching as a nit comb. Puckle's doesn't splash about in the entrails but swims into the bloodstream and settles down to the medical business." "The only reason Fisher bought the tonic," Dr. Sollows said later in Ankerrow's, "was that the drummer spoke well. In any case nothing could have resurrected Genova. She'd spent too many years digging a grave with her teeth."

Genova's appetite aside, two days after the funeral, Fisher's letter appeared. "To the friends of Genova Breeks," Fisher wrote, "a tender heartfelt acknowledgement for their kind and last respects to the departed one. Genova fancied sweets, and her earthly shell didn't float into the air. To the pallbearers who toted, bless you. To Pudsey Wallace who made the wreath of white carnations with blackberries squirreling along the top spelling 'Crossed Over,' bless you. And Pudsey, it will please you to know that after the shoveling was done, I took the wreath home and plucking off the berries, made a fine cobbler, just the thing to strip away thorns from grief and buck up a body who had spent fifty-four minutes and thirty-seven seconds on his feet in a graveyard. To Mahala Hiscake who prepared Genova for dancing with the King by pounding her into her wedding dress and who restored her youth by spading up the wart on her chin and turning her hair red again, bless you. And thank you, too, for putting the hearing aid in Genova's right ear. Genova was deaf as a beetle, and although the device didn't help her hearing, she was proud of it, buying it mail-order from Memphis and paying as much for it as I would a Holstein heifer. To Isom Legg, bless you for digging such a fine, deep grave and for sprinkling Chase's Bug Dust in it then covering it with a tarpaulin the night before the funeral to keep out possums and coons. And lest grief make me forgetful, thank you for spraying a quart of chicken blood on the mound after the service. Nothing keeps moles away better. To Nurse Nibs, bless you. You noticed Genova's bed was resting across the floorboards instead of parallel to them. Once you shifted the bedstead, dying took holt and within an hour Genova had shucked her mortal coil. To Enny Thickness, thank you for the handsome funeral cakes just dandy for two bites, four inches in diameter and an inch tall with one of Genova's initials, *G* or *B* icing each bite. I took a bag home and ate two with my cobbler. Nobody can make a tastier chocolate. Smith Countians, make Enny your baker when one of your dearly beloveds slams the screen door to her earthly mansion and tosses the key down the well. To Slubey Garts whose preaching gave Smokey the lockjaw and blew away the clouds of discord that long had lowered over the sky of wedded felicity obscuring the Star of Happiness, bless you. And lastly to the boys at the Roost, bless you for that basket piled high with heavenly fruit: Burr's New Pine strawberries; Stump the World and Yellow Red Rareripe peaches; General Hand and Blue Violet plums; and those pears, Tyson, Brandywine, Summer Doyenne, and Flemish Beauty. And boys, since I won't be having any more dialogues with Genova, there will be more opportunities for polylogues with you at the Nest, starting tomorrow night at eight sharp. I'll bring the cards. Yours Respectfully, Fisher Breeks."

No one accompanies me to Carthage. Once or twice Eliza has asked about a trip, but after I have guided her through a paragraph, her attention wanes. Doings in Carthage satisfy me, though, and I would be happy spending all my vacations in Smith County. For Vicki and Edward Carthage is the last of pea time, the first of frost. To keep family happy, I beat trips into the batter of school vacations. "We are not tourists, Daddy," Eliza said last week. "We live here. We are travelers. We make journeys not trips." Be Eliza's emendation as it may, I booked a trip to Adelaide and the Flinders Ranges during the vacation following the first term at school. In part I arranged the trip in hopes that activity would force Vicki out of melancholy. I suspected dismantling her parents' home in Princeton would make her gloomy, a mood not easily dispelled by routine. Four days after Vicki returned from the United States, we flew to Adelaide. We stayed in North Adelaide in apartments owned by Rodney and Regina Twiss, their company called North Adelaide Heritage Group. Accommodation cost $1,895 for six nights, $315.82 a night, a small price for startling Vicki into smiles.

We spent the first night on Tente Street, until 1996 a fire station. Constructed in 1866 as a shop, the building became a fire station in 1904. Parked at the foot of Vicki's and my bed was an International Fire Engine built in 1942 and sent to Australia by the American government during the Second World War. At the foot of the children's bed, a red fire pole ran through the ceiling. Red and white striped awnings covered the door to the station. On the wall hung maps outlining Adelaide's fire districts. About the room stood extinguishers. Helmets hung on hooks, one resembling headgear worn in the Trojan War, or at least film versions of the war. On the front of the helmet was a silver badge, two axes quartering it, the letters S, F, A, and B, each appearing in a quarter and standing for South Australia Fire Brigade. Draped over a rack were blue wool uniforms. We put on helmets and jackets and posed for photographs in the truck. Few tenants resisted the lure of the engine. "What a tale to tell folks back home, especially our grandson age six," a man wrote in the guest book. "Had read about the Fire Station back in Wales," a woman wrote, "never for a moment thinking we would stay in it." "Our three boys, aged four, six, and eight have literally polished the fire engine by crawling all over it," a woman from Chichester, England wrote. "At last all those Fantasies fulfilled," wrote an American. For adults who did not ride the engine back to childhood, fantasies were ordinary. "You should have seen my wife on the seat of the fire engine in her red negligee," wrote a Californian. Besides families with children the

Fire Engine Suite attracted honeymooners. Four times we changed rooms in the Heritage Group. The night before leaving for the Flinders, we stayed in the Residency Suite above the fire engine. Occupying the suite below was a newly married couple, "not young," Vicki said, "honeymooners old enough to afford a red engine."

If the Inn was quaint, the Residency was posh, consisting of two bedrooms, a living and dining area, and a modern bathtub with pipes that shot knots of water at bathers, massaging legs and backs. In the Residency I sampled the tub. Never had I bathed with water pounding me like knotted rags. I did not bathe long. Because the tub used so much water, I was uncomfortable. "Bathing is irresponsible," I said. "Come on," Edward said, "don't be such a fuddy-duddy." While we stayed on Trente Street, an American flag flew from a balcony atop the station. In fact many people who signed the guest book were Americans, inhabitants of New York, Illinois, Maryland, California, Montana, and Washington. Most lived in affluent suburbs: Bloomfield Hills, Michigan, Upper Darby, Pennsylvania, and Breckenridge, Colorado, for example. Writing "Storrs, Connecticut" in the book pleased me. "That will tear a run in the silk stocking," I said.

We spent four nights in Buxton Manor, three of the nights in the Butler's Apartment, the other in the Garden and Loft Suite, the former consisting of two bedrooms, a kitchen, sitting room and yards of hall; the latter, three bedrooms, kitchen, sitting room, and porch facing a rose garden where Vicki and I drank tea and listened to wattlebirds rummage through trees. Built in 1909, the manor was brick. So much orange had been baked into the brick that from a distance the house looked like a clay bank. Here and there ornamental cords of brick gripped the exterior like roots. Along the front a chimney rose straight as a right of way, near the ground sinking into a firebox that clung to the wall like a shed. Above walls the roof pitched sharply into gables, terra-cotta tiles coating it dusty red. In the apartment some bedsteads were brass; others, Victorian, their headboards gabled. In both sets of rooms kitchens were vast, and willow plate ran through cabinets like molding. At the end of each day in Adelaide, Vicki and I sat in the kitchen, drank tea, and ate toast slathered in butter. In the morning Vicki cooked breakfast. The children only ate cereal topped by bananas, but to fortify myself for the day's roaming, I ate an English breakfast of tomatoes, toast, eggs, and bacon. The first night in the Manor I pondered describing appointments. "Don't," Vicki said; "the flat reminds me of Princeton and the antiques I sold for nothing." "Right," I said and dropped my pad on a coffee table, the legs of which were elephants, their trunks rolling like small hills and tusks curving upward like basins.

Food is more important for travelers in a city than for travelers in the country. City days resemble school days, and galleries and museums smack of classrooms. The bush erases schedule, and travelers meander more, their lessons arbitrary and idiosyncratic, not hung on walls or printed on cards. In the city travelers peruse signatures of exhibits. In the country travelers relax. In Adelaide we ate lunch hurriedly, often in arcades, Regent or Adelaide. While bolting mounds of Chinese food or pita bread stuffed with vegetables, I studied guidebooks. At dusk school adjourned, and we returned to our rooms. Because I cannot master bus routes, we walked Adelaide. Indeed I always walk when I visit a city. "Is walking spiritual with you?" Eliza asked after a long day of traipsing. "Not spiritual but philosophic," I said. Real philosophy runs deep; I prefer shallows, places where stones flicker and minnows whisk. Still the pace of walks seems human. After I have hoofed through a day, I like the world more. Every morning before turning down Montefiore, King William, or Frome, we roamed North Adelaide: Buxton, Mills Terrace, Molesworth, Tynte, Archer, Gower, Childers, and Barnard. Cast iron hung from balconies like antimacassars. Gray ricks of tea tree fences bordered sidewalks. Never had I seen bluestone cottages, and I admired the hard simplicity of the color. While Eliza and Edward strode ahead, chatting about returning to Storrs and eating doughnut holes at Sugar Shack or walking the dogs around Horsebarn Hill, I stared at stones, the blue hypnotizing me. Ash and sweet gum turned roads into naves, and breezes twirled olive leaves. After dinner we also walked

North Adelaide. One night a boobook owl clung to a white wooden sign on Tynte. "North Adelaide Medical Centre 183," the sign said.

Rarely does visiting a city disrupt routine. In the bush time seems fabrication, and routine erodes. In Adelaide, as in Perth, dinner was important. Every night we ate in North Adelaide. The first night we ate at the Oxford, a restaurant on O'Connell Street. The restaurant was a bare room stainless with steel. I had spatchcock chicken. "Cornish hen by a fancier name," Vicki said. When Edward and Eliza asked for water, the waiter brought bottled water imported from Italy. Despite the restaurant's trendy minimalism, a machine in the lavatory dispensed condoms, the "Arouse" brand with a "Pleasing Coral Tint." Dinner cost $108. "The fewer the decorations, the higher the price," Vicki noted. The next night we ate in the bar of the Wellington Hotel, first licensed in 1851. Vicki and I had racks of lamb. "My sort of place," Vicki said. Twice we ate pasta for dinner. For dessert at Cibo Eliza had a slice of chocolate cake and a bowl of ice cream, this last two scoops of chocolate atop two scoops of cookies and cream. Vicki and the children seasoned meals with ice cream. After pasta and an evening stroll, once we ended at Café Paesano, Eliza having caramel atop roasted almond; Vicki tiramisu and nougat; and Edward, more conventional with strawberry and chocolate chip. Guidebooks called Adelaide a city of churches. For us it was a city of restaurants.

Arranged in grids, the city was lovely. "If we return to Australia, let's come here," Vicki said. Every morning we stood on Montefiore Hill and looked across the Torrens River. Beyond the river the city rose like a crystal garden. Usually we walked the riverbank, crossing the Torrens at the footbridge behind the University of Adelaide. Along the bank white poplars grew in clumps, and ornamental grasses waved like paintbrushes. Crested pigeons scudded the grass, and wood ducks dabbled in the water, black manes falling off the heads of males.

In cities we always visit zoos, and the first morning in Adelaide we walked to the zoo. In comparison to that in Melbourne, the zoo was small and homey. Crowds were also small, and instead of pushing against each other, forming snags of children and strollers, people ambled. When I was a boy, I caught snakes by the handful. The Reptile House stood near the front gate of the zoo, and I hurried inside. Scales on green tree snakes resembled prisms, breaking blue into yellow and turquoise. The forest cobra was my favorite snake. Except for splotches of vanilla under the lower jaw, the snake was darker than bittersweet chocolate. "Did you go inside?" a simple woman asked as I left the Reptile House. "Yes," I said. "I love snakes." "Ugh," the woman said, backing away, "I can't stand them." Before leaving the zoo, Eliza bought a stuffed snake. Fifty-one inches long, the serpent was a blend of rattlesnake and boa constrictor. While the tip of Curly's tail was black, rounded like wampum, and contained a rattle, its body was green and yellow, mottled for the floor of the jungle. The inside of Curly's mouth was pink. While two white fangs hung down like small tusks from Curly's upper jaw, a black tongue lolled from the lower.

Much as I cannot pass a reptile house without going inside, so Vicki always buys souvenirs at zoos. In addition to Curly she bought a turquoise shirt and two teacups. On the front of the shirt three rosellas perched in a gum tree. On one cup bilbies frolicked gaily; on the other, numbats. We spent most of the day at the zoo. A meerkat stood on top of a rock scanning the sky for predators. The breath of a pigmy hippopotamus smelled like sweet mash. Taller than my thigh, palm cockatoos dozed on dead branches, scarlet waxing and waning across their cheeks. After lunch keepers freed tamarinds, and they scurried through trees. Looking like kegs, tapirs dozed between the roots of a fig. Vicki and I meandered aviaries. In one an eclectus parrot said, "Hello." In another Vicki stroked a red-tailed black cockatoo, chucking it under the beak.

After leaving the zoo, we explored the Botanic Gardens, the first of two visits to the garden. Gardens undermine acquisitiveness. Amid trees and flowers possessions lose allure. If politicians spent time in gardens, the world would be better. Wonder drives resentment out of mind when one looks at Abyssinian bananas, leaves big as stoves, mid-veins coursing red through them. While

Edward and Eliza kicked mock oranges, I burrowed under the yellow skirt of a cypress, the Adelaide gold variety. Leaves on Moreton Bay chestnuts gleamed like mirrors, while those on pepper trees dangled in mobiles. On an Irish strawberry tree candelabras of green bells dangled upside down. We strolled through the Palm House, a large doll's house of clear and blue glass, urns atop white columns binding corners together. Peaceful doves spilled onto the lawn of an Italianate garden. In a greenhouse stepping stones of water lilies crossed a tank, small goldfish flicking like mica around them. Twenty-two Moreton Bay figs formed an alley, their trunks thick ribs, roots shovels pushing up stone and slowing walking. In the conservatory screw pines tottered over tines of roots; pleats pressed fan palms into sharp formality, and from chenille plants flowers hung in woolly red ropes.

Travel makes one aware of the fleeting nature of life. For a moment the Botanical Gardens belonged to me. But as we crossed the Albert Bridge and climbed up Frome, the rough threads of traffic forced me to concentrate on asphalt. Nonfiction does not mirror experience. At best paragraphs mold artifacts that can be placed on mantles and whose presence evokes parts of experience. When not walking to and from Buxton Manor, we wandered museums: the Migration Museum on Kinore, on the North Terrace, the South Australian Museum and the Art Gallery of South Australia. In the courtyard of the Migration Museum, Vicki and I drank cappuccinos, the stone buildings around us swept quiet by time, voices from the old lying-in hospital transformed into silent photographs. In the South Australia Museum while Edward and Eliza roamed, marveling at dinosaur bones and giant spider crabs, Vicki and I watched films taken by anthropologists showing Aborigines hunting the bush.

Travelers are drawn to what interests them at home. Indoors I sought the out-of-doors. In the Art Gallery of South Australia, I spent a morning amid landscape paintings, my favorite being H. J. Johnson's famous *Evening Shadows, Backwater of the Murray, South Australia.* In the sky behind a gray fog, yellow flickered into green. Four river red gums towered over a still pond. Weight bent their trunks, and shattered branches looked like stumps. On the right side of the canvas, a tent opened, the entrance a larger version of a hole in a tree. To the left a figure stood by a pool; in front a broken limb sagged through the water. If the water rose or the log rolled, the person would vanish. "Life before chainsaw and bulldozer," Vicki said. In Tom Roberts's *A Break Away!* a horseman tried to turn a flock of sheep away from a water hole. Although sheep would inevitably pile against each other causing some to drown, the painting was romantic. Pasted against a blue sky and orange ground, the hard life of drovers softened. Paintings that appealed to me seemed parts of a postcard world. The canvases depicted outsides rather than in, wordless places far from classrooms. In *A View of the Artist's House and Garden, in Mills Plains, Van Dieman's Land,* flowers bloomed, their petals meticulously drawn. Beneath the blossoms the ground unrolled into a fertile mattress. In John Lewin's *Fish Catch and Dawes Point, Sydney,* fish spilled in slabs from a basket, their colors and shapes making the world endlessly alluring.

Age increases appeals of clarity and silence. Cities are forever in flux. Traffic jerks; signs blare; buildings rise and fall, and around cafés talk billows like smoke. I enjoy imagining life apart from fret. No longer do I pause long over the fashionable or the clever. Attached to a wall in the museum was a life-sized chartreuse rhinoceros, constructed out of aluminum and fiber glass. On seeing it, I thought of a shopping mall, one bustling with youth lured by the glittering, artificial moment. Even when I drifted beyond landscapes, I didn't stray from the traditional, pausing, for example, before J. W. Waterhouse's Pre-Raphaelite depiction of Circe. Circe stood beside a pool, her dress slipping off her right shoulder, in her hands a platter, water overflowing in green strings. Blue rippled moody over the canvas, creating the impression of dream. "Don't you like this, Eliza?" I said, pointing to the painting. "Not really," she said.

Rarely do travelers free themselves from the expectations of others. Acquaintances tell travelers what they should do and see on a trip. After trips travelers endure quizzing. If one has missed a tourist site, people express disappointment and imply the trip was incomplete. An hour north of Adelaide land splits into a green seam forming the Barossa Valley, South Australia's famous wine-making region. Friends said a visit to Adelaide had to include a trip to the valley. Northeast of Perth grids of wineries cover the Swan Valley. Although we had driven across the valley several times, Vicki and I hadn't stopped at a vineyard, wine and traffic being a lethal brew. In Adelaide I booked a day's bus trip through the Barossa. For the four of us the trip cost $290, including morning tea, lunch, and, among other things, stops at three wineries. Renting a car would have cost less, but I wouldn't have been able to sample wine. Moreover, whenever I drive through an unknown region, Vicki proves an unsatisfactory navigator, and tension rises to shouts. With eyes only for the road and cars hugging my bumper, I pass interesting places before Vicki locates them on maps. Lunch inevitably becomes burdensome, the difficulty of choosing a restaurant reducing meals to sandwiches. Such concerns aside, however, only the elderly and Japanese, as Edward put it, took bus tours. "Well, then," I said, "I will be comfortable, for once among people my age." Edward was right. Most people on the bus were over sixty, and the rest were Japanese.

At 8:40 the bus picked us up at Buxton Manor and after stops at hotels on Brougham and North Terrace delivered us to the terminal on Franklin. We idled in the terminal for twenty minutes waiting for other buses to deliver tourists. When we left, all seats in the bus were filled. Freed from the anxiety of driving and trying to please family, I enjoyed the day. Moreover groups foster anonymity. In the Porongurups when I stopped at a winery, I was the only traveler present, and feeling pressure, bought wine. On the tour because I was faceless amid a crowd, I sampled a case of wine and bought nothing: at Grant Burge, port, Shiraz, and cabernet sauvignon; at Kaesler, merlot and a Shiraz from vines planted in 1893 and selling for thirty-eight dollars a bottle; and at Richmond Grove, port, merlot, and Shiraz.

The bus traveled through Tea-Tree Gully and Williamstown to Lyndoch, on the way stopping at Barossa Reservoir to allow people to stretch. At the reservoir the dam curved for 140 meters. A walkway ran across the top. If a person stood beneath the curve at one end of the dam and pressed himself against the wall and whispered, people at the far end of the dam could hear him. I wanted to whisper to Edward and Eliza, but a throng of Russians plugged both ends, ignoring other visitors. In Lyndoch we stopped at a bakery for coffee and bienenstich, a custard cake topped with honey. Small towns pocked the Barossa. Many houses were stone and in the light gleamed like gold. Vineyards swept across low hills, perming the landscape. "Think how much insecticide growers spray each year," Eliza said. "And fertilizer," Edward added. "I'll bet cancer is epidemic." The bus paused on Mengler Hill, a lookout eight kilometers from Tanunda. Slabs of granite and marble cluttered the slope below the car park. The stones were sculptures, poetic rather than realistic. "This stuff would make a five-year-old throw up," a man said. The sculptures didn't bother me. Behind the parking lot, however, stood the Barossa Pioneer Memorial. Engraved on the memorial was a statement from Joshua, "The Lord has given us this land." "And because the land is ours," I thought, "we can do whatever we want to it." Believing one is chosen leads to despoiling. Still beauty blunts thought, and as I stood on the hill, I longed to walk the valley. We did walk Murray Street in Tanunda. At the Wine and Visitor Centre, Vicki bought a tea towel for $7.50. On the front appeared a mural. A cooper made a barrel; two men pruned vines, and grapes tumbled into a trough.

The bus stopped several times. At Angaston Vicki bought dried fruit at the Angas Park Fruit Company, and I picked up a dozen apricots covered in white chocolate. Because the candy had passed the date for sale, the price had been reduced from twelve dollars to eight. Although the candy was old, the flavor was fresh. That night Vicki and I ate the apricots, reckoning that taking them to the Flinders would be a nuisance. On the trip we ate lunch at Kaesler Wines. Tour participants were given a choice of kangaroo or chicken. We chose kangaroo, awash in juniper sauce. Lunch was good, and Vicki and I spiced the meat with wine. During the day the bus covered much of the valley, Roland Flat, Angaston, Tanunda, and Nuritoopa. We saw enough to make us want to stay a week, but also enough to satisfy us if we never returned. At five-thirty the bus dropped us at Buxton Manor. Leaves were falling from sweet gum, and the sidewalk bloomed in yellow stars.

Trips are islands of order. Instead of the unknown travelers explore the planned—landscapes shaped by guidebook and bank account. At home people struggle to force days into schedule. They fail. Hours swirl and spin plans into snares ragged with flotsam. No matter the weight of the suitcase a traveler carries, the burden is relatively light. School does not whip days into white-caps. Faucets do not drip through the night like cash registers, and clutches do not bark and grind expectation to dust.

At 8:16 on the twenty-third, Toby fetched us from the fire station. In February I booked a vacation with Ecotrek, seven nights and six days walking the Flinders Ranges. In addition to Toby and us, six people took the trip, providing conversation and cama-raderie. Two couples were in the group, John and Joan, John a retired accountant born in Hungary, Joan his wife, born in Australia and a retired librarian. Bill and Debbie were the second couple. Bill was British by birth. He had owned a glass company but had retired to play the organ. Debbie, Bill's wife, was an American who came to Australia two decades ago to teach school, but who now ran a consulting business. Two single people were also in the group. Nicky flew from Scotland for the tour. A caterer for a large corporation, Nicky was deaf, not something that hindered adventuring, however, for she had ridden a bicycle along the west coast of India and into Arabia. John, the other single person on the tour, was sixty-three years old and the number two ranked triath-lete in his age group in Australia. With the exception of marriage he'd experienced many things: soldiering in India and Malaysia, flying planes and crashing in Australia, climbing in Nepal, and scuba diving the world, so far as I could tell. At the moment John was caretaker of a nursing home. He was a licensed electrician and plumber and "knew bit about carpentry." John gamboled up ridges, keeping pace with Edward and Eliza. "They must be athletes," he said to me one evening. "They never breathe hard." "Daddy," Edward asked, "could John have done all the things he says?" "He never married," I said. "Then he had the time," Edward said. Twenty-four years old, Toby was guide, repairman, cook, and nice, unflappable guy. In June he planned to fly to California and spend the summer working at a boys' camp.

We rode in an eleven-seat Hiace Toyota commuter van. Toby and Nicky sat in the front in bucket seats. Behind the driver were three rows of two bench seats. Because a sliding door opened on the left side of the van, not until the third row was a seat buckled to the left side of the Toyota. Behind the three rows of seats was the rear seat. Vicki, a child, and I usually sat on the third row of seats while the fourth family member always sat on the back row. Bill and Debbie sat on the row behind the driver. John and Joan usually took the second row, although they sometimes hurried to the car and sat in the back to spell us. From Adelaide to Wilpena in the Flinders, roads were paved. We stayed, however, at Oratunga Station, sixty-four kilometers beyond Wilpena, all the driving beyond Wilpena on unpaved corrugated road. Shock absorbers did little to smooth travel. The van bounced across corrugations, the tail of the vehicle slamming like a door. Dust billowed, and windows shook. When the van crossed grids separating sheep stations, metal thrummed. A hail of rocks pounded the undercarriage, beating hearing senseless. Glass banged, and at times seats seem to lift from the floor. Never had I enjoyed travel less. One morning we left Oratunga at 8:03. We arrived at Wilpena Pond at 9:09, shaken, as Vicki put it, out of "sense and muscle." Some days we spent four hours in the van. I hated floodways because the rear of the van pounded the ground. To deaden the grind of metal, I memorized the names of creeks: Patterton, Wockerwirra, Enorama, Deadman's, and Orparinna. I counted kangaroos. Herds of euros, grays, and reds stared at us from fields. One evening on the way back from Wilpena, I reached 126, but then at Bulls Creek the van hit the pavement like a forearm, and I stopped counting.

Time in the van was agonizing. From distorted retrospect, however, I would endure the van for the sake of a second trip to the

Flinders. Beyond Adelaide land opened into broad thighs. Hills rose slowly like bare knees, perched on them sheds, scabs of trees flaking around them. Kestrels hunched on dead limbs or lanced the air. Wheat stubble shadowed fields, and flocks of sheep drifted over the shaved land. In the Flinders topsoil was thin, and overgrazing had reduced much land to red pebble. Instead of sheep, station owners had begun to invest in tourism, converting shearers' quarters to paddocks for city dwellers. I wandered the land around the quarters at Oratunga. Sheep had peeled grass away, their paths aging the ground into crease and gully. Scattered across the land were hunks of bone, lower jaws looking like scythes and spines like broken baskets. Wool pooled about dead sheep. From a distance the animals looked like hay, the wire binding their flesh having rusted like the land itself.

On the way to the Flinders, we stopped in Port Augusta and ate lunch in a small park, our table donated by the Port Augusta Garden Club. Toby handed out quiche, slices of which the children and I dumped into a garbage can. On walks we carried the makings of lunch. Lunches were simple, sandwiches, stuffed with hummus, tomatoes, cheddar cheese, celery, carrots, lettuce, and Philadelphia Cream Cheese. I usually ate half a sandwich. For dessert we had fruitcake, a brand, Vicki noted, which cost $5.99 a bar. We drank water that we carried with us. Because of exercise not ingredients, sandwiches tasted good. At night at Oratunga Toby prepared dinner, a stew or pasta with chicken. In Hawker Toby filled the van at Hawker Motors, and Vicki bought postcards. In the men's lavatory an ardent lover had carved his and his girlfriend's initials into the plastic cistern atop the toilet. "DR," I read, loves "KA," the *loves* not a word but a heart, the left ventricle swollen with affection.

Often the more barren a landscape the more one notices. Our rooms in Adelaide were so rich with appointments that thinking about describing them made me dull. At Oratunga simplicity awakened. The shearers' quarters was a white block building with a tin roof. One end was divided into six rooms, each room opening to the outside, three facing east, three west. The other end con-

sisted of a kitchen and dining room. Vicki's and my room faced
west and measured twelve by ten feet. Linoleum covered the floor.
On either side of the door was a narrow window. Pushed against
side walls were twin beds. Between the beds stood a small table
with a Formica top. A fluorescent light was attached to the ceiling.
On the wall above the table hung the only decoration, a square
mirror, a foot on each side, the edging black plastic. Beyond the
door a concrete sidewalk led to showers twelve paces away. To the
left of the door stood a small water tower. The shower building
was also block and rested on a slab. Inside were three showers and
two sinks. Blocks separated the showers from each other, and curtains hung in front of each shower stall, enabling men and women
to bathe at the same time. In another small building beyond the
showers was a toilet. A second lavatory stood on the other side of
the quarters near a shearing shed. I did not use the bathrooms,
preferring instead a rocky gully from the bowels of which I could
watch birds. Only once did I enter the lavatory, this at the children's urging in order to see a huntsman spider that clung to a wall
like an orange birthmark. Northern pine bristled on the western
side of the quarters; on the east red dirt spread like a pond. A hundred yards away stood a palsied windmill. Nearby were paddocks,
a cistern, and the tin shearing shed. Low hills bowled across the
distance, all irregularly thatched with northern pine, the slopes
torn, looking as if wind had ripped off swatches of trees. Every
night I awoke after midnight. Usually I walked around the quarters and strolling to the windmill watched stars flare across the sky,
their tails bright feathers.

The dining room was thirty by twenty-four feet and so bare it
seemed clean. At one end stood a pine sideboard. Atop it every
evening Toby set two boxes of wine, each four liters: Morris Pressing Style Dry Red and Renauld Premium Varietal Chardonnay. I
had never drunk wine from a box. Nevertheless the wine went
down nicely after a fifteen-kilometer hike. A wood stove stood
halfway along the eastern wall, to its left a wicker basket of
firewood, to the right two leather and five green plastic chairs, in
front of this last a brittle rug. On each side of the room were a win-

dow and a door. Nailed to the west wall was a cork bulletin board. Tacked to it were flyers advertising "The Great Four Wheel Drive Journeys of the Flinders Ranges" and in Blinman, the Old Schoolhouse Tearoom. A brochure celebrated the virtues of the Port Augusta Campus of the Open Access College. On the front of the brochure appeared a young girl with blue eyes and brown hair in bangs. The girl wore a yellow dress and talked into a two-way radio. Outside the room in which the girl sat stood two gum trees, their trunks white and creamy, the ground beneath them baked hard.

In the middle of the dining room was a wooden picnic table, its legs heavy pipe. On each side of the table ran wooden benches, their legs also pipe. A cheesecloth lay atop the table, swatches of blue, pink, and orange gathering then spreading like wings. At the north side of the quarters were the kitchen and pantry. Toby cooked, but all walkers did chores, chopping vegetables or washing dishes. At one end of the kitchen stood a stove that burned bottled gas. A generator supplied electricity for everything else. Toby started the generator as soon as we returned from walking, generally at six. At ten he switched it off, not something I noticed because I was always asleep. We clumped together in the dining room like furniture, our conversation decorating emptiness with knick-knacks. Fragile, the words fell from memory as soon as I left the Flinders.

In the Flinders iron lace did not seduce. Instead of racketing around bluestone houses, sight fanned outward. Amid the vast open life drifted past glittering like krill. At Oratunga red-capped robins congregated in northern pine. From stubble around the shearing shed, bronzewings clattered into flight. Mallee ringnecks beat through trees, their calls softer than those of ringnecks in Perth, their greens and yellows paler, almost as if the dry land leached color from them. In patches beyond Sacred Canyon a flock of Adelaide rosellas foraged the hard scrub. South of Parachilna on the shoulder of Route 83, a wedge-tailed eagle tore a dead fox, hoeing flesh from the body. Near Wilpena little corellas turned a field into a campground of diminutive white tents. One afternoon at Oratunga I counted thirty-eight galas in a dead cypress. The next afternoon I counted eighty-four, the tree suddenly a pink confection of cotton candy. Every morning a willy wagtail hunted insects atop the stock tank. One morning eight blue-winged parrots joined him, his black tail scything back and forth in front of them. Above a dry wash a pair of mulga parrots perched on a limb. A young dusky woodswallow bustled brassy from grass along Bunyeroo Creek, the bird's flight, unlike its call, a soft melody of brown and white. Grey-breasted white-eyes skipped through pines, trills punctuating movement. In Wilpena Pound a pied butcher-bird pinched a caterpillar round as my index finger from the ground, and a white-browed babbler hopped through roots. On top of the Saddle at Wilpena, a yellow-fronted honeyeater stapled itself to the stalk of a yucca. At Blinman Pools black-fronted dotterels mottled the edge of the water, one moment tottering in old age, the next frolicking like youth.

On treks I walked alone in order to escape the mist of conversation. I usually followed so far behind that creatures flushed by the group had returned to feeding. Solitude frees imagination, and instead of molding myself around remarks, I tried to see the shape of the world. Beneath a cradle of rocks high above Blinman Pools, honeycombs hung white against a bluff, sharp as rudders in an orange sea. Red kangaroos studied me, and skinks pulled nubs of apple from my hand. Above Wilpena Pound a painted dragon dozed, only cocking his head when I sat nearby. Along banks above Yulna Creek, the webs of golden orb weavers glowed between trees. In the webs spiders hung head down, their black and white legs spread wide forming saucers. Tied above them were bundles of prey looking like the lumpy tails of scorpions. When I touched the backs of spiders, they shook their webs, and sunlight blinked golden, bright enough to startle and confuse predators. Near a heeltap of water a king brown stretched like a root. Stippled with yellow, brown scales shingled the snake. In the Flinders I saw only one other snake. Returning to Angorichina after following Blinman Creek, I climbed a ridge above the pools. Spinifex grew in cushions between rocks and small ledges. Rocks themselves were thick and spread across the ground like hard sleet. Crevices chan-

neled ridges, forcing me to bend over so that I looked like a walking elbow. Eventually I shuffled down a ridge, having become nervous that by stitching back and forth I'd lose my way. Near the
bottom of a ridge, a brown snake poured itself into a thicket of
reeds. To avoid the reeds I would have been forced to climb
through bales of fallen trees. I was tired, and so I broke a branch
from a tree and after stirring the reeds, hurried through them
down to the creek.

In the Flinders we occasionally explored the man-made: the old
tuberculosis sanitarium at Angorichina, now a tourist village, and
the North Blinman Hotel, its walls papered with business cards.
Because I wanted to see the cards, I persuaded Toby to stop outside the hotel, and I treated the group to beer. Ruins crumbled
throughout the Flinders, shucks of houses and outbuildings, kernels of life long vanished. Man comes, tills the land then breaks
apart in old age. At Kanyaka ruins were almost a village. At Sacred
Canyon Aborigines carved symbols into rocks. Later visitors
chalked designs nearby. "Why not?" Vicki said. "Drawings are
signs of life." In caves above Blinman Pool visitors imitated Aboriginal drawings, stamping white hand prints and whirls onto
stones. Now a shadow of its past, Blinman once thrived as a cop-
per town. The mine became the largest in the Flinders and was
worked until 1908. One morning while Eliza and Edward flew over
the ranges in a light airplane, I roamed the ruins. Tunnels transformed a hill into an underground barn, loft collapsed and stalls
akimbo. On the hill boilers rusted. Clumps of iron lay half-buried
in dirt, and slag heaps gleamed frozen and black. The biggest heap
contained sixty thousand tons of slag. Below the heap pepper trees
bloomed, drawing symphonies of bees. The mines operated
twenty-four hours a day and spewing racket and fumes, turned
Blinman into a prosperous Hell. After leaving the mines, I walked
down Blinman Road to the cemetery. Light dug sharp under my
skin. The graveyard was bare, and tombstones tottered dizzily.
Engraved on the stone of Jane, the wife of Barnard McPharlin was
the epitaph, "Weep not for me my children dear, / I am not dead
but sleepeth here. / My days were short / My griefs were less. / I'm

gone from you to happiness." Actually Jane lived a long time, fifty-eight years. In contrast Beatrice Ann, the Henerys' daughter, died at twenty-two months. "Thy will be done," her memorial stated baldly. The stone over the grave of J. W. Morrison, killed in a mine when he was twenty-one years and ten months old, was "Erected By His Loving Mother." Across faces of stones flowers snapped; doves carried olive branches in their beaks, and anchors hooked crosses in the sky. On March 3, 1872, Mary Ann Murray died. Mary Ann was three and a half years old. Two weeks later on March 17, Mary Ann's two-year-old sister Lily died. On February 14, 1885, Ellen Glass died at fifty-three. Ellen was a spinster and loved God with the passion of the Song of Songs. Although the language on her stone was biblical, never had I read a similar epitaph. "She being dead yet speaketh, sown in / weakness, raised in power, let him kiss / me with the kisses of his mouth for / thy love is better than wine, and I / will give her the morning star."

Each day we walked between ten and twenty kilometers, the average being slightly over fifteen kilometers. I wore short pants, the cargo variety bulbous with pockets along the thigh; thick gray socks; Rocky Boots, 10 wide, bought in Connecticut; a long-sleeved shirt; sunglasses; and a floppy blue hat purchased from the Australia Cancer Society in Perth. I did not wear underpants, fearing they would chafe the insides of my legs. I also bathed my lower legs, especially calves; backs of my hands; and neck and face with sunscreen. Around my neck I hung binoculars, the case hanging down my chest, my stomach pushing it into a bounce when I walked. On my shoulders I carried a backpack stuffed with two pairs of glasses, one for reading, the other for distance; oranges and apples; a tube of sunscreen; pad and pencil, and two, sometimes, three liters of water. Eliza began each walk in a sweatshirt. As days warmed, she took off the sweatshirt, and I added it to the heap in the backpack.

Most mornings we got up at six-thirty and were on the road by seven-thirty. The first day we drove to Aroona Valley, settled in 1851 by Frederick Hayward. I stood on a knob at the head of the valley. In the distance rose the A, B, C, and Heysen ranges, the first soft and close as teeth on a zipper, the other harder, gullies pinching ridges into tents. Above the knob sheets of light streamed into the valley, some of the sheets silver, a few yellow. In the mountains blue shadows covered gullies in capes. In the open rocks hunkered red and orange. Lower slopes of mountains were scruffy with trees. In the middle of the valley, river red gums fenced a creek. Beyond the creek the valley floor withered into gray. From the Aroona Valley we walked the Heysen Trail to Red Hill Lookout, following a road blazed by firefighters. The hill grew shale not trees. Valleys fell away from the hill in skirts then rolled upward into dry red mountains.

Although hills eroded into calluses, they attracted me. Above Willow Creek I climbed the lookout. Once there I wandered to a nearby knob, far enough away from others so that I inhabited silence. From a lookout mind, not eye, absorbs view. So much lies before a person that he realizes certainty is a fiction shaped by life in lowlands, places in which appointments of landscape obscure the distant. Oddly, however, hilltops do not separate me from people, no matter that I'm alone. The absence of crowds triggers sentimentality and infuses me with good feeling for my fellows, not something that occurs in a city. In cities I avoid huddles of people and fret myself into distaste. High places also comfort by exposing a person to his insignificance. Atop a mountain one slips the bars of envy, and for a moment, inhabits a self in which ambition seems silly and ceases to foment dissatisfaction. For a moment one sits undefined and indefinable—just a person on a rock.

We descended Red Hill and for several kilometers followed Yuluna Creek. Tracks filigreed sand and dirt, and kangaroo droppings gleamed black as beetles. Under ledges dirt daubers plastered rails of nests. High water rolled blocks of stone through the creek bed. Brush caught on the trunks of river red gums, and branches stabbed through each other, forming joists that storms eventually turned into huts. Floods wrung trunks into tension, twisting them around like a mangle. I watched a pair of goats pick their way up a red bluff. To see, a walker must stop. Even then schedule reduces sights to snapshots, most discontinuous, the negatives always lost: fossilized rocks, once tidal flats, their surfaces rippled; emus plodding through high grass; quartzite at Brachina Gorge, the stones forming walls of red brick; in Sacred Canyon, tufts of rock isotome, precarious in crevices, leaves jagged, the flowers white post horns; and across low hills pale lemon-scented grass, the plants dry but the fragrance still tingling when I crushed blades.

We spent part of a day on the Bunyeroo and Wilcolo Creek bush walk, 9.5 kilometers. For luck I sliced the foot off a dead kangaroo. I chewed horehound and crammed feathers into my hatband, white feathers from a corella and green from a mallee ringneck. One afternoon we meandered Blinman Pools. River red gums were as massive as steam engines, and oleander thick as wallets. We spent two days roaming Wilpena Pound, a weathered pelvis ringed by purple mountains. I began each day's walk with coffee at the Wilpena Visitors Centre, the two worst cups of coffee I drank in Australia, and maybe the world. The first day we walked the St. Mary Loop, some seventeen kilometers. We climbed into the Pound through the Saddle, a depression in the mountains. At times the climb was almost straight up. As I pulled myself along, I wondered if a heart attack would bowl me over. "Grandfather Ratcliffe died at sixty-one," I thought, "and I'm fifty-nine." Climbing the Saddle, Vicki said, "I had three heart attacks but I survived." Beyond the Saddle the walk wound through the Pound. I trailed everyone by several hundred yards, disappearing into thickets of sheoak and black tea trees. I crammed sheoak cones in my pockets. Later the valves opened, and the winged ends of seeds protruded, nutlets remaining hidden until a breeze lifted the wings. Seeds were brown and tea-colored. Including the wing each seed was a quarter of an inch long. Wings jutted out from nutlets at an angle, making seeds whirl the air. I chewed several seeds but could not detect flavor. Actually I ate a handful of prunes before chewing the seeds, and the prunes probably masked taste. I am not sure why such small things interest me. Maybe the seeds intrigued me because they were concrete, not abstract like memories. Moreover

I am willful. I walk slowly and studiously notice the small, in reaction to others who trot forward on an escalator of words. Often distance becomes the only measure of a walk. In meandering off trails to pluck cones from sheoak, I may have been trying to escape the yardstick. Of course no walker sheds awareness of the kilometers that spool a day. The longer I walked, the better I felt about myself. "Tattered I may hang on my frame," I thought one night at dinner, "but I can still stride the hills."

On the twenty-ninth, we left the Flinders, returning to Adelaide, driving through Melrose, Wirrabara, Laura, and Clare, land fat, first with wheat then with vineyards. We spent that night at Buxton Manor. Early the next morning we flew back to Perth, arriving at 10:30. The following day school began. Three days later I spoke to creative writing students at the university. "Study the world around you," I advised. "Why," Vicki asked that night, "does routine pummel experience from mind?"

All the Fun

After enumerating the problems of middle age—difficulties with wife, children, and job; an aging house and prostate, the one losing shingles, dry rot undermining the other—Frank asked querulously, "Why does Sisyphus get to have all the fun?" At seven the next morning I spoke at Christ Church Grammar School, addressing the eighth-grade Father and Son Breakfast. In the talk I rolled out mossy words of encouragement, preaching the virtues of books and study, sports and music. "Don't become upset," I advised, "if you do not become the best person in your class in your favorite activity." "Work brings rewards. Genius is diligence. Participation builds a self-sufficient, muscular character." I told silly stories about my amateurish self. The previous Sunday I ran the ten-kilometer Challenge Run at Perry Lakes Stadium. Some five hundred and fifty people ran. Parents pushing baby carriages passed me. Few people my age and no one pear-shaped ran. No other runners were in sight when I crossed the finish line, neither in front nor behind, and the announcer had leisure enough to announce my name. "Was I embarrassed?" I said. "A little," I answered, continuing; "by the end of the race, I was bent over like a paperclip. Still I felt good, not simply about myself because I ran ten kilometers, but also about the great gift called life." In the next paragraph I plugged laughter. "Remember," I said, "that if gloom covers you like a cloud today, tomorrow will be sunny."

Speaking to a range of ages is difficult. "Standing here," I began, "amid muffins and orange juice makes me feel like a vitamin, one dispensing milligrams of this and that—A, B, and C, 3 percent of a child's daily requirement of uplift, 150 percent of the adult male's." Despite the calculation only briefly did I address fathers. "Enjoy the unfolding years," I said; "marvelous things will happen." "Sometimes, though, being Daddy will be tough. For the good of our children, you and I do what we think right. Later time will prove our actions wrong. That is the heartache of being human: to do things selflessly with good intentions and in the process hurt others."

As soon as the words stopped, children rushed to class and fathers hurried to work. Before leaving a member of the Parents' Association presented me the customary bottle of wine. Actually the wine was better than usual, a 1992 cabernet sauvignon from Coonawarra "famed for its rare Terra Rossa soils," Rosemont Estate's "Show Reserve" and "Museum Release." In Melbourne in 1993 the wine won Gold in "Class 16." In 1995 at the International Wine Awards in Zurich, it harvested another Gold. Because the wine seemed a barrel above the ordinary, I asked the proprietor of Mosman Heights Liquor Store to estimate the price. "I don't carry that wine," he said, "but my guess is $31.95." Alas, I cannot rise above plonk, and after a taste I consigned the bottle to Vicki.

For years I have organized days around ordinary fare. Good wine might undermine expectation. Instead of lifting and pushing I might grow careless and swishing imagination back and forth let duty slide. I spent much of May planning July, our last month in Australia. On the fifth of July Eliza, Vicki, and I fly to Darwin. We stay four nights at the Mirambeena Hotel. On the morning of the ninth, World Expeditions fetches from the hotel and for seven days and six nights a guide takes us through Kakadu National Park. Late on the sixteenth we return to the Mirambeena. The next afternoon we return to Perth and spend five nights in a university apartment on Myers Street. On the afternoon of the twenty-second, we fly to Sydney. We spend six nights there, staying at the Russell, a small hotel on the Rocks. On the twenty-eighth we fly to Fiji. Because our plane arrives at dusk, we spend a night at Raffles

Gateway Hotel. The next morning a launch takes us to Castaway Island where we lounge for a week, food paid for in advance. On the afternoon of the fifth, the launch returns us to the mainland and the airport at Nadi. That evening we fly to Los Angeles. After an eleven-hour layover we take the red-eye to Hartford. Although the details were soporific, planning kept me up nights, making mind break out in hives.

Because Edward decided to spend the summer working as a counselor at a boys' camp in Maine, I arranged his departure in early June. After making sure that Edward finished examinations at Christ Church, I booked a flight for him on Air Malaysia. Because the plane stopped in Kuala Lumpur, I purchased transfers to and from the airport, breakfasts, and two nights at the Mayflower Concorde Hotel, on the ground floor of which was "Hard Rock Café, Kuala Lumpur," matter for a T-shirt. I arranged for a graduate student to fetch Edward at the airport in Hartford and drive him to Storrs. I restarted my automobile insurance so Edward could drive. When she was in the United States, Vicki tried to schedule a physical for Edward, a requirement for Middlebury College. When Vicki attempted to arrange the physical, Ken Dardick's June schedule was filled, so she tried to book a date in August. Because the computer at Mansfield Family Practice was not able to schedule physicals more than three months in advance, Vicki was unsuccessful. "You mean," Vicki said to the secretary, "that I cannot book a physical now. When we return from Australia in August, Ken will be fully booked." "That's right," the secretary said. "In other words I will have to fly home at the end of May to schedule a physical," Vicki said. "I guess so," the secretary said. "This really pisses me off," Vicki said and slammed the receiver down. "You do something," Vicki ordered when she returned to Perth. I contacted Ken directly, and on June 6 Edward has a physical and gets a shot for bacterial meningitis, this last just part of the ball I rolled up the hill. Before Edward left Perth, I gave him a wad of Malaysian money. I compiled a list of hints for him, for example, informing him that he could purchase a bus ticket from Willimantic to Portland, Maine, at Bev's, a café on Main

Street in Willimantic. I wrote a check for his expenses in the United States, including the cost of the physical. I photocopied my health insurance card and explained its use. Sisyphus had life easy. Every day for a fortnight I rolled Edward's departure through my mind, pondering what he would need. Of course much remains to be done. In August after the end of camp, I have scheduled appointments for Edward with two dentists and a dermatologist. Edward's wisdom teeth need pulling, but that can probably wait until Christmas vacation, as can an eye examination. Francis, my other son, is in Germany. He plans to return to Connecticut early in September, half a week before returning to Princeton. I dare not think what I must do for him. I won't worry much about him until after I figure my income tax, filed late because of spending the year in Australia. In any case I have kept receipts for expenses. "Don't be sure, Sam," Vicki said the other night. "I'll bet you don't have records for half the big expenses."

The trip home resembled a puzzle, pieces of which I trimmed into pattern. I spent two mornings in Perth at the Qantas office. One morning I stood at the counter while the clerk closeted herself with the manager. On returning to the desk she said we could not stop in Sydney. Permission to stop took three telephone calls from home to the Qantas headquarters in Sydney. Between inquiring about hotel rooms in Sydney and actually booking them, whole floors vanished. Suddenly World Expeditions changed the date of the Kakadu trip. Overnight, some kayaking I pondered disappeared from a catalogue. On Fiji many resorts filled, and I got the last bure on Castaway Island.

I planned to leave Kalgoorlie Street on July 5, the day we left for Darwin. When we returned on seventeenth, I intended to stay in a university apartment for five days. Initially Kempton Azzopardi said no university flats were open in July. On a flat's suddenly becoming available, I walked to the office to pay in advance. "I cannot take your money," a clerk said. "Our computer program does not allow for advance payment. You can't pay until after you have spent a night in the flat." Because the flight from Darwin to Perth did not land until evening, I asked Sue in the English department to fetch keys for me and put them into my mailbox. Sue is not a computer, and she agreed to pick up the keys. Between forcing pieces of the puzzle into place, I fretted like a band saw, pondering alternative trips, one to New Zealand, for example. Seven years ago we visited Sydney. This year we are returning because Eliza forgot the city and wanted to see it again. "How will we spend days there?" Vicki asked. "Maybe we will go to the Blue Mountains," I said, adding that the Botanical Gardens were lovely and worth wandering. "I'm not going to the Botanical Gardens every day," Eliza said.

Now that pieces of the trip are wedged together, I must settle other matters. By the third week in June, I must pack my books and send them home. I hope they can be sent through the university post office. Even though I will pay the postage, Sue thinks mailing them through the university will be difficult. At the beginning of July I will sell the car and deposit the check in my bank account. The check should clear before we return from Darwin. On July 18 I will pay the rent for the flat on Myers Street and close my account at Challenge Bank. A manager told me closing the account and receiving a check for the money remaining in the account could be accomplished in an hour. I hope so. Soon I must pay the last house bills: gas, electricity, water, and telephone. Also I must ask Leasing Elite to refund my housing deposit on July 18, so I can cash the check before leaving Perth. I want to pay cash to the Russell, and I am not sure how much money I will need in Sydney and Fiji. I prefer paying cash because I don't like credit card bills. "But suppose you lose the money," Vicki said. "What will you do, and how much are you taking in cash?" "I can't answer either question," I said and left the house for a jog. After the run my arthritis was almost as painful as worry. During the jog I thought about the date on which I should stop receiving mail. "The Australia Post on June 20 and email on 17 July," I said aloud when I returned to the house. "What?" Vicki said, cooking lamb kebabs. "Nothing," I said.

The next morning I went to the university. Raymond had sent an email from Storrs and on the first page of his letter mentioned the Slough of Despond three times. "That's age," Nigel said then quoted an old rhyme. "Great fleas have little fleas upon / Their backs to bite 'em, / And little fleas have lesser fleas, / And so *ad infinitum.* / And the great fleas themselves in / Turn have greater fleas to go on; / While these again have greater still, / And greater still, and so on." After chatting with Nigel I walked to Barrett's and to cheer myself bought a chocolate cupcake. After the purchase I ambled back to the university. Traffic was backed up from Stirling Highway along Broadway. I ate the cake as I threaded cars at Cooper. A woman driving a white Holden munched a blueberry cupcake. We noticed each at the same time. We smiled and raised our cupcakes in a sugary toast. Immediately thereafter the traffic bumped along, and the Holden disappeared. I finished the cake and wiped my lips on the back of my left hand. For a moment, though, the woman's smile lingered. Years ago, I mused, she would have pulled to the curb, thus icing a tale.

For the last fortnight fair girls who might have stopped but who instead passed out of my life had occupied my thoughts. Early in May memories of Alice brightened dreary moments. I had known Alice in graduate school. She was warm and decent, and I had a crush on her. One night she came to my room to ask about an assignment. We almost touched, but religion slammed between us blocking hands and affection. Alice was a Catholic, and I, a lapsed Episcopalian. Today such differences are inconsequential. In the 1960s the difference seemed vast. I had not seen Alice since 1970, but in dry moments between planning the departure from Australia and running errands, I sentimentalized the undone and wondered what life with Alice would have been like. At the end of a fortnight, I skimmed periodicals in the university library. When I picked up *PMLA,* the journal fell open to the obituary page. I read the names. Two-thirds the way down the page appeared Alice's name. She died this past August. "Shit," I said and sat down. That night girls with whom I attended graduate school shimmied through memory. In the green years of youth, all bloomed bright: Sarah, whose two children died in a car wreck;

Cathy dead of breast cancer at thirty-eight; Bridget, killed by breast cancer at fifty-two; and Callie, still alive after a bone-marrow transplant. Not drudgery but the gift of life itself seemed heavy. That night I had two odd dreams. A flock of blackbirds perched in a cherry white with flowers. Suddenly the birds blossomed red and feathery as azalea. Just as quickly they tumbled from the tree, dying and turning black as they fell. Once all the birds lay on the ground, flowers rained from the cherry, the petals mildewing in the air. Next I dreamed I slipped off the bed and became wedged between the wall and mattress. My friend Ellen, still alive, thank goodness, rushed into the room and placing both hands on my chest, fingers spread like leaves, pushed down so hard I couldn't breathe. Although I struggled for air, I sank, the weight on my chest too heavy to dislodge. Then, all of a sudden, I was awake and gasping for air.

All hope of sleep having been exhaled, I went into the living room and read *Sard Harker,* an adventure novel written by John Masefield. Two days earlier I checked the book out of the university library. Age has transformed my reading. Rarely do I read any fiction other than mysteries or tales of improbable adventure. Generally I confine myself to nonfiction. I read randomly, however, not with the optimistic purpose of youth, innocently believing book guides for hacking paths through the maze of years. No matter the hours I spend roaming library stacks, I eventually check out books written by old acquaintances, authors with whom I have been familiar for decades. I first read John Masefield's novels twenty-one years ago. Vicki's father read them as a child, and on shelves in the farmhouse in Nova Scotia, I found *Dead Ned* and *Alive and Kicking Ned,* novels which Edward read after I encouraged him, thus insuring that some day years hence he will read more of Masefield. I finished *Sard Harker* and *The Bird of Dawning* before sunrise. After breakfast I thumbed the title pages, jotting down notes of vast insignificance, something I have done since childhood. The "Student Fund" paid for the purchase of both books. On February 28, 1940, the books became part of university holdings, *Dawning* being volume 42,436, *Sard,* 42,437. The numbers were written by hand. The writer used a pen with a broad nib that he turned sideways in order to make thin strokes. Thus 4 consisted of two slender vertical down strokes and a thick broad horizontal slash. The next two digits in each number, the 2 and the 4, were joined, the bottom of the 2 rising in a flourish to the top of the 4, giving the numbers a Chinese appearance. "What do you think about these numbers?" I asked Vicki. "Nothing," Vicki said, adding; "You aren't going to write about them, are you?"

Breaking habit is impossible. If Sisyphus's rock had been stolen, he would have pined into shadow. If given the choice between dozing comfortably, laurels wreathing his brow, or pushing a larger rock, he would have hightailed it to the slope. The race at Perry Lakes was my second run. My number was 519, something I always note, and I finished the course in an hour and twelve seconds, shuffling through a kilometer every six minutes. During the last two kilometers I tried to catch a heavy woman, but she was thirty years younger and galloped off on hearing the thump of my shoes.

The week following the run at Perry Lakes I ran the Lake Gwelup Fun Run, a community run around a small lake northeast of Scarborough Beach. The run consisted of two races, once around the lake for a 3.2 kilometer course, or twice around for 6.4. I ran the latter. My number was 161, and my time was thirty-six minutes and twenty-two seconds. Curtains of rain fell during the race. Since I don't own running shorts, I wore a bathing suit. Although the rain was cold and made me uncomfortable, I did not chafe, having greased the insides of my thighs and my nipples, this last a necessity for all middle-age male runners except the anorexic. In this race I did better, passing a woman thirty-five years younger than me 250 yards from the finish, then holding her off at the end even though the sound of splashing grew loud behind me. Proceeds from the race were donated to the air-conditioning fund at the local primary school. Despite the rain the community turned out in force, scores of dogs on leads and classrooms of thigh-high children in hand. "Rosie O the Clown" painted faces. In defiance of the weather a sunflower waved from the top of

Rosie O's cap. Children went for rides in a vintage fire engine, more balloons waving above them than umbrellas.

The race started at Gwelup Community Cottage. Inside the cottage boosters sold coffee and tea. Three lemons cost a dollar, and tables were shelves of cakes, carrot and apple being the most popular. Slower to sell were slices of chocolate cake, two artificial cherries topping each piece; cupcakes smothered by rainbows of sprinkles; and fudge, on each piece candies shaped like raspberries, most green, yellow, or red, turning the fudge into stop lights. After the race I changed clothes in the back seat of my car. I put on blue jeans and a sweatshirt. I did not wear underpants, and although I replaced running shoes with sandals, I didn't remove my damp socks. By the end of the race puddles had become wading pools. No matter how carefully I walked, my socks were sure to be soaked. Parents operated a sausage sizzle. A sausage cost two dollars. I bought one sausage, heating it with onions and barbecue sauce and wrapping it in an eiderdown of Wonder bread, the supply of buns having run out.

After the race a drawing was held for prizes, all donated by local businesses. Balcatta Animal Hospital donated a one-year "Fit for Life policy." "That's a good prize," I said to a woman, "but I think I'll just stick with my G.P. He has examined my dewclaws since 1978." Crème Aveda Concepts Salon donated two thirty-minute "Aromatherapy Body Massages." "The perfume of love. I'd like that," the woman said. Winners chose their prizes, selecting from over fifty items: a sixty-dollar lunch donated by Funtastico Restaurant in Subiaco; from the Great Escape, passes for the all-day waterslide and Wacky Putt; bouquets from Gwelup Flower Shop; a river cruise for two from Captain Cook Cruises; and from Odin Auto Parts in Balcatta, a battery recharger. Even I won a prize. By the time 161 was drawn, however, pickings were slim, and I won "10 free cuppas" donated by the Dome Café in Karrinyup.

After the race I felt exuberant. That afternoon I searched my notebooks and found an epitaph that fit my memory of Alice. "She was a mortal, but such gifts she bore / About her that we almost deemed her more; / For every day we saw new graces start, / To touch our love, and bind her to our heart." "The verse is lovely," Vicki said, "but why apply it to someone you didn't see after 1970?" "I don't know," I said. "That's not an answer," Vicki replied. "Replies aren't always answers," I said, then quoted another verse I'd found. "Call it madness, call it folly, / You cannot chase my grief away. / There's such a charm in melancholy, / I would not, if I could, be gay."

Prissy

"Daddy," Eliza said, on my declining to accompany her to the movie *Moulin Rouge*, "you are prissy." "Very prissy," Vicki added, going out the door. I am not prissy. I prune life so days don't grow spindly. Never have I sampled wares peddled by street corner pharmacists. I've not seen an adult movie or purchased a blue magazine. I haven't broken bread in a tabernacle that treats women as things. "What do you believe, Daddy?" Eliza asked last month. "A lot," I said—not so much as I once did, however. Institutions I used to respect now seem rotten. The Pharisees on the Supreme Court are not people whom I would greet at the front door. "Don't you have patriotic feelings?" Eliza asked three nights ago when I snapped off the television, exasperated by buffoonery in Washington. "Certainly not!" I exclaimed. "Has global warming cooked your brain?" Absence makes youth enthusiastic. Australia has narrowed Eliza, provoking her to celebrate everything American, a condition that returning to Connecticut will purge from her system.

Of course I might be the narrow member of the family. Not since childhood have I wanted anything for Christmas. I have bought no new clothes for fifteen years. "Your jackets and suits are so worn," Vicki said last night, "that when you dress up, you look like a hairball." Yesterday Vicki, Eliza, and I went to downtown Perth. While they shopped, I went to the Art Gallery of Western Australia. In galleries strangers talk to me. As I stood before

Lucien Freud's *Naked Man with a Rat,* an old woman asked, "How could you elect that man president?" "I didn't," I said, after which we discussed the glow throbbing under the skin of Freud's nudes. In museums I usually spend much time in front of one or two objects. Studying objects stamps them into memory and creates the illusion of ownership. At the gallery I coveted an epergne manufactured in 1875. A rug of silver dirt covered a rocky outcrop. Between stones two eucalyptus trees twined together like scissors, tips of their blades breaking into leaves. Between the handles a tree fern waved loosely. An Aboriginal man climbed one of the gums, pursuing a possum. To climb, the man jabbed spikes into the trunk of the tree and created a ladder. Below, his wife warmed herself at the embers of a fire. A kangaroo pelt covered her from the waist down. Above the navel her breasts sagged like rotten mangos. To the woman's right a hound raced around the trees. Behind the dog a bearded man galloped on horseback. The man wore a stovepipe hat. In his right hand he held a throwing stick; in his left he held the reins to his horse. For its part the horse was springing over a fallen limb, the tip of the limb a rail. Ahead of the man a second hound pursued a kangaroo, an emu bounding ahead. "If this epergne were on a dining room table," I mused, "no one would ever think about politics."

The paintings I study are landscapes, windows through which I escape the suburban present. Arthur Streeton's *Hillside* hung in a hall in the Centenary Gallery. Only ten inches square, the painting provided a moment's wandering. A grassy hill slumped like a shoulder across the canvas, high on the left, low on the right. Amid the grass grew thimbles of buttercups. Above the hill the sky split loose and pale blue then tightened to purple. In the distance the ocean slumbered in a low mist. Cattle drifted along the hill, three brown and one white. Atop the hill other cattle trudged down to a river looking like buttons. Along the slope trees clumped in brown brushes. A sandy path switched through the grass. Beside the path stood a woman. A bonnet perched on the woman's head, and in her right hand she grasped a walking stick. She wore a long pink dress, a red belt cinching the waist.

For eight minutes I ambled the hill, chewing blades of grass, and tipping my hat to the woman. She knew me, and we smiled. The time I spent on the hill invigorated me. Afterward I explored Carillon Arcade and felt energetic enough to shop. City Menswear was going out of business, and I rummaged racks looking for a teaching jacket. Unfortunately the store was out of my size, forty-three long. I chatted with the manager. All suits in the store were dark—blue, midnight gray, or black. "Business uniforms," the man said. Despite appearances created by movies like *The Castle* and *Priscilla, Queen of the Desert,* Australians are conformist, not simply in dress but also in thought. "When America orders," the woman in the gallery said, "Australia jumps."

Across Hay Street Mall was Tony Barlow, a branch of City Menswear. Pasted to Barlow's window were placards advertising a sale "10% to 60% off," the 10 percent being minute, the 60 huge and blaring. Clothes in the store were duller than those in City Menswear. Buying, though, was in the air, and I wandered Murray to Jim Kidd Sports. My running shoes pinched, buckling my toes backwards into blisters. At Kidd's I bought a pair of Aesics, size 11, "Motion Control," Gel MC-Plus, a discontinued line. I don't know what the letters mean. Last night I wore the shoes for the first time. My toes did not blister, but this morning the sides of my feet ached, the shoes having changed the way my feet hit the ground.

"Gloom, if genially presented, and without rancor, is an enjoyable emotion, as well as being quite plainly the best approach to our national predicament," Auberon Waugh wrote in the *Way of the World,* a collection of newspaper columns he wrote for the *Daily Telegraph.* When hours cloy, I head to Carthage. Carthaginians are not prissy. While Eliza and Vicki watched *Moulin Rouge,* I traveled to Tennessee. Turlow Gutheridge met me at the bus station. An epidemic of bathtub drownings had plagued Maggart. "That just goes to show," Turlow said, "that folks ought to learn about a new thing before using it." Last month Googoo Hooberry had his sinuses irrigated in Chattanooga. On returning to Carthage he described the city to the lunchtime crowd at Ankerrow's Café. In the window of Buntin's Imperial Marble City, a funeral supply house, was a little, pink coffin, "so small," Googoo said, "that it couldn't possibly be intended for a living soul." In Carthage Death enjoys his work and never takes a holiday. Last week Mathuzalum Guppy preached at Horn Dunch's funeral. Horn was a handyman, a polyartist, as he dubbed himself. He rebuilt tractors, hung cabinets, and dug wells. More than any other chore, however, Horn liked repairing watches. At the funeral Mathuzalum wound remarks about a watch metaphor. "Christianity," he said, "was the mainspring of Horn's being, and the Decalogue, the regulator of his actions." "The Bible set Horn going, and his compassionate hands did not stop until he relieved distress, no matter the hour." "For Horn life was a round of good deeds; prayer turned the key to his character and kept his motions regular."

"Time dented the case of our dear brother and striped away the fobs of appearance," Mathuzalum concluded, "but I can give you a lifetime guarantee that the Master Clockmaker took Horn's soul into His shop. There He cleaned, repaired, and wound Horn anew, setting the springs of eternal life turning for the world to come, beyond lint and the ticking of time, forever and without end." In the past Mathuzalum's sermons had been memorable only for failings of grammar and thought. In speaking to the high school at Alice Wells, Mathuzalum twice said, "than they used to was." In the same talk Mathuzalum stressed the importance of education. "If Noah had been a reader," he said, "and had owned a copy of The Handbook for High Water, published by the Tennessee Valley Authority, he'd have managed the flood better. A dam here, a dam there, and Noah wouldn't have had to build the ark. All that water would have flushed out into the Tennessee River and vanished without disturbing so much as a stalk of Silver Queen."

The superiority of the funeral sermon to the rest of Mathuzalum's prose made me suspect that Mathuzalum relied less upon inspiration than usual and more upon a library. For two days I rummaged forgotten sermons in Reid Library. At the end of the second day, I found Mathuzalum's source, a sermon preached in 1833 by Aenid Eusden Wodswill at the funeral of Cowper Hopkins, a watchmaker in Selborne, England. The plagiarism did not bother me. Instead I admired Mathuzalum's ingenuity and wondered how he'd unearthed the manuscript, Carthage being far from beaten bookshelves. Even more interesting was Wodswill, and I spent another two days trying to discover information about him. I found out little. From 1832 to 1837 Wodswill was a curate in Selborne. All that I learned about his life before 1832 was that he graduated from Cambridge University, attending St. Catharine's College. After 1837 he vanished. The funeral sermon seems to have been the only prose he published. He wrote poetry, however, and although I couldn't locate any of his poems, I dug up the titles of four: "Poor's Benny's Walk," "A New and Newer Version of The Policeman's Daughter," "Hot Codlings for Breakfast," and something puzzlingly called "The White Beetles."

The bite that turns paragraphs acidic often makes the writer bilious, "prissy," in Eliza's terms. Appreciating the contemporary is difficult for the middle-aged. As a person ages, energy decreases. In order to keep up some interests, a person must dissociate himself from others. In middle age criticism comes more naturally than appreciation. To prevent myself from becoming too curmudgeonly and my remarks from clouding Eliza's optimism, I walk. Glimpses of tree and flower awaken wonder, and when I return home, I am mellow. Along Palmerston paddlewheels of red rolled around poinsettia. Cape daisies splotched curbs, and the new leaves of lupin spun through blankets of sour sobs. In the back yard spray of gold carpeted the fence. Pincushion and rose mallee still bloomed. "I wish we could grow a rose mallee in Connecticut," Eliza said later. One afternoon I sat for two hours on the back porch and watched birds forage the eucalyptus hanging over the garage. Rainbow lorikeets jangled upside down; red wattlebirds squawked, and ravens growled and cleared their craws. Singing honeyeaters seized blossoms and shook them like mops while brown honeyeaters darted about like pencil stubs. My magpies flew onto the porch, and I fed them chicken scraps. Later that afternoon I walked to Freshwater Bay and stood at the end of Keanes Point Jetty. Twenty feet away a pair of dolphins chuffed through the water. That night a mouse appeared in the sitting room, scooting across the rug like a windup toy. The next morning Vicki and I walked Kings Park. Blossoms on Ashby's banksia smelled like hay, and flowers were coppery on Teasel banksia. On large-fruited net bush, tips of flowers looked like they'd been dipped in red watercolors. A white-browed scrub wren bounded from limb to limb, and a red wattlebird dug into a Hooker's banksia. That afternoon Vicki and I drove to Fremantle and ate lunch near the markets on Henderson Mall. We ate at EMC. The letters stood for enchiladas, muscles, and chips, and I ordered muscles soaked in coconut milk and lemon grass. "A good day," Vicki said, eating chicken curry. Later we went to the Bakehouse and sweetened the meal with beetroot cake. That night, as Mathuzalum might have put it, the master clockmaker rewound the mouse and set him going in the living room again. "Look at that mouse," I said to Eliza. "Uh, huh," she said, putting her feet on a stool and reading *Martin Chuzzlewit*. "Dickens's characters are familiar," I said. "Every night on television, I see Jefferson Brick, General Choke, and Mr. La Fayette Kettle." "I haven't gotten that far," Eliza said. "Just you wait," I said.

Going

Yesterday a reporter from the *Sunday Times* interviewed me at the university. Before returning home I walked to the bookstore and picked up five boxes into which to pack books and clothes. That afternoon I borrowed Patrick White's novel *The Vivesector* from the Cottesloe Library. "That will be heavy going," a woman in the library said. "Each year I start one of White's novels. Unfortunately I never finish." I checked out *The Vivesector* because I knew the book would be heavy going. Near the ends of long stays, people ponder what they have missed. For the most part I have lived within family, Perth only furnishing decorations for days. Reading White, I kidded myself, might deepen thought and appreciation.

During my first months in Perth I roamed Mosman Park and Peppermint Grove. After Edward left Australia in June, I started walking the alleys of Peppermint Grove. "Do you think truths lurk in alleys?" Eliza asked. I wanted to say *yes,* but I knew better. "No," I answered, "the groomed reveals more than the unkempt." In Peppermint Grove trees leaned over alleys transforming them into arcades. Graffiti sprawled across walls, letters bent out of recognition, looking like plates broken from metal watchbands. Mould spread through paint like eczema, and wooden fences slumped wearily, slats broken like old clothes hangers. Ratty with twigs, gutters sagged under roofs. Heat pumps throbbed beside garages, and sidewalks crumpled into mounds of concrete slabs. From above a wall a bauhinia dropped purple flowers. In the dirt petals turned brown and looked like strips of cardboard. Dogs barked behind corrugated fences, the sound more lonely than startled. "Did you see anything wonderful in the alleys?" Eliza asked last night, putting down *Martin Chuzzlewit*. "Yes, chickens," I said. "Behind one house is a chicken coop. I love the sound of chickens." This morning a photographer took a picture of me. I stood behind a round bush of lavender and stared poetically into the distance. "L'homme fatale," Vicki said, "coming through the lavender." "Sure," I said then quoted a parody of Longfellow's "Psalm of Life" sent to me by a librarian in Kentucky. "Lives of honest men remind us / That to wrong we mustn't stoop / That we mustn't leave behind us / Footprints 'round the chicken coop."

Affection for a Machine

In a letter to C. F., a neighbor in Storrs, I lamented that institutions rarely rewarded loyalty or affection. "When I was twelve," C. F. responded, "I spent days on a Ford Jubilee tractor. She was the crown jewel of tractors, and I loved her. She was ten years old, worn and tired, and I spent long hours keeping her running. One evening after a trying day of wrenches and gaskets, I walked into the kitchen. My father sat at the table sipping coffee. 'How did things go?' he asked. 'You would think that after all I've done for that tractor she'd treat me better,' I said, sitting down. 'Son,' my father said, putting down his cup and staring at me, 'let me give you some advice. If you go through life loving a tractor, you're going to be disappointed.'"

Disappointment disturbs but also invigorates. Devotion to place or institution makes one a conformist. Not belonging keeps a person uncomfortable and alert. Indeed only eccentrics, as non-conformists are often called, change society. For my point of view not oddity but aesthetics undermine the seductions of place. Nowadays on rambles I notice architectural monstrosities. Some are small, a garage door on Globe, for example, the sight of which nauseates me. Painted on the door are colored squares, tipped on their sides to create a diamond pattern. To the right of a stack of three dark blue squares totters a column of two pale blue squares, at the top and bottom of which are triangles of half squares. To the left of the dark blue squares stands a column of white squares, this, too, consisting of a pair of squares and two half squares. To the left of the white column appear three pale blue diamonds; beyond that, dark blue, two squares sandwiched between two triangles. At the corner of Palmerston and Keane, a wall surrounds a faux adobe house. Both house and wall glow pink and luminous, "fleshly terra-cotta," Vicki calls the color. "If we stayed in Perth," I told Vicki, "we'd have to move. The house gives me hives." "My God, you have become sensitive," Vicki said. "I suppose it is an allergy triggered by aging."

Taste and knowledge cause allergies. Only the immature believe, as Oscar Wilde put it, that self-love is the beginning of a lifelong romance. Last week a young mother wrote me, basting her letter with niceness. "You have made an impact like the proverbial stone in the pond. It may have started as an influence on one, but has affected the course of events in many lives. This is what I find curious. How can one person inspire others? How can it be done in one lifetime?" Alas, for me niceness smacks of the artificial or the unobserved. Moreover when stones splash into ponds, they rarely cause ripples. At least I don't see ripples. *Inspiration* itself seems a word that people use when nothing else comes to mind. At worst the word forms part of the stock vocabulary of panhandlers and snake-oil salesmen, that is, politicians, motivators, preachers, and teachers peddling cure-alls for the incurable. Of course not all letters cause mind to slip into a diabetic coma. Last week John, who had been part of our group in the Flinders, sent me an account of a hundred-kilometer race he ran as a member of a four-person team. All team members ran the hundred kilometers. John's account was typed and consisted of one paragraph ninety-two lines long. Punctuation and spelling did not matter. "This part of the trip was quite an experience, walking through the scrub on Mr. Lofty at night. Go and try it sometime," John began on line 41. "The trail markers were very hard to follow and on a number of times we were geographically embarrassed. We were walking through the trees when this horrible roar let out. It sounded like somebody had got a gorilla by its nuts I jumped 2 metres in the air and took off down the trail like a Jack rabbit, much to the amusement of the rest, who pointed out it was only a koala bear. Have you ever heard one? We saw roos, owl, foxes, and many other creatures. I said look theres a owl, I was corrected and told it was a tawny frog or something. I said if thats a bloody frog it can certainly jump it must be 30 feet up that tree."

The frog was a bird, the tawny frogmouth. John's strength was description. Later in the letter and race, line 62, he wrote, "We passed through some marsh land via way of a very flimsy plank walk. We past chicken farms piggeries and even saw a calf being born. Dave impressed everybody with his knowledge of the smells of different dung. Thats chicken crap he would say, and thats goose crap its got a much sweeter smell. I said I cant smell it but it sounds like a lot of bullshit to me." After I read John's letter to Eliza, reading favorite parts twice, Eliza said, "I've begun to understand Mother." "It's about time," I said, picking up a pencil and jotting down the remark.

As impressionist painters tried to capture light, so I labor to grasp transient days. To do so, I struggle to remain free, if not from love, at least from mechanized living, the sort of life that hunts inspiration or devotes years to tractors. For Vicki's and my twenty-second wedding anniversary, I ordered a chocolate mousse cake from Martineau's. "There was an accident this morning," Cathy said, when I appeared at the bakery. "Our delivery man piled so many cake boxes in his arms that his sight was blocked. When he turned, he knocked your cake off the refrigerator shelf." "Yes," Jane said, "then he stepped on it." I bought another cake, in the process hearing a story that jollied the day. The next morning Vicki, Eliza, and I ambled Cottesloe Beach. Waves broke soft and sudsy. Silver gulls spun above the sand, and cormorants skipped over the ocean. In scrub a bobtail bathed in the sun. Near a wooden walk an old man stripped to his bathing suit. Knots of bones bulged from the man's shoulders, and his ribs flared weak as twigs. The man plucked a small clot of chewing gum from his mouth and stuck it atop a post. After a short dip the man returned, dried himself, dressed, and then searched until he found the gum. At North Cottesloe Eliza raked sand for shells while I watched currents brush algae into bangs. That afternoon Vicki and I sat on the shoreline at Freshwater Bay. A crown toby turned through the water. A school of silver fish ricocheted around the bay, driven by little cormorants and followed by silver gulls. While Vicki fed bread to a pair of black swans, I watched a praying mantis pick its way up my sock. On the slope under Mosman Hill, a flock of black and white cockatoos gathered in trees, their cries high whinnies.

Two days ago Vicki and I took the 9:30 ferry from Fremantle to Rottnest. At the bakery I bought a bun stuffed with apple. The cappuccino machine only gave me two-thirds of a cup, so I took a sip then refilled the cup, the excess sloshing over the lip. I paid for one cup and told Vicki to fill her cup twice. "I felt odd about doing that," she said later. "I didn't," I said. "I paid for a full cup, and I got a full cup." After drinking the coffee, we rented bicycles and circled the island. Near Bickley Swamp mountain ducks clumped on the ground, looking like baskets, their necks handles, heads grips. Red-capped robins plucked insects from the railway right of way. Breasts of the birds glowed like the sun. In contrast necks and heads of red-necked avocets wading the shallows of Lake Herschel were muted, claret thickening to brown. Although we fed apple to a skink at Cape Valamingh, birds appointed the day: ring-necked pheasants; pied stilts dozing, heads shelved under wings; oyster-catchers; chestnut teal; kestrels hanging in the air like puppets; and white-fronted chats, bobbing along the shoulder of the road near Strickland Bay. We saw four ospreys. Their nests perched atop rocks and were so big they looked like stumps. At day's end we drank a second cup of coffee at the Dome Café. A quokka drifted under our table searching for crumbs. The fine for feeding quokkas was fifty dollars. Vicki handed me a macaroon. I spilled crumbs into my lap then brushed them onto the ground. The quokka didn't notice. On the way home on the ferry, I sat below deck near the bar. Workers from the island flocked to the bar, most of them heavy-set and drinking Emu bitter or Jim Beam in a can. A woman with Chinese letters tattooed on her right shoulder blade and above her left hip ordered a Victoria bitter. "How far did you cycle?" Eliza asked at dinner. "About twenty-eight kilometers," I said. "We had a super day."

The excursion was only partly responsible for my feelings. The day had been Eliza's last at St. Hilda's. She received good grades, in three classes finishing first in eleventh grade, in the other two, third, in chemistry, for example, three out of seventy-three. Even better, in history class friends presented her a basket brimming with mementos. "Don't forget us," Sally wrote on a card. "Come back for university," Jane urged. Contents of the basket tugged at affections. Although I paid $150 to enroll Eliza in the old girls' association, I knew memory would weaken and friendships would vanish from recollection. Never again would Eliza see Perth. The only things she'd cart home that she would not forget would be the paragraphs I wrote. Still the presents touched me. Clutching the handle of the basket was a small gray koala, two and a half inches from head to bottom. He wore a blue vest, on the back of which was printed "i love AUSTRALIA," the *love* being a heart not a word. Inserted between the koala and the handle was a small Australian flag. Inside the basket lay the koala's cousin, brown and wearing a red instead of a blue vest. On the back appeared the same affectionate statement, the *I*, however, being a capital not a small letter. Instead of a handle the brown koala clung to a blue pen decorated with orange kangaroos. The pen, flag, and koalas were made in China, these last selling six for $3.50 in the E-Shed in Fremantle. Also in the basket was another koala from China. This bear was bigger, three and a half inches separating his left hind paw from his right. His ears were white, and his nose was a black plastic jellybean. He, too, wore a red vest. Printed in white on the back was AUSTRALIA. In his left arm he held a small Australian flag.

An outback of creatures lurked amid the presents. A joey looked apprehensively out of her mother's pouch. Tied around the mother's neck was a red ribbon, AUSTRALIA printed on it in yellow. Sticking out from the left corner of the mother's tail was a label reading, "Made in China." Among other animals in the basket was a small echidna wearing a white diaper, the name *Millie* stamped on the diaper. Originally Millie commemorated the Olympics and above her name rose the Olympic torch and the words "Sydney 2000," the golden arch of McDonald's curving over the words. Another echidna looked like a brown beanbag. With a carrot nose and eyes like peas, the echidna did not resemble Millie. Still it was a relative, for it, too, was "Handmade in China." A packet contained ten envelopes and ten "Australia Notecards," these from South Africa. Sundry animals frolicked across the cards: wombats and platypuses, in addition to koalas and echidnas, then an aviary of birds, kookaburras, galahs, cockatoos, and lyrebirds.

Wrapping a mug in black, green, and red bunting were the words "PERTH WAS SO EXPENSIVE MY FRIENDS COULD ONLY BUY ME THIS LOUSY MUG." The mug was "made in Taiwan." Among other presents were postcards, on the front of one a photograph of downtown Perth, on another the Aussie Ocker Alphabet. In the alphabet *F* stood for Fair Dinkum, meaning honest or true. While *C* stood for chook, a chicken, *K* meant kark, to die, and *L,* larrikin or troublemaker. A black kangaroo bounced across a mustard-colored coin purse. A second black kangaroo scampered across the middle of a boomerang. Sixteen inches from horn to horn, the boomerang was made in Australia. From a key ring dangled a gold swan, its belly stuffed with opal shavings, this, too, manufactured in Australia. In the basket were two jars of Vegemite, "Australia's Favorite Spread" and "One of the World's Richest Known Sources of Vitamin B." Near the Vegemite lay an Uncle Toby's Muesli Bar, the "Crunchy Anzac." From the Great Australian Roadside Company came a square yellow sign, seven and a half inches on each side. Printed on the front of the sign were a battered outhouse and the words "The Great Australian Dunny" and "Outback 50 Metres." Accompanying the sign was a piece of paper on which was printed the definition of *dunny* in English, French, Spanish, and German. "The bush dunnyseat," the paper explained, "was often made from one slab of timber, the piece cut out could be used as a bread board." On the outhouse itself boards opened like seams in trousers. While five flies clumped together on toilet paper, three dozed on the edge of the privy. Other flies swam through fragrance which seeped from the dunny in four places: the tin pipe sticking out of the roof, through a hole in the side of the dunny, and from the door, both bottom and top. Eliza's friend Claire burned two CDs containing popular songs. Other girls drew the covers. Green letters trailed across the first cover, proclaiming "Top Aussie Pop Songs!!" Beneath the words waved the Australian flag. On the other cover green letters alternated with yellow. "i reckon you're a full-dodgy random," the cover stated. In parenthesis appeared, "Note: often used amongst friends." Below the note was an explanation. "Aust. coll. I believe you are a strange or untrustworthy person whom I am not well-acquainted with." What were strange were the songs and the names of the groups who sang them. Killing Heidi sang "Weir," and Ice House, "Great Southern Land." Regurgitator sang "Polyester Girl"; Prawns with Horns, "Let's Go to the Beach"; Spiderbait, "Glokenpop"; and Frenzied Rhomb, "Never Had So Much Fun."

Many girls signed an address book. Hallmark published the book, and it was printed in China. On the cover of the book a bouquet of four and one-half blue flowers and four leaves lay on a pale yellow square. Printed on sides of the square were "Little forget-me-nots," this despite the flowers' resembling periwinkle. Inside the front cover Didi drew a heart and wrote, "Best wishes for the future. We hope your time in Perth will remain close to your heart always." The inscription made me sad. "If the presents made you weepy," Vicki said, "why did you write down where they were manufactured?" "I don't know," I said. "Age does peculiar things to the affections."

On the Way

In Western countries people solve problems. They set goals and climb ladders. At day's end, however, life seems out of joint. Achievement loses significance, and doubt obscures accomplishment. Instead of stamping footprints into the sands of time, maybe life would be better if one sank anonymously into the soil itself, reaching a natural equilibrium, so much so that identity would be a symptom of imbalance. Instead of quantifying life as a series of measurements, wouldn't man and his host, the earth, fare better if societies celebrated harmonies, silences in which people floated contentedly and did not thrash toward achievement? Universities foment the spread of numbers. Presidents demand that faculties quantify duties and achievement. Rarely does a faculty member opine that the most important things in life cannot be reduced to numbers: hatred, love, the first daffodil of spring, a child's warm hand, or the jagged edge of anger or of grief. Such matters lie beyond mathematics and as a result slip from educational concern.

Travel disrupts. In so doing, travel frees people from measurement. For me experience never smacks of the mystical. Still, occasionally, in an out-of-the-way nook, the noose of ambition loosens, and for a moment I enjoy indefinable pleasure. For a brief period I seemed webbed in harmony. Of course thought or a voice eventually snaps the dragline, and the web sags. Moments, however, invigorate, and so I travel. Later I write in hopes of transferring my pleasure to another or at least that is what I think now. Tomorrow may provide a different explanation. Be that as it may, however, early on July 5, Vicki, Eliza, and I left Perth for Darwin and the Northern Territory.

Activity dominated the week before we left. I arranged for the phone to be cut off and the final bill to be mailed to me in the English department. I shifted the name on accounts for gas, electricity, and water back to Leasing Elite. I packed books and oddments into five boxes. John at the university mailroom shipped them air freight to Connecticut. Postage was $658. The books were making a third journey across the Pacific, the cost of the trips amounting to more than I paid for them. On July 2 Vicki and I carted suitcases, boxes, and sacks to the university, converting my office into a storeroom. We made two trips, transporting three suitcases the size of refrigerators; six cardboard boxes containing foodstuffs Vicki thought she might need when we returned to Perth on July 17, and finally four plastic carry-alls, the names on the bags Myer, Fremantle Souvenirs, Gallery, and Pure Australian Clothing Company. Contents of the plastic bags were diverse: sweaters, shoes, tea towels stamped with goannas, and shirts, on one shirt, the seal of the University of Western Australia on the left breast, a black swan afloat in the middle. On July 3 I drove the Mitsubishi to Mazda City, and Rod Evans purchased it, paying, as he did seven years ago, almost the price I bought the car for in September. Vicki thought I should have sold the car on July 4, the day before we flew to Darwin. "Suppose a problem arises on the fourth," I said, "then what?" Vicki resembles her father. The week after Francis's birth I bought two insurance policies on my life. "Don't waste money on insurance," Vicki's father advised. "Suppose I die," I said. "Who will care for your daughter and grandson?" "You won't die," he said. "Nothing," Vicki said, "will happen to the car if you sell it on the fourth. You worry too much." I am overly cautious. Three times before leaving Perth I visited the Challenge Bank, going to a different branch on each occasion, and asked if I'd be able to close my account in one day.

In part reaction to Vicki's ways provokes my planning. Never does she pack ahead of time. To no avail I urged her to add two boxes to the five we took to the university and mailed home from Perth. As a result whenever we travel, bags are heavy as barbells. To Darwin we took three duffel bags, one of which we stored in the hotel during our excursion in Kakadu. The duffels looked like blue hornworms, gorged with belongings. In addition we carried backpacks, Vicki, two in fact. Mine functioned as a shoulder safe. Into it I stuffed the five hundred pages I wrote during the year; a manila envelope containing last year's tax return; two packets containing receipts, these for hundreds of bills ranging from school tuition to chits for birthday cakes; and a folder containing Eliza's grades from E. O. Smith in Storrs, reports from Exeter Summer School in New Hampshire, and marks from St. Hilda's. In a plastic case were plane tickets and vouchers for our room in Darwin and the trip to Kakadu. In a pocket in the bag, I put two notebooks, nine ballpoint pens, two six-inch rulers, and three pairs of glasses, for sun, distance, and reading. In another pocket I put a jar of hand cream. After a day of walking my left heel splits and bleeds. At night I fill the cracks with cream. At the top of the pack, I stacked binoculars and five books: *A Field Guide to the Birds of Australia,* 460 pages of plate and description; Greg Miles's *Kakadu Wildlife;* Ian Morris's "natural history guide," *Kakadu National Park;* and finally both Fodor's and Frommer's guides to Australia "2000," both hefty handbooks, the first 624 pages, the latter 706. Folded over everything like the roof of a Quonset hut were two large manila envelopes. During the trip I filled the envelopes with maps and tourist brochures. When I booked a taxi to cart us to the airport, I ordered a station wagon. Before we returned to Perth, memorabilia fleshed out the bag even more, so much so I thought it would split like a chrysalis, spilling contents into the air. Whenever we moved, worries about transporting bags undermined sleep, beating good mood into exasperation.

Despite chores that minced days, I didn't always hoe and chop. Some afternoons I sat in the living room and tinkered with words. In May Vicki sent $250 to Rachel as a high school graduation present. The last week in June Vicki received a postcard from Rachel.

She wrote fifty-five words, each word costing Vicki $4.545, in, I pointed out, American dollars. I did not include the address in the computation since the girl's mother addressed the card. The card itself advertised Pacific Bell's "call forwarding." "FOUND YOU!" sprawled across a red oval. In smaller letters above the open space for writing appeared a paragraph. "CALL FORWARDING fiNDS YOU! With *Call Forwarding* from Pacific Bell, calls to your home phone can find you at the office, at the beach, at the game—anywhere. Simply forward your calls to your mobile phone or pager. So get *Call Forwarding* and never miss a call. To find out more, call 1–800-PAC-BELL." The paragraph consisted of fifty-three words. "Two less than Rachel wrote," Eliza said, then added, "but who would want to be found on the beach or at the game?" "Or in the sack?" Vicki said. "Good Lord," I said and began reading a poem sent to me by a student. In March I taught a class in which the woman was enrolled. In class I said lies were essential in nonfiction. "To lie is sublime he said," the woman wrote, recollecting my advice, "and our duty to do / to satisfy every kind of Deity." "Daddy," Eliza asked, "why do you say such things?" "Because Truth matters," I said. Later that night I handed Eliza a review of one of my books. The reviewer observed that I was "not possessed of a sensibility that is needlessly trammeled by facts." "High praise," I said.

During the last week in Mosman Park, I roamed the neighborhood, hoping that tramping would press place into mind. Alas, little can repoint the memory of an aging male. Early one morning I strolled south along Palmerston. At Lochee a young woman pushed a wheel chair. A decrepit man sank into the chair. He wore white jogging shoes, and his legs were tightly pressed together. The woman turned onto Palmerston and walked behind me. The man sat silently. Only when the woman started across the road thrusting the chair toward Freshwater Bay Nursing Home did the man move. Then he began to sway and moan, the sound rising heavy as soot. That afternoon I strolled to Coles with Vicki. While Vicki bought salad makings, I sat outside the store on a green bench and dozed in the sun. "Practicing to be old?" Brenda Walker, the novelist, said, seeing me on the bench. "I'm not practicing," I said. Two days before leaving the house, Vicki and I drank a final coffee at Cappuccino by the River. "Saying goodbye to this life will be hard," she said, watching cormorants glide around Keanes Point. That afternoon I walked to the post office and mailed two cards to Edward. Afterward I walked to Rewind and returned *Vlad, the Impaler*, the last movie we watched at home. The day was July 4, and that night we lit sparklers in the backyard. The sparklers were a combination of mitten and star, each point of the star a fat finger. We had two sparklers apiece. We lit the sparklers in the middle, and while flames curled around the fingers, we spun about the yard, waving the sparklers, creating arcs of light and shouting, "Good-bye Perth."

On the morning of the fifth, I sowed the backyard with hamburger meat for the magpies. "The Last Breakfast," Vicki said. I hid the key to the house in the refrigerator in the garage. Then I dragged the bags onto the front porch and waited for the taxi. That afternoon we landed in Darwin. Evergreen frangipani bloomed along the highway leading to town from the airport. Overhead kites looped and skidded across thermals. We stayed at the Mirambeena, a hotel on Cavenaugh Street. Every morning I strolled along Cavenaugh toward the harbor and ate breakfast at the Roma Bar, toast, eggs sunny side up, tomatoes, bacon, and cappuccino. Eliza drank a cappuccino with me then went to an ice cream parlor on Smith Street where she bought a smoothie. We roamed downtown night and day. In a shop off the Smith Street Mall, Eliza bought a pink bikini. The owner of the shop wrote two receipts, one for the actual price $95, the other for $45. I showed Vicki the latter. "The suit was a bargain," I said. "Trust me to find sales, even in women's stores."

Eliza, Vicki, and I explored Darwin, roaming Bennett, Harry, Chan, Woods, Peel, and Searcy. We rummaged souvenir shops. Vicki bought a wardrobe of shirts, all presents, crocodiles toothy across the chests. I explored stores searching for Aboriginal art. At the Museum and Art Gallery of the Northern Territory on Fannie Bay, I studied paintings from Arnhem Land, all crosshatched on bark. A pair of black rock wallabies curved thick into each other like halves of the moon. Stone axes sprouted from the knees and elbows of Namarrakon, the lightning spirit. I coveted a painting depicting three spirits from the rock country. Tall and thin, the spirits could slip through cracks like breezes. My favorite painting depicted Moon Dreaming, the Moon's head, neck, and pelvis luminous, legs on each side of his body bent like springs. Compared to the holdings of the gallery, shop art was derivative and mechanical, smacking of the marketplace. Still, morning and afternoon I searched. Finally at Aboriginal Fine Arts at the corner of Knuckey and Mitchell, I saw a painting that appealed to me. The canvas was fifty-five by seventy-five centimeters. The Rainbow Serpent coiled around five eggs. While the background of the painting was black, the snake's scales were ochre and white. When I was a boy, I roamed my grandfather's farm in Virginia, turning over rocks and lifting boards in hopes of discovering snakes. Time has not changed me much, at least not mentally. In Storrs I place slabs of plywood in fields. Snakes find them and doze beneath them. "That's the painting for you," Vicki said; "it's good." The artist, Ivan Namirrikki, lived in central Arnhem Land and was the ceremonial leader of his clan. For two days I studied the picture. On the third I bought it. I started a flood of buying. At the gallery Vicki bought three wooden birds and a dot painting, *Bush Plum Dreaming.* For Eliza I got a shell necklace, this free, part of my bargaining for the painting. Seven years ago I bought little in Australia, suspecting I might return. My days in Australia being numbered, I purchased the painting as a berm against the erosion of memory.

After browsing shops, we sat on benches in the Smith Street Mall, watched people, and ate ice cream, our favorite being mango swirl atop spotty dog. Swedish and German tourists eddied around clumps of Aborigines. On benches slumped men worse for drink, their faces sinking inward, cavernous and rotting like fallen fruit. American sailors strode past in running shoes, their thighs thick as drainage pipes, conversations clacking. Because we had spent eleven months in Australia, we felt superior to tourists. "I am not a tourist," Eliza said. "I have spent an eighth of my life in this country."

We roamed town. Grasshoppers big as mops thrummed across the path to Stokes Hill Wharf. Black and white butterflies floated through scrub. Black-tailed godwits tipped through mud along the shoreline. Small freighters settled in the harbor. Heat seemed to suck rust up from the water, and I imagined steamy trips to ports pinched dark by mangroves. At the dock we wandered exhibitions of pearls and coral then ate prawn sandwiches on the wharf. Sunlight clung to us like a wool suit, and I drank a beer. On the way back to town, we entered tunnels built to house oil during World War II. Water leached through the middle of the tunnels, and looking like remnants of mouse, spider webs hung from walls. Heat sapped energy, and Eliza and Vicki napped in Bicentennial Park, Vicki on a bench and Eliza on the grass. Straw-necked ibis raked the ground, and peaceful doves bathed in the sun, the birds looking like gravy boats borrowed from a dollhouse. At Lyons Cottage, built in 1925 for the British-Australian Telegraph, a docent urged me to walk to Doctor's Gully and watch the fish feeding. The woman was heavy and was scheduled for a knee replacement. "The operation is safe," I said; "it's killed only one of my friends." "Lord God," the woman said.

Near Doctor's Gully a golden-backed honey eater flew into a yellow flame tree. "Gold in gold," Eliza said. At the gully people tossed bread into the water. Like runoff at storm drains fish swirled in clouds: catfish, and diamond-scaled and green-backed mullet. Milkfish thick as bottles spun about, their lips soft, almost skimmed. Two reef herons patrolled a beach, now and then darting into the water. Rays swept the sand: shovel-nosed, fantails, and blue-spotted. Above the shore green ants wove leaves into wallets. When my mouth grew moldy, I plucked ants from trees and bit off their abdomens, the taste lemony and cleansing. Trees differed from those in Perth, and I recognized only a few: cerbera; coastal sheoak; beach hibiscus; stinkwood, the wings of each seed two paddles; and weeping wattle, the flowers bridal trains of yellow. We spent an afternoon in the Botanical Gardens. Cannonball trees bloomed above Rainforest Gully. A yellow-spotted monitor stood bronzed atop a pile of wood chips. In the gully I ran my hands over the rough leaves of sandpaper figs and listened to orange-footed scrub fowl scraping through brush. We sat in plastic chairs near the plant display house and watched rainbow bee eaters slip from limbs. At the foot of a slope bottle palms grew in rows, the bottoms of their trunks white-washed. Below Heritage Lawn a tree snake wound through the slats of a bench. In the light the snake seemed orange twine. A pale lizard pasted itself behind the upper slat of the bench, the end farthest from the snake. Quickly the snake rose upward like a vine, its head a tendril. When the snake rolled under the upper slat, the lizard fell to the ground. Immediately the snake dropped on it. Seizing the lizard, the snake began swallowing the lizard headfirst. To force the lizard down its throat, the snake slide up a nearby tree, at first wavering off the ground like a sapling. Once in the tree the snake wrapped itself around a limb like a rope. From the snake's mouth the tail of the lizard waved back and forth, and a woman standing nearby seized a stick in order to hit the snake and free the lizard. "Don't do that," I said and stepped between her and the snake. I watched until the lizard became a soft lump behind the snake's head. The snake swallowed the lizard in less than nine minutes, and I wished I'd timed the meal carefully. "What a treat," Vicki said. "That makes the day special."

Later we crossed Gilruth Avenue and walked to the art gallery. During our visit we went to the gallery three times, in part to calm mood. In galleries the whirl of living unwinds, and life straightens. Landscapes are my favorite paintings. In Theo Hansen's *Lake Near Blackburn,* reeds blackened the corner of a small lake. Light glanced off the water in yellow scrapes, and behind the reeds a path wound through a dusky wood. At the near edge of the lake, a rowboat sank waterlogged in shallows. Across the lake hunkered a cabin, clouds bunched dark above. As I looked at the painting, mind slowed, and I drifted comfortably into shallow thought. The museum also contained several exhibits, a gallery, for example, devoted to Cyclone Tracy that smashed much of Darwin on

Christmas Eve 1974, and then a dry dock of boats in the maritime gallery. Although I lingered amid the boats and studied photographs taken in 1974, what clung to mind were paintings and then a stuffed bat, a northern blossom bat in the section of the museum devoted to natural history. "Gosh, I'd like to see that bat in the wild," I said to Eliza. "So would I," she said.

I don't travel to ride in cars. On trips I spend much time walking. Small vans cruised Darwin, however. For two dollars the vans carried people about the city. Twice we hopped vans, but generally we walked. One night we walked to the Asti Motel on Smith Street and ate at Tim's Surf 'n' Turf. I ate a "New York Cut" steak and drank two Victoria bitters. Two nights later we ate at Twilight, a restaurant on Lindsay Street, not far from the Mirambeena. We sat outside and watched a possum climb palms, the only wild possum we saw in Australia. After dusk alcoholics and the fragrance of flowers drifted across streets, the former collapsing on grassy waysides, the latter sugaring the air, drawing imagination away from the ragged bundles on the ground. By night Darwin smacked of an earlier time, say, fifty years ago. Pickups rumbled along empty streets. Outside a strip joint near Bennett, vulgarity racketed. At evening's end we bought ice cream cones then stopped at Woolworths where Vicki purchased snacks, orange juice, croissants, and dark chocolate. In the morning she stuffed the chocolate into the croissants, and I stored them in my backpack. Darwin's size appealed to me. The Chinese driver who took us to the airport at the end of our stay disagreed, however. "When I came to Darwin fifteen years ago, I loved the town," he said. "Now eighty thousand people live here, and the city is too big for a good life."

The more uncomfortable a hotel room the more a traveler rambles. *Frommer's* said rooms in the Mirambeena had been refurbished in 1998 "to a high standard," noting that each was "a decent size." Our room, number 50, was sixteen feet long and eleven wide. Wedged into the space were four single beds, each thirty inches broad. Three beds lay along one wall, one parallel to the wall, the heads of the other two pushed against the wall, their bodies at right angles to the first bed. Between these last two beds a

SAM PICKERING

mirror hung on the wall. Along the opposite wall running from the door to the end of the room were a wooden dresser, a small refrigerator, a wardrobe on top of which sat a television, and lastly the fourth bed. On this bed we stored two duffel bags. The other bag and our backpacks sat on the floor in the middle of the room. Walls were gray, and the floor was tile. A circular fan spun below the ceiling. An air conditioner jutted out over the door to the bathroom. The machine leaked, and water splattered on the floor. The transom over the entrance was the only window. The room, however, wasn't dark because a fluorescent light was attached to the wall above the dresser. Two small tables stood near the first two beds along the wall, one at the head of the first bed, the other at its foot. A plastic lamp stood on the second table. The bathroom door was beside the entrance door. On the back of the door was a second mirror, and in the bathroom a window opened onto concrete steps.

"I'm not going to spend time in this closet," Vicki said when we arrived. "Good," I said, "we are here to enjoy the city." On Saturday we went to Fannie Bay Racecourse for opening day of the Darwin Cup Carnival. I asked a clerk at the reception desk what time races began. "Eight-twenty," she said. When I questioned the hour, she said, "I ought to know. I worked at the track, and I had to be there at 8:20." At the Roma Bar I bought a newspaper. The first race was scheduled for 1:30, the seventh and last at 5:10. We took a van to the course and sat in the grandstand. For $20 I bought a bottle of Yellowglen champagne. "The wine," the label stated, "displays melon, pineapple, and citrus characteristics." During the afternoon we munched potato chips and apples that Vicki bought at Woolworths. After the fifth race I ordered a ploughman's platter for $8.80. During the races galahs flocked on the infield, and whistling kites banked overhead. I wandered the grounds and watched grooms hose down horses after races. "No Alcohol Beyond This Point" warned a sign tacked to a fence. On the opposite side of the fence, a heavy man leaned back in a plastic chair. On the ground beneath the sign, but on the proper side of the fence, stood a beer can. Occasionally the man reached under the fence and seizing the can, sipped beer. Afterward he placed the can back under the sign.

We made three $2 bets on each race, Eliza's bets to place, Vicki's and mine to win. We selected horses named Rose of Tirol, Tordean, and Alkoomi. Two of my picks won, Rockhound paying $18.60 in the fourth race, and Cover Girl, $11.20 in the third. We finished the day $1.20 ahead. "I like horse races," Eliza said as we walked toward Dick Ward Drive. "So did my mother," I said. "Touts loved her and gave her tips. At Hialeah she manufactured money."

We arrived in Darwin on Thursday night. That evening we went to the Mindil Beach Sunset Market. Held every Thursday, the market consisted of scores of food, arts, and crafts stalls. Hundreds of people wandered the market. Most brought dinners, sat on the beach, and watched the sun set across Fannie Bay. Buskers played an orchestra of instruments: saxophones, piano, fire sticks, and didgeridoos. Two women played duets on flutes. A wind ensemble gathered in a green space. A man plucked a banjo while a red-winged parrot perched on his left shoulder. Two girls in cowboy boots and straw hats played country music. One girl of the girls wore a sundress; the other, blue jeans. Another busker imitated a statue, moving only when someone dropped a coin into a hat at her feet. The busker stood on a wooden box. She'd painted her back and face white, including lips and the inside of her nostrils. She wore evening gloves and a long white dress scalloped at the back. Her hair was blue, and thin black lines circled her eyes like the edges of shells. Her shoes, however, did not suit the costume. She wore brown leather school shoes, the soles thick rubber treads.

Strings of lights swung over stalls, and the market resembled an old-fashioned circus, not packaged and confined to a building, but out-of-doors, crowds milling and drifting willfully. For twelve dollars a person could buy a cap at Create-A-Cap. "Order While-U-Wait" a sign said. The man in charge of the stall dozed, marijuana blowing about him in a sweet cloud. Eliza and Vicki bought sarongs at a clothing stall. Another stall sold crocodile heads, sixty dollars for the head of a saltwater crocodile, forty dollars for a freshwater. Eliza bought a back scratcher, paying twenty dollars for the front foot of a crocodile mounted at the end of a stick.

Food stalls abounded, many Asian, others selling possum, crocodile, kangaroo, and witchetty grubs, this last being sold out when I inquired. Instead of grubs I grazed on cuttlefish, baby octopus, curry puffs, shrimp, and quail. Eliza was less adventuresome and ate chicken and cashew nuts over rice then crepes stuffed with feta and tomato salsa. The night was hot, and we drank a gallon of blended tropical drinks, only the lime and pineapple clinging to memory. We arrived at the market at five o'clock and left at 8:45. We promenaded back and forth and soon recognized other walkers, so much so that by the end of the evening they nodded to us whenever our paths crossed. "Darwin is a nice place," Eliza said later in bed. "Provided I did not have to stay in this hotel, I'd like to live here." "Part of the reason you enjoy the town so much," I said, "is because the room is dreadful. If the room had been fine, we wouldn't have seen much."

Kakadu

At 7:15 in the morning on July 9, Paul picked us up at the Miram-beena. Paul worked for World Expeditions. For eight days he would guide us, the last two days along the Katherine River, the first six through Kakadu National Park, a World Heritage Landscape east of Darwin consisting of some twenty thousand square kilometers, often called "God's own country." Paul wore black shorts, a bat-tered hat, no shirt, and no shoes. No matter where we walked or climbed, across rocks that would slice rind off a hog, he remained barefoot and shirtless. He was, Vicki guessed, between thirty-two and thirty-six years old. His hearing and sight astonished me. At times his vision seemed to curve, allowing him to identify birds beyond bends in the Katherine River. Never have I met a guide who knew land and creature better. He was so capable that I suspected bullies must have persecuted him as a child. "He is compensating for something," I said to Vicki. "Psychobabble," she said, "he is smart, athletic, practical, and hard-working. That's why he is capa-ble." I admired Paul, but I was not fond of him. He was too con-trolling and too optimistic. "Every experience," he said one night, "is a good experience." "What do you think about that, Daddy?" Eliza asked. "A fine outlook," I said, swallowing a rejoinder.

Four people besides us went on the trip: Helen, a young British anesthetist, who had roamed the world since she was sixteen and then Cecilia, a mother almost my age, and her two daughters, Clau-dia, and Melissa. Thirty years ago Cecilia emigrated from Switzerland to Australia. Claudia was a first-year university student studying mining, and Melissa was sixteen and in her second year of high school. Before the trip Eliza worried that she would be lonely without Edward. By trip's end she and the two girls were laughing companions. In part a trip is a microcosm of life. For days a group lives elbow to elbow. People learn the secrets and habits of others. Then suddenly the trip ends, and the companions of today are forgotten by tomorrow, recollected only in photographs. The melancholy one experiences on leaving a group is not caused so much by affection for individuals as by the awareness that human encounters are ephemeral, even those of a father and a daughter, the emotional stuffing of the past sixteen years of my life.

Paul drove a white Toyota Land Cruiser. Theoretically the cruiser could carry eight people, two in bucket seats in the front, one of these the driver, then three each in two bench seats behind. The last bench, however, resembled a ricer. Occupants wedged themselves into place, knees pressed hard against the seat in front. Moreover the floorboard slanted upward at the rear of the cruiser, forcing legs high, pushing chests against thighs, every bump in the road compacting flesh and bone. Quickly legs cramped, and veins behind knees throbbed. When I sat on the back bench, my head bumped the roof of the cruiser, forcing me to lean forward and stretch like a long-necked turtle if I wanted to see beyond the cruiser's interior. After thirty minutes in the rear seat, occupants' legs locked, and people in front had to pull them out of the car.

Attached to the back of the cruiser was a green van that Paul had soldered into shelves and cabinets. Behind flaps that hung down from the sides of the van, small boxes contained tools and utensils. A cooler contained food. Everything had a set place: tents, medical kit, and duffel bags, for example. Whenever someone mentioned natural dangers, say, snakes or water buffalo, Paul responded, saying that the highway was more dangerous than the bush. He was right. A sudden stop would have broken the knees of people in the rear seat. Had the trailer smashed into the back of the car, people lodged in the rear would have been decapitated.

For dinner the first night Paul cooked a side of beef. To reach

Gunlon campground, Paul drove two sides of a triangle, south from Darwin along the Stuart Highway then north up the Kakadu Highway. The drive swallowed the day, and we arrived at Gunlon late in the afternoon feeling tired and boxed. Unpacking muscle and mood took time, and we ate sparingly, so much so that Paul concluded our appetites sputtered on two cylinders. As a result future meals kept us lean. Once for breakfast he cooked bacon and eggs, but generally our choice was limited to dry cereal: Crunchy Nut Sultana Bran or Lowan Multiflakes with Tropical Fruit. With the breakfast I drank coffee, not billy-brewed and granular in the stomach, but instant coffee, thin as birds' legs. Lunches consisted of sandwiches and crackers thick with cheese, avocado, tuna fish, and bean sprouts. For dessert people ate fruit: honeydew melons, apples, oranges, and pears. Vicki and Eliza were stalwart trencher-men, marching through bastions of bread. For my part I ate like the forlorn hope. Heat sapped my appetite, and instead of eating I roamed during lunch. Typically dinner started with crackers and a dip: onion, hummus, or yogurt with avocado. For a main course Paul might serve burritos, stuffed with red cabbage, beans, and Gouda cheese; for dessert, tinned peaches, and to drink, coffee.

During the day temperature climbed into the eighties, and humidity was as heavy as mud. Every morning I put on the same outfit: hiking boots that supported my ankles, thick socks, cargo shorts, a long-sleeved shirt to protect my arms from the sun, and a floppy hat that hung over my nose and cheeks. Humidity twists underpants into rough knots, so I did not wear them. Before a hike I plastered the inside of my thighs with zinc oxide to prevent my legs from chaffing. I also bathed my face, hands, neck, and calves in sunscreen. Lower legs aside, Vicki, Eliza, and I wrapped our bodies in protective clothes, turning ourselves into walking mum-mies. Near the end of the trip when we kayaked the Katherine River, Eliza wore socks on her hands to protect them against the sun. Unlike us Paul never accommodated himself to weather. To him melanoma resembled snake bite, a threat swollen out of ratio-nal proportion.

On my shoulders I carried a black backpack. Inside I stuffed a bathing suit, towel, socks, binoculars, and a liter bottle of water. In the pockets of my shorts, I carried a pencil nub, two ball point pens, and a Belgrave notebook, six by four and one-quarter inches. Pages in the notebook were lined, and the notebook was bound in thick cardboard. The notebook was sturdy, not the loose pad I usually carry, a fact that proved fortuitous, as my penchant for falling into pools would have stripped pages from an ordinary pad. When the notebook became soaked, I separated pages from each other with leaves from eucalyptus or paperbark, bloating the notebook but not separating sheets from binding.

Along the highway to Pine Creek woolly butt, stringybark eucalyptus, and pandanus palm grew rough and tweedy. Fire had reaped spear grass, but here and there grass sliced pale and sharp across a paddock. Termite mounds rose in heavy flutes. I snapped a finger off one, and grass spilled out. Immediately termites flowed to the wound and began building clots. Across the broken land turkey bush bloomed purple. Yellow burst from kapok, and ghost gums clumped in weak stands, their trunks anorexic. Burning paddocks weakened trees, preventing them from aging into muscle. Almost all large trees were dead, their trunks hollow shells inhabited by termites. Termite colonies spilled from the forks of limbs, from a distance looking like animals dozing in the sun. Great white egrets, spoonbills, and jabirus gathered at a waterhole. Whistling kites floated low over burning savannah, and a brown falcon slung himself toward the road then pulled up into a loop. Along the Kakadu Highway smoke clung to the asphalt in soiled bandages, kites flaking up from the roadside when the cruiser approached. Flame lapped the bush, tongues leaping out suddenly then dropping and burrowing into logs.

We stopped at Pine Creek. At the roadhouse I bought a mango smoothie for four dollars. So thick that sunlight didn't melt it when I stood outside, the smoothie was the best I had in Australia. Heat wrung water from us, reducing visits to the lavatory, not a concern for Eliza but important for a middle-aged man cramped in the back seat of a car. Not far from Pine Creek Paul turned off the highway and followed a track north through savannah, eventually parking near a thicket of monsoon forest which grew in a collar around a small creek running from the Mary River. The creek slid over rocks into a deep hole. I swam across the hole and let water massage my back. Throughout the trip I swam under waterfalls, at Gunlom, Koolpin, and finally Edith Falls. Sometimes water fell like boards and knocked me about. Occasionally reaching a waterfall was strenuous, particularly at Edith Falls when I swam alone and my feet cramped. Signs notifying swimmers that crocodiles might lurk nearby did not deter me. Instead warnings made nervousness ripple pleasantly, lending credence to the deception that I was adventuresome.

Gunlom campground was near Waterfall Creek, a tributary of the South Alligator River. Beyond the campground a sandstone plateau loomed like a red cloud, sun drilling it white and yellow. A track wound up the face of the plateau to Gunlom Lookout and a chain of sunken pools. Eliza and I climbed the face and walked to the edge of the waterfall. The landscape spread like a hand, and I stretched and unwound. Later we pitched tents, Vicki and I sharing one and Eliza sleeping by herself. Raising a tent is no longer twenty minutes of stobs and ropes. We hooked, threaded, and erected the tent in three minutes. Sweeping the floor of the tent in the morning took more time than raising it. While silver-leafed paperbarks bent in gentle curtseys over Waterfall Creek, salmon gums rose in whisks over the campground. Leaden flycatchers pirouetted from their branches. Northern rosellas blew shrieking through leaves, and shrike thrushes perched on limbs tossing their shoulders, calls cracking like whips. Pigs rooted just beyond the camp. Two nights later one rolled in front of the Toyota looking like a muddy black barrel. Paul said that if he'd been alone he would have clipped the pig's rump, breaking a back leg, after which he would have cut the animal's throat. Paul had little use for pigs, horses, and water buffalo, feral animals that he said should be "re-educated," that is, slaughtered. At night bats swung above the campground squeaking like hinges, bringing to mind childhood and country summers in Virginia. Unless event bashes character

SAM PICKERING

like a mallet, one usually doesn't stroll far from youth, the interests of the boy becoming those of the man.

Early the next morning Paul drove southeast to Koolpin Gorge, the last eight kilometers on a dirt road. Off the main road tracks sliced into scrub. Beside them buildings collapsed into kindling and sheets of tin, while machines weathered out of shape and function. Several tracks led to abandoned uranium mines. Although cleanups had been spotty, signs rarely warned people away. Near Koolpin a flock of red-tailed black cockatoos shifted raucous through bush. Buffalo tracks potted the road almost to the campground. The next morning Paul jogged before breakfast. Rounding a bend, he startled a buffalo and himself. The following morning I got up early in hopes of seeing the buffalo. "You are lucky the buffalo was somewhere else," Vicki said, adding, "you damn fool." No matter the years man behaves stupidly. Willingness to take physical risks seems to characterize late middle age, this, alas, at a time when strength and coordination have deteriorated into memories.

Camping was restricted in Koolpin, and we had the southern part of the Mary River District to ourselves. By ten we had set up camp and were climbing ridges into Koolpin Gorge. Koolpin Creek flowed through the ridges and down to the South Alligator River. On the way the creek fell through waterfalls, at the bottom of which pools spread into small basins, forming an emerald necklace. Settings around the pools varied. While rock beveled some sides, along other sides paperbarks draped over hips of white sand. Atop rocks flat as tables Merten's water monitors lay like forks. Rock hole frogs snapped in and out of sandstone pools, these last small, some no larger than kitchen pots. A common tree snake wrinkled between pools. To prevent the fear that he assumed we felt, Paul quickly identified the snake. Paul tried to defang Kakadu. In doing so, he flattened the frisson of alarm that makes days pleasurable. He also underrated our abilities. Although my bosom hung pouting and swollen over my chest and my stomach shook as I walked, making me look like a laundry bag, I wanted days to stretch muscle and capacity. I did not want to think Kakadu safer than a botanic garden.

Because Paul misjudged our abilities, the final four days of the trip were pedestrian. The last two days we kayaked the Katherine River, both afternoons reaching our destination at 3:45, long before fatigue sapped interest. In part the group was responsible for Paul's judgment. Vicki didn't hike the chain of pools on Koolpin Creek, preferring instead to stay in one place and observe quietly, and alone. For my part I lingered behind in hopes of escaping the chatter that inevitably reduces the extraordinary to the mundane and shackles imagination to convention. Moreover I'm uncoordinated. In Kakadu I slipped from a crease along a ledge and fell backward into a pool. The ledge was only two feet above the water, and I tumbled between two boulders, dampening clothes and notebook but not enthusiasm. Later while canoeing, I overturned, not in difficult rapids through which I slid easily, but at a knee that twisted around a tree. In truth I enjoyed the spill and bounced downstream eager for the next bend in the river. Although I lost sunglasses and a hat when I rolled over, forcing me to wrap my face in a tee shirt in order to protect my skin from the sun, I didn't do badly. In fact I managed to seize my eyeglasses with my teeth, something, I told Vicki, few people aside from circus performers could accomplish.

Reservations aside, however, I saw creatures at Koolpin I'd never seen before—at the edge of woodlands, chestnut-quilled rock pigeons and a red-browed pardalote; and in water, grunters, gudgeons, and archer fish, black stripes in quivers along their scales. In a monsoon forest a day moth clung to a leaf, its upper wings spangles of blue, orange flashes pricking lower wings. Between muddy stones bladderwort burst in small bouquets of orange and yellow. Other sights were familiar. Small red dragonflies turned twigs into sparklers, and double-barred finches combed grass. At night eastern curlews howled ghostly and melodramatic from riverbanks.

The second day at Koolpin was the most strenuous and best of the trip. At 8:41 we left camp, heading for Freezing Gorge, only a six-kilometer trip, but as a guidebook put it, "a strenuous walk on an unmarked track over difficult terrain." We returned at 6:02. The first portion of the walk crossed woodland. Woolly butts tilted spindly. Amid yellow blossoms green fruits dangled from kapok; orange flared through northern grevillea, and here and there red scones glowed on kurrajongs. Fire reduced spear grass to splinters, and walking was easy. A black whip snake curled around a rock. An agile wallaby bounced down a slope. In Kakadu we saw antilopine and black wallaroos, the latter dark humps in escarpments. Beyond the woodland massive rocks rolled upward, a stream weaving between them. I leapt from rock to rock, trusting balance and the soles of my boots. Three times I removed my boots in order to cross the stream, once swimming, holding my boots over my head. In damp corners grew anwolbon and anbinik trees, barks of both appearing battered like my hide as I clawed upward.

A giant cave gecko clung to the underside of a boulder that leaned against a sandstone wall like a strut. Between boulder and wall was a keyhole through which I pushed, rolling my hips like bearings so they wouldn't jam. The day was humid, and late in the morning we reached a shallow pool shaped like a pelvis. In the open water was green, but it turned black in sockets under rocks. We stopped and swam, shadows in the sockets pulling me like strained tendons. At lunch calls of friarbirds rang from a wood. Higher up the escarpment a peregrine falcon stuttered. Canopus butterflies wavered palsied; mud wasps fretted yellow and black, and Arnhem flies spun around us like bulbs on Christmas trees, red eyes and blue tails flickering, backs snapping green and orange.

After lunch the climb became difficult. While Eliza bounded over gulches, Vicki and I wedged feet and hands into cracks and levered ourselves upward. A descent seemed to follow every ascent. By afternoon I dropped through descents like jelly melting through a strainer. Webs of tent spiders swung from ledges, centers sagging in goblets. From seams in rocks basket ferns groped upward, leaflets dried but spread imploringly. Like hands in prayer the walls of Freezing Gorge pressed together over a stream and like the Litany towered through colors that repeated themselves, red, yellow, and gray, all stony in the afternoon. A keelback snake dawdled from the side of the gorge, its tail rooted in a crack. For much of its three hundred yards, the stream was shallow, and I walked, in the process bashing toes on rocks and banging shins against sunken logs. Near the end of the gorge, the bottom dropped out of sight along a wall, and I swam. Above me slabs of rock leaned from the wall. Perhaps someone responsible for college tuition should have avoided the gorge and spent the day in a woodland. Still the climb was tonic, deluding me into stripping a decade from my age.

For the next two nights we camped at Mardugal. The exciting part of the trip was over, albeit we were now exposed to mosquitoes, the most dangerous creatures in Kakadu. Despite sealing the tent carefully, mosquitoes turned my feet into sacks of raisins. The mosquitoes were small. Perched on legs, they stuck out straight from the skin, looking like Spanish needles, seeds caught in hair, not insects. At Mardugal I went to bed early, usually at eight o'clock. I also woke early, at six in time to wash dishes for breakfast. At dinner conversation lagged, only the scratching of bandicoots or one night a dusky rat invigorating words. During the day we visited famous sites, doing things done by groups taking bus tours. We climbed Nourlangie Rock. Below the rock the country slid into a skirt of billabongs and forest then rose into a stone ruffle. I like lands that at first glance seem comparatively bare: deserts, bush, and plateaus rocky as the bows of rusting ships. In the cramped valleys of New England, trees snag body and mind. Even if thought twists loose and begins to float, a limb soon hooks it. Atop Nourlangie Rock imagination can drift and curl like a line tossed by a fly fisherman. For a moment as I stood on the rock, I longed to escape responsibility. I imagined returning to Australia alone and driving from Darwin to Cairns. Names of the towns along the way spun in a dance: Mataranka, Roper Bar, Cape Crawford, Borroloola, Burketown, Croyden, Mount Surprise, Ravenshoe, and Mareeba. To be a good husband or father, though, one must purge feverish imagination, and so I doused myself with bird-watching. At Anbangbang billabong I watched green pigmy geese floating on the water, the distance white with lilies, whistling kites yawing above, pale bars under their wings rudders. At Cahill's Crossing the East Alligator rolled slowly, its surface thick as mud. Across the water shelves of stone rose into steps, beckoning one into Arnhem Land. Before I dreamed about elsewhere, I shifted vision. Almost at my feet an archer fish rose and sank in the water as if attached to pulleys. An egret stood on a mud flat. From the front the bird resembled an aged man with no shoulders, all flesh gone to belly, his legs bony, feet slippered. I sat beneath a cluster fig and watched kites. Suddenly one fell from a tree and plucked a sandwich from Vicki's hand, just as she was about to take a bite.

At Ubirr I roamed the galleries of rock paintings by myself. I'd had second thoughts about the Rainbow Serpent I purchased in Darwin. Aside from books, almost never have I bought anything for myself. After buying the painting, I felt indulgent. Galleries at Ubirr, however, made me glad I purchased the snake. "If Ivan Namirrikki ever paints a long-necked turtle, I'll buy it," I thought. At Ubirr I climbed Nadab Lookout. The floodplain was lush. Amid the green, blue lily pads of water opened like pockets, and egrets stood out in white slivers. I walked to the northern edge of the lookout and hid behind a bale of rocks. Below me finches rattled though ghost gums, and for a moment I was alone.

Late one afternoon we rode a boat through the Yellow Water billabong. Estuarine crocodiles floated through the billabong waterlogged, eyes and snout knobs above the surface. Other crocodiles lay beached under pandanus looking like old shoes, lasts sprung, heels pushed to the sides in fat rumples. A pair of sea eagles clung to a dead tree. Suddenly they lifted into flight, their wings beating heavy and dark above thick white undercarriages. Night herons stalked shorelines sharpening themselves into arrowheads. A pied heron crooked a leg and studied the ground. In the distance whiskered terns swarmed over the water thick as gnats. Burdekin ducks gabbled in cohorts. Magpie geese stared, their necks walking sticks, and plumed whistling ducks jostled through each other looking like earthenware. Jabirus, brolgas, and straw-necked ibis stalked high grass. Rainbow bee eaters flew lariats, and a lemon-breasted flycatcher darted through scrub. Wild horses grazed a plain; nearby a black pig rooted. Overhead a wedge-tail eagle surfed the air. My favorite birds were kingfishers, the azure, its breast an orange rag shaking on branches, and the forest, a blue skull cap on its head, black binding its eyes, a blue cape iridescent over shoulders, and white falling like a scarf over its breast. While peppermints stood atop shags of roots, lotus sagged like the seats of caned chairs. For a long time the horizon nibbled at the sun. I didn't notice, however, until the sun turned into a wafer and slipping into the water, dyed the sky purple and orange.

Age changes concerns, the number of birds one sees during a lifetime mattering more than honor or achievement. Be that as it may, however, the next morning we left Mardugal and drove to Katherine. While Paul bought groceries and filled the cruiser with gas, I roamed downtown, wandering Lindsay, First, Giles, Warburton, and Katherine Terrace. At Tommo's Bakery on Giles I purchased a cup of coffee and the worst mud cake I'd ever eaten. The cake was so bad that I dropped it into a garbage bin after two bites, the second bite only a nibble, taken to confirm the impression of the first. After stocking the coolers Paul drove to Shady Lane Caravan Park on Gorge Road. There he left the trailer and picked up John, a passenger, and four Bushranger fiberglass canoes. After we launched the canoes in the river, John drove the cruiser back to Shady Lane. Two days later he met us at Carbeen, a chin of land jutting into the Katherine River. Although the canoes were heavy with camping gear, paddling was easy. While everyone else used kayak paddles with blades at both ends, I used the traditional Indian paddle with one blade, the J stroke of camping days forty years ago leaping to hand.

Because canoeing was easy, we drifted to lose time. Wattles swung over banks in yellow eddies. Behind the wattles horehound dried into scratchy rods. I watched four blue-faced honeyeaters dash into the river. Afterward they flew into a tree and preened. Sulfur-crested cockatoos shrieked, and yellow orioles burbled. Shining flycatchers twisted song into silver screws. At dusk families of blue-winged kookaburras hacked notes out of metal, and barking owls made me think hounds had slipped their traces. During a flood, water had tossed logs thirty feet above the ground where they lodged across branches supported by rails of limbs. We slept on sandy spits. Although I dug and smoothed holes for my hips, I slept poorly. Throughout the first night I watched shooting stars and followed the Southern Cross as it ticked through the dark. Early in the morning pale light pierced pandanus and paperbark, creating cutouts: a bobcat; a crocodile, a derby hat pushed down on his head; to his right a man in a soft Cavanaugh, and beyond him a wallaby stooping over a waterhole. "It was a euro," I told Eliza at breakfast. "How did you identify him at night," she asked. "Come on, Eliza," I said. The second night small green beetles migrated into my sleeping bag and crawling up my legs danced on my stomach, occupying me so that I did not see cutouts. The last morning Vicki explored burned land behind our camp. Smoke drifted in fingers from ashes. A wallaby stood on a bank above a waterhole, the sun carving the animal's reflection golden into the water. Amid ashes Vicki found a license plate. The back of the plate was greasy and charred. Stamped into the front of the plate in black letters was HOTNOT. Beneath in smaller letters appeared "N. T.—OUTBACK AUSTRALIA."

Because I did not expend much energy on the water, I ate little, at breakfast the last day, for example, having only two cups of coffee, for lunch eating an orange and two bites of a vanilla and mango ice cream bar Vicki bought at Edith Falls. The last morning we pulled the canoes atop a small ridge near Carbeen, the pulling more strenuous than paddling. John appeared with the cruiser, and at 8:31 we left the river. Deep ruts cut the road, and riding in the backseat was unpleasant. At 9:25 we reached asphalt, Paul having stopped once to examine a dead rat he saw beside the road. We reached Shady Lane precisely at 10:00. At 10:49 we left. Ten minutes later Paul stopped at the Shell station on Katherine Terrace, and I dashed off to buy new sunglasses, along the way dropping a handful of postcards off at the post office. At 11:11 we were back on the road. At 11:58 Paul turned off the highway toward Edith Falls, this despite everyone's saying we preferred to hustle back to Darwin. The printed description of the trip said participants could expect to "arrive back into Darwin around 5:00," and Paul was determined to stretch the day to fit the description. At Edith Falls great bowerbirds sat in trees and whistled. At 1:11 we left the falls, stopping at 2:23 at Emerald Springs. Parked on the shoulder of the highway opposite the roadhouse were eight road trains. The trains had taken cattle to Darwin, and above them hung a cloud musty with the fragrance of stock pen. A sign on the roadhouse said, "$2.00 Showers to None Patrons," the *none* a misspelling of *non*. At 2:43 we left Emerald Springs, only to stop at 3:35 at Adelaide River, as Paul tried to wring minutes from the afternoon. At 3:51 we left Adelaide River and at 5:08 reached the Mirambeena. Goodbyes were crisp. Because the last days were not strenuous, participants had the leisure to wander their own worlds instead of sharing experiences. At the hotel we showered, then walked up the street and ate at the Twilight, ordering six appetizers instead of a main course. Afterward we strolled the city, Eliza topping dinner off with an ice cream cone, spotted dog on top of black raspberry.

Interim

On our return from Kakadu we checked back into the Mirambeena, room 48, the twin of 50. The next morning rain fell in shutters. I didn't have a raincoat, so Vicki removed a garbage bag from the duffel. "I travel prepared," she said. She punched a hole through the top of the bag for my head, and slipping into the bag, arms inside, pasted to ribs, I strolled to the Roma, feeling flat as a sandwich board. Eliza accompanied me. She drank a cappuccino at the Roma then went to Smith Street and bought a smoothie. After breakfast we returned to the hotel and fetching Vicki spent the morning browsing galleries. That afternoon we flew back to Perth. In May I tried to shift tickets so we could fly from Darwin to Sydney. The cost was too great, so we returned to Perth for six nights.

We arrived at 7:30. Because I had relinquished the house and its $495 weekly rent, I booked us into a university apartment at 17 Myers Street. Seven years ago we began and ended our year at 17 Myers, and the symmetry appealed to me. The realtor refused to give me a key to the flat before we flew to Darwin. "You can get the key," she said, "the afternoon you move in." Because I was going to be in Darwin, Sue, the secretary of the English department, agreed to collar the key and leave it in my mailbox in the English department. Sue is wonderfully reliable. Still I worried that the key might have gone astray. We took a taxi from the airport to Myers Street. After depositing Vicki, Eliza, and the bags at the door of the apartment, I ran to the university. A key was in the mailbox. Unfortunately it was not to the flat on Myers but to a third-floor apartment on Caporn, three blocks away, the flat on Myers being, a note from the realtor explained, "not ready." After studying a map, I ran to Caporn, found the apartment, and after making sure the key fit the lock, returned to Vicki and Eliza. Shouldering backpacks and pulling duffels, we trekked to Caporn. We deposited the bags inside the door then walked back to the English department. Three trips and ninety-four minutes later, we had removed the boxes and suitcases stored in my office. Vicki then went to a late-night grocery at Broadway Fair and purchased dinner, cornflakes, milk, and bananas.

I scheduled five days in Perth in case plans for leaving Australia went akimbo. All went smoothly, however. On the twentieth I closed my bank account, the balance being returned to me as a check in American dollars, $12,503.88. I also withdrew $9,000 in Australian money to cover expenses in Sydney and Fiji. The year had not been cheap. Of the $70,000 I deposited in the Challenge Bank, I spent $55,000. Moreover before leaving the United States I purchased plane tickets that cost $11,000. In Australia itself I paid for many things with charge cards, primarily school tuition, the moneys amounting to another $15,000. "How could we afford that?" Vicki asked. "What we couldn't afford," I said, "was not living." When the door slams behind me, I don't want to regret life missed for the sake of dimes and dollars. Early the morning of the eighteenth, I walked up Hampton and paid for the apartment. Then I took a taxi to Leasing Elite on Richardson and signed papers so I could retrieve the house deposit the next morning. The next day Leasing Elite gave me a check for the deposit. The agency telephoned its bank two blocks away, and I walked over and cashed the check. The following day at the post office, I paid final bills for gas, electricity, and telephone.

For a parent life rarely runs smoothly. After taking examinations at Christ Church, Edward left Perth on the first of June. In the middle of the month, he rode a bus to Portland, Maine, and was spending the summer nearby, working at Camp Timanous in Raymond. On our return to Perth a letter from Edward greeted us. "Camp is wonderful," he recounted, adding that during spare time he read *Joseph Andrews,* E. B. White's *Essays,* and Robert Frost's poetry. "I'm studying Frost," he wrote, "to get ready for Middlebury. I can't wait for school to begin." Edward's letter was not the only mail waiting our arrival. Aaron, our house sitter in Storrs, emailed a copy of a letter the dean of admissions at Middlebury sent Edward. After being admitted to college, Edward loafed through his last term at Christ Church, spending evenings writing short stories and starting a novel. Consequently for grades he received one A, one B, and three Cs. The A was in English, his teacher telling him he was the best English student in school. One of the Cs was in "Small Crafts," boats, not arts, the other two in computer courses. In the letter the dean stated that because of his final grades Edward's admittance was being reconsidered. Applying to college from Australia had been taxing enough. "Now this," I said to Vicki. "Well, the truth is that Edward didn't study much at Christ Church," she said. "Shitfire," I said, muttering about impacted, old-maidish academic behavior. "What does the last semester of high school matter?" "Daddy," Eliza said, looking worried, "will you take care of this for Edward?" "Sure," I said. The next morning I sent an email to Middlebury, saying that I was responsible for Edward's grades. I said I took him out of school for trips, stating I thought travel in a foreign country more educational than textbooks, particularly for a second-semester high school senior. In passing I mentioned other colleges that admitted Edward. Lastly I treated the matter as inconsequential. "You needn't worry," I wrote reassuringly, "Edward will be a distinguished student." "Just what I need," I said to Vicki later, "a bout of college colitis to go with the herniated tit hefting those bags gave me." After writing admissions at Middlebury, I emailed a copy of the director's letter to Edward. "Please contact Middlebury," I suggested, "and straighten this out." Edward wrote both Middlebury and me. "If Middlebury axes me, I will go in the army or get a job.

I don't much care. This past year was the worst in my life, and I never want to hear the word *Australia* again." "Well," I said to Vicki, "the dean accomplished one thing. He ruined the memories I worked so hard to give Edward. The stupidity of educators never ceases to amaze me. I'd like to chop the balls off that [and here I used a word that I am not going to print]." "Don't you think Edward a turd for writing you such a letter?" Vicki said. "Sure but sons always behave like dog ends," I said. The night before we flew to Sydney, Middlebury wrote Edward and told him not to worry about the review. "What unnecessary turmoil!" Vicki exclaimed.

Two other letters greeted me in Perth. "Hi," a girl wrote, "I am doing my senior thesis in high school on the topic of the enlightenment, specifically the ways in which humans can reach enlightenment. I've heard about you from several sources and you seem like a fantastic candidate for sharing your knowledge of the higher states of human existence." From the University of South Carolina, a "seeker" asked me to inspire her, explaining, "my crayons have always fallen upon the paper differently just as yours do." My replies were gentle and commonsensical. Middlebury and Edward tired me, however, and at the end of my two letters, I said fatherhood left me little time for either drawing or higher existence. "Aren't you the sweetie now?" Vicki said after I wrote the girls.

Flying directly to Connecticut from Perth would have been easy. Later, though, I knew I would regret missed opportunity. Still I had to force myself to book stops in Sydney and Fiji. "Think of the stops as digressions," Vicki said; "you have always meandered." "A decade ago when people nominated you for college presidencies, you managed to tie acceptances into knots. Have you ever had a straightforward goal in your life?" "Not an acceptable one," I said.

The flat on Caporn consisted of two bedrooms, lavatory, small kitchen, and a combined living room and dining room. Unfortunately after two nights in the bedroom, welts the size of quarters mottled Vicki's legs. I thought the swellings delayed reaction to mosquito bites in Kakadu. Not Vicki, she reckoned bugs infested the bedroom. I scanned floors and walls but could not find fleas or bedbugs. Nevertheless when we departed, Vicki left a note behind suggesting that the flat be fumigated. Sentimentality reduces itches. I spent the greater part of my days in Perth rambling the university campus, savoring limestone, kookaburras, and date palms. I ate a last Broadway pizza and drank a final cappuccino at Barrett's. Although Sue knew when I was leaving, I asked her not to tell anyone. Farewells make me uncomfortable. I prefer silent leavings. I gave Sue money to purchase wine at Christmas for the English department dinner. In the mail boxes of four people, I left books. But I told no one good-bye. "The deeper the feelings, the quicker the going," I said to Vicki.

Vicki spent much time hoeing suitcases, weeding out clothes. "Can't we mail two more boxes home?" she asked. "No," I said. Every morning Eliza ran for an hour. During days she ate "a lot of tuna fish and watched the Tour de France bicycle race on television." Twice she and Vicki took buses uptown, buying clothes, I concluded gloomily, to replace those thrown away. On the twenty-first we went to the Monet and Japan exhibit at the Art Gallery of Western Australia. Japanese woodblock prints startled Eliza. "I lose myself in their blues and grays," she said. Instead of the exotic Monet's paintings brought the familiar to mind. Looking at the light slipping through the stone arch in *The Manneporte (Etretat)*, I thought the brush strokes of nouns and verbs, arches through which mood sometimes slid cleanly but more often than not glanced aside, losing the eyes of readers. As the *Haystacks* changed through seasons, so my books changed as I aged. The blue and white of winter, I thought, now fast covering the fall. Other paintings brought distant places to mind. While *A Cart on the Snowy Road to Honfleur* evoked January in Connecticut, *Cliff Walk at Pourville* recalled Nova Scotia and our farm at Beaver River, Monet's ragged bluff, our drumlin, pared sharp by tides flooding the Bay of Fundy.

I purchased a catalogue of the exhibit. I hid it in my backpack and didn't show it to Vicki until we returned to the flat. "We don't have room," she shouted. "It's a present for Edward, now that he is back in Middlebury," I said. The next afternoon we flew to Sydney. I forced the catalogue into my duffel and took out Charles Dickens's *Pickwick Papers* to read on the plane. "The Pickwick Club will make me smile," I said to Eliza, "and I won't think about Perth."

Sydney

We stopped in Sydney because of Eliza. Seven years ago we visited, and I knew the city well. The prospect of lugging bags to and from a hotel sapped my enthusiasm. "But, Daddy," Eliza said, "I don't remember Sydney, and I really want to go there." Not only does Eliza usually get what she wants, but eventually I want what she wants. A shuttle bus carted us from the airport to the Russell, a hotel in the Rocks, a peninsula enclosing the western side of Sydney Cove. In 1788 the First Fleet anchored by the Rocks. Unlike downtown Sydney in which buildings loom over streets like bluffs, scale in the Rocks is human and walkable, most buildings, Victorian and three-story, old warehouses now hives of restaurants and stores. Day and night we roamed streets exploring alleys and cobblestone paths: Cumberland, Argyle, Kendall, Playfair, Suez Canal, Gloucester, and Nurses Walk. Life beneath skyscrapers is digital, and away from the Rocks, we walked fast, heels clicking like minutes. In the Rocks time circled; our pace was slow, and we meandered shops. Because schedule did not stamp hours, we browsed ourselves into purchases, forgetting the bloated condition of our bags.

At the corner of Globe and George Streets, the Russell was over a hundred years old, the building housing the entrance to the hotel having been built in 1887. Above the door a turret capped two stories. To the left stood a chimney looking like the handle of a spatula. Boulders Restaurant occupied the first floor of the hotel.

From the door a staircase climbed to a small lobby on the second story. Our room was on the third floor, two buildings to the right under a roof garden. The hotel lacked an elevator, so Vicki and I carried the bags to our room—up twenty-four stairs turning in a half-circle to the lobby then walking through a narrow hall to the right, walls papered gold, a blue carpet on the floor, boards creaking, warped into sudden rises and falls. At the end of the hall we went down six steps, turned left down a short hall then climbed ten steps to a landing. At the landing we reversed direction, climbed ten more steps, and walked along a hall to our room, the stairs numbering fifty. We stayed in the Suite, a double room through the windows of which we could see the Circular Quay. Eliza slept on a rollaway bed in the sitting room. The Suite cost $285 a night. Included in the price were continental breakfasts in Boulders. Instead of bundling out on the street to eat then returning to our room to brush teeth, we ambled stairs at our convenience, pausing in the sitting room on the first floor to glance at newspaper headlines. "A perfect location," Vicki said.

We arrived in Sydney on a rainy night. Indeed rain fell throughout our stay. Cold did not bother me, and on streets I was often the only person wearing short pants and a short-sleeved shirt. When not walking, I talked to clerks, the chat warming days. The first night we ate in the Rocks Café. We sat at a table next to a bay window at the front of the café. During the meal a drunk suddenly staggered through the door. Shouting "I'm the one," he dropped his trousers and mooned customers, a thick seam of red hair dividing his bottom. Almost immediately the bartender opened the door with one hand, grabbed the man with the other, and kicked him into George Street. The kick was strong, and the man tumbled like fruit spilling from a cart. The bartender strode into the street and slapping the man with his open palm rolled him across the pavement. When the man's companion, also drunk, remonstrated and bent over to pick up his friend, the bartender kicked him in the head and knocked him over. "What a dinner," I said, "chicken Caesar salad, Hahn's beer, cappuccino, and mocha chocolate cheesecake." We ate well in Sydney although entertainment did not season subsequent meals. Twice we cooked steaks and drank red wine at Philip's Foot, just up George from the Russell. At Boulders we ate kangaroo before going to the opera. Another night we had pancakes at Pancakes Café. Eliza and I also had tea and cakes at Renaissance Patisserie on Argyle Street, Vicki choosing to absent herself from sweets. We sat in a courtyard and munched *tranche au chocolat*, if one munches cakes with French names. Around us house sparrows, Indian mynahs, and red-whiskered bulbuls picked through bricks snapping up crumbs. On the road eating imposes order on days. Twice we ate lunch at the Gumnut Café on Harrington: mushroom soup, garlic bread, and toasted coconut bread slathered with lime marmalade. We sat in a small room, crammed against the single window. Outside, tourists rushed by, leaning so against rain that they themselves seemed vaporous. Behind us on the wall a poster depicted gumnut babies sipping a drink through straws. Pupils in the babies' eyes were round and black, rings of blue and white circling them. Aside from the top of the nut that perched on his head like a cap, the boy baby was naked. The little girl wore a skirt bright with yellow stamens.

During one lunch Eliza asked, "What are the five functions of an endoskeleton?" Before I spoke, she answered the question: support, movement, protection, storage of calcium, and production of blood cells. To keep mind active, Eliza forever asks herself questions. At the end of the meal, she said the alphabet backwards. She said it faster than I can say it forwards. Since then as a party trick, I have asked her to say it backwards several times. No one else in the family can do it. In truth Eliza gets her way so often because she's bright. Not only do I not want to thwart curiosity, but Eliza is fun, forever breathing life into dry participles of conversation.

Rain pinned us to the Rocks, and every day we explored stores. Built in 1882, the George Street North Police Station housed Australian Craftworks, small rooms linked by halls and resembling attics. In Burberry in the Galleria across Globe from the Russell, I brushed my right hand across a coat priced at five thousand dollars. "I'm not buying this," I said to the clerk, embarrassing Eliza. "I just want to touch it." Visual equivalents of Harlequin romances filled the Billich Gallery housed in the old Bethel Union Chapel. In contrast to the building's hard stone walls, paintings in the gallery were fleshly, looking soft battered vegetables, tomatoes or parsnips. While nudes watched a soccer game in one painting, in another naked golfers frolicked along a fairway, their buttocks golf balls. At Original and Authentic Aboriginal Art, I looked at *Mimi Spirits* painted by Billy Dullman. Priced at eighteen hundred dollars, the painting was beyond my pocket. At Hogarth Galleries a nine-foot limb had been carved into a snake. Each scale on the snake was distinct. The saleswoman said the snake cost twelve hundred dollars. That afternoon I returned to the gallery in hopes of talking the price to eight hundred. "I'm afraid I made a mistake," the woman said; "the snake costs twenty-five hundred dollars." "Yipes," I said. In the gallery Vicki bought presents, mostly scarves and shirts. On the other hand I shopped at Gannon House next to the Patisserie, eating then buying presents, an inlaid box and a wooden wombat the size of a fist.

For myself I bought a landscape by David Lake. The painting was the second I purchased in Australia, and for a moment I imagined myself a collector. In the painting a white cottage sat abandoned. The roof of the cottage sagged, and weeds hid the foundation. In the distance clouds stained a blue sky. Light in the painting was thin as old glass, the last pane clinging to the window of a broken barn. "The painting evokes the outback," I said to Eliza. Along with two blouses Eliza bought a puppet from the Puppet Shop in the basement of a building off George Street. Scores of puppets dangled like spiders from the ceiling, making customers bob and weave. Eliza's puppet was a white horse, thirteen inches tall, four inches broad, and eight inches from tall to chest. Flowers bloomed across amid the horse's coat, all red and yellow with four petals. "Now my suitcase is a stable," Vicki said.

Despite spending hours close to the hotel shopping in the Rocks, we walked a great deal: George, Market, York, and Hyde Park. One night we walked the raised path beside the Cahill Expressway. Cars scuttled past, and lights flickered like frost across buildings. We spent a morning roaming boutiques in the Queen

Victoria Building. A wholesome governess stood outside a lingerie shop, a blonde boy balanced on her shoulders, her eyes fixed on a trapeze of garters and straps. In the Strand Arcade I darted into Coombs Shoe Repair. For six dollars and fifty cents a cobbler mended a strap on my left sandal. The shop resembled a pantry. Five men worked in it, three in the back and two at the counter. Customers streamed in. "This is about the only shop like this around here," a man said. A woman brought in pumps elevated by six-inch heels. The shoes were loose, and the woman wanted new holes in the straps. "How can you walk on those heels?" I asked. "When I stalk love," she said, "comfort is not important."

One morning we explored the Botanic Gardens. Trains of tour buses parked on the shoulders of roads leading to Mrs. Macquaries Point. Japanese schoolgirls swept over the point, moving in unison like minnows. One group wore black Mary Janes, white knee socks, navy skirts and blouses, over the latter white handkerchiefs hanging like pinafores. Another group wore black penny loafers, not a single coin visible; blue socks, skirts, and sweaters, under the sweaters, blouses with round collars shaped like horseshoes. In the garden tree camellias appeared rouged, covered with blossoms pink and pudgy as cheeks. In contrast flowers fell from rose apple in pale unkempt sprays. High above paths flying foxes lolled and twisted, chattering discordantly. Over rice paper plant black seeds swarmed busy as ants, and on tree germander color drained into brown veins. From cedar of Lebanon limbs opened widely, platters of foliage at the tips. On coastal cypress needles clumped in thick humps. Bark on black tea trees shredded into shingles, and dark lines ran through trunks of pepperberry trees.

In gardens the eye shifts and blinks like a shutter on a camera. Near the pond I glanced back at the town. Buildings marched with signs: HUDSON, AXA AUSTRALIA, AMP, RENAISSANCE, ZURICH, LUFTANSA in yellow, and WESPAC, the W in red. Eventually, however, the battalion dissolved, and buildings seemed only blocks, edges of some beveled, other edges mirrored into illusion, but still blocks. Birds congregated about the Main Pond, black ducks, minas, dusky moorhens, and on the grass a lone pied currawong. At the restaurant ibis were nuisances. They filched food from tables, French fries being the snack of choice. A German tourist bought a chicken Caesar sandwich. He put the sandwich on a table and walked back to the counter to fetch coffee. Before he returned, an ibis brushed the sandwich off the table and raked ingredients across the ground.

The morning spent in the garden was sunny. Most days were overcast. One afternoon during a heavy rain, we took the ferry to the Taronga Zoo, "the *Lady Northcott* ferry," Eliza reminded me. Perhaps the best time to visit a zoo is during a rainstorm. Water swept people from walkways. If a person dresses to be almost comfortable, which I did, wearing shorts, hiking boots, a cap, and finally a garbage bag over his shirt, he will have the animals to himself. At the zoo Eliza wandered away from us. I didn't worry about her vanishing amid a crowd. No matter where she roamed, she was the only person in sight. Three blue-winged kookaburras flew into the chimpanzee enclosure and perched on ropes. Around the corner three other blue-winged kookaburras hunkered cold in a wire box. To escape damp, gorillas gathered in their shelter. The enclosure resembled a cage, a side of which was glass. The glass stripped privacy from the apes and transformed observers into peeping Toms. Zoos always make me uncomfortable; yet, when I travel, I visit zoos. The diversity of life startles me, and always I learn something. A bite from a fierce snake, I read, can pack enough venom to kill two hundred thousand mice. One of Eliza's favorite animals is the sun bear. In the zoo a bear paced an enclosure, the path it trod worn to a channel. A businessman rescued the bear and two fellow bears from a restaurant in Cambodia, the animals' paws being items on the menu. Behind a log in the enclosure containing a Sumatran tiger lay an orange ball. A stuffed lizard clung to a stump in the cloud leopard's enclosure. "Why do you notice such things?" Vicki asked. "I just do," I said. More than any other exhibition, I enjoyed Creatures of the Wollemi, a large aviary containing animals and birds. Vicki, Eliza, and I were the only people in the enclosure. Wallabies stared at us from boulders. A platypus dived into a pool, and birds spun through the air like tops.

One morning we went to the aquarium, taking the ferry from Circular Quay to Darling Harbour, this time the *Borrowdale*. As the ferry slid under the Harbour Bridge, Eliza said, "Sydney is my favorite city. I am so glad we came here." Because aquariums are confined to buildings, rain increases attendance. Only in empty spaces does tolerance flourish. Despite signs imploring people not to thump tanks, Japanese pounded glasses. As I studied an octopus collapsed like soggy paper, a Moslem backed into me. He then turned around and with his left hand pushed me back so he could take a picture of his son, his two daughters ignored, behind them his wife, a lump of coal in black. I almost spoke, but instead I walked away and was soon distracted by a sign saying the mortality rate among people stung by cone shells was 25 percent. As age begins to restrict my doings, I notice confinement. Cages and aquariums make me think of wheelchairs and people beached on sheets. In a small tank a large barramundi hung still as a sign. About the fish a pig-nosed turtle flapped, swimming up and down repeatedly. Below a lungfish lay like a log.

After eating a sweet roll in the Botanic Gardens, we crossed Cahill Expressway and went to the Art Gallery of New South Wales. On exhibit was "Renoir to Picasso," some eighty-one "Masterpieces from the Museé de Orangerië" in Paris. Few of the paintings appealed to me. No matter the effort I expend, I cannot appreciate Renoir. To me his women resemble fruits ripened into decay. The only painting I coveted was Cézanne's *Apples and Biscuits*, fourteen apples pink and red atop a sugar chest. Behind the chest green shifted lightly through wallpaper. To the right of the apples lay two-thirds of a plate, two biscuits in the white bowl of the plate, a thick blue line binding the edge.

The gallery owned many landscape paintings. Unfortunately as I climbed stairs leaving the exhibition, lights went off, and guards cleared the gallery. In cities we always visit museums. Displayed at the Museum of Contemporary Art was "What Elephants Paint," some fifty canvases painted by elephants with their trunks. The canvases were startling displays of color. Proceeds from sales went toward protecting the Asian elephant. Most paintings were priced at $660. Of the rest three cost $770; five, $990; three, $5,000, and one lollapalooza measuring 305 by 550 centimeters, $20,000. The artists ranged in age. While Arun was born in 1973, Juthanam was born in 1993. Born a year later, Ganesh began painting in 1999. On the second floor of the museum appeared enlargements of twelve photographs of Red Square taken with a Polaroid camera by Mikki, a chimpanzee. "What do you think, Daddy?" Eliza said. "Clearly the work of a chimpanzee," I said. On the third floor was an exhibition of Robert Macpherson's art. Adorning four walls of a big hall were 156 signs, each 122 by 91.5 centimeters, white paint against a black background, for the cognoscenti, Dulux Weather-shield's acrylic on Masonite. On the signs appeared words found by road and wayside:

TUB FIREWOOD
GRINDER AGED
MULCH. IRON-
BARK

I liked the signs. Reading them brought country to mind, matters suitable for an urban gallery but not an urbane dining room.

During the week we also visited the Australia Museum. In the gem collection was a garnet found in Raymond, Maine, the village near the camp where Edward worked. Minerals startled me, but I did not know how to look at them and spent more time studying the museum's collection of skeletons. The skeleton of a python resembled a white fern. A man sat astride a horse, both skeletons, the composition entitled "The Bone Ranger." "Domestic Bliss" was a tour de force of skeletons. A skeleton sat in a rocking chair. In the skeleton's left hand lay a leash. The leash was attached to a collar loose around the bony neck of Towser, a dog. Perched in a cage next to Towser was the skeleton of Old Polly, a parrot. Hanging on the wall was a frame enclosing the words HOME SWEET HOME. Below the frame the skeleton of a cat pursued that of a rat, this last about to scamper through a hole in the wall. Next to the skeleton in the rocker stood a lamp, the shade leaded with panes of milky glass.

SAM PICKERING

Resting on the skeleton's pelvis was a book. Although I twisted my bones, I couldn't read the title of the book. The book, however, discussed human anatomy and was open to a section entitled "Sprains and Dislocations." Traveling strips away the pretence of years. On the Rocks I led the family to the Toy Museum. In the museum cases of dolls leaned against sandstone walls. The only toy, I coveted, though, was "Ham and Sam," a team of wind-up minstrels eighty years old. While Sam strummed the banjo, Ham played the piano, the sheet music for "Dixie Blues" before him.

At night we roamed Sydney Cove. Lights transformed tall buildings into collarbones tarty with rhinestones and wrists shaking with opals. We spent three evenings at the Opera House, in the Drama Theatre seeing Sheridan's eighteenth-century comedy *The School for Scandal* and in the Opera Hall, Donizetti's *L'Elisir D'Amore* and Giordano's *Andrea Chénier,* this last the opening night of a new production. I went to the opera to create cultural recollections for Eliza. Opera did not visit Nashville when I was a boy, and I didn't see an opera until I was twenty-two, *La Traviata* in Sofia, Bulgaria. Once at the Tennessee Theater I saw a road company production of *Damn Yankees.* Of course I know that the more one stuffs into memory, the more one forgets. Still maybe some of things to which I've introduced Eliza will grow into interests that in years ahead will enable her to escape melancholy.

At dawn on the twenty-eighth Vicki and I carried bags downstairs to the curb outside the Russell. An airport shuttle picked us up, and later that morning we flew to Fiji. On the plane I read Gabrielle Lord's new thriller *Death Delights.* Just before the plane taxied down the runway, Eliza said, "Thank you for taking us to Sydney. I had a wonderful time. I hope Fiji will be as much fun." "It will," I said.

Fiji

In May I spent two evenings studying the "Qantas Holiday Guide to Fiji." I wanted to spend a week marooned on an island. Because Vicki is conservative with money, I told her we would stay three days. Once I've made a booking, Vicki invariably enjoys herself and wants the holiday to last for months. I narrowed my choice to the Mamanuca Islands east of Viti Levu and the airport at Nadi, most of the islands two hours by launch from Denarau Marina, itself a thirty-minute bus ride from airport hotels. One of my choices, the resort on Tokoriki, consisted of only twenty-nine bures (huts). With sixty-six bures the resort on Castaway was larger. "A much sought-after island resort," the brochure said describing Castaway. "Altogether, the facilities and activities are perfect for couples, honeymooners, and families alike." "That first place is too little," Vicki said. "Eliza would have more fun at a larger resort." "We'll see," I said. Deliberations proved beside the point. Tokoriki was booked, and I got the last bure available on Castaway, an inland bure, all huts on the beach having already been reserved.

We landed at Nadi at dusk on July 28. After I exchanged Australian for Fijian dollars, we rolled three of our bags to the storage room at the far end of the airport. Before leaving Perth, I booked a transfer to and night at the Raffles Gateway Hotel. The name *Raffles* smacked of the derring-do of boys' novels: lazy ceiling fans; jaded men in white suits, circles of yellow stains beneath their armpits; paths coiling through banyan trees bony as catacombs; villainy on a spit of sand walled in by mangoes, roots clutching mud like fingers writhing in pain. The actual Raffles was a comfortable quadrangle. A gecko skittered across the ceiling of our room when we turned on the light. "We are in Fiji," Vicki said, watching the gecko shake into shadow. At eight the next morning we boarded a bus for Denarau. We stood beside the highway a hundred yards from the hotel. Drivers honked in hopes of pocketing cab fare and making going to work profitable. The bus stopped at a score of hotels. Buildings were gray, almost Soviet, the walls slabs. Most people on the bus were young backpackers. Instead of German or Swedish as in Darwin, they were Californian. Throughout the year the trips children took startled me. Children now explore places far beyond the realm of my childhood. Eliza doesn't think her experiences extraordinary. Practically every day during the past year, I marveled at being in Australia. Sometimes I worry that in so multiplying possibilities of travel affluence has undermined, not awakened, imagination. Places that once furnished days with dream are now catalogued and shelved among the commonplace.

I enjoyed the slow bump to the marina. A sign hawking Adidas stood in a field of sugar cane. The bus stopped at a railway crossing, and a sugar-cane train clicked past. A miniature engine pulled toy cars. The train was long, and I wish I had counted the cars. "When I was a boy," I told Eliza, "I counted cars." "What was the longest train you ever saw?" she asked. I couldn't remember, but in the back of my mind empty coal cars rolled through northern Virginia, "Norfolk and Western" white on the sides. Before arriving at the marina, the bus stopped at the Sheraton. A golf course surrounded the hotel. Although age and means have subdued discontent, the leveler in me occasionally rises from the past. I longed to drive a bulldozer down the fairways and dig real divots. Two hours later I was on Castaway Island, enjoying the good tourist life, all ire vanished.

The resort sat on the northwest end of the island. Behind the resort land rose into a ridge. Paths zigzagged through woods then sliced through high, sharp grass along the crest of the ridge. Like wrinkles goat trails furrowed the wood. Four times during the week I explored the ridge. To the north the sea unraveled in a green rug. On the horizon islands crumpled into blue shag. Near me a white-breasted wood swallow perched on a dead limb. Beneath him dry grass shingled the hillside. The bird plucked insects from the air, swooping from the tree, its silhouette stubby, belying the bird's quick flight. One morning Vicki and I met honeymooners. The day was hot and humid, and perspiration drizzled from us. "Too hot for," Vicki said, after the couple swayed past arms linked. "Yes," I said, interrupting then pointing up, "look at the frigate birds." High above us two lesser frigate birds soared effortlessly, tails scissored, long wings bent into levers, their breasts white as clouds. Although I had never seen a frigate bird before, I recognized them.

Two reef herons fished the shallows beyond North Beach. They stood atop flat rocks, so still and gray, they seemed sculpted. Comparatively few birds roamed the shore. Every morning before breakfast I sat on the porch of our bure. Mynahs gleaned the ground, their bright yellow feet looking like rain boots. While foraging, they rubbed calls into hard kernels of sound. Families of red-headed parrot finches flickered into hibiscus hedges then dropped to the grass. While bodies of the birds were green, their tails were crimson. Gray-backed white-eyes shuffled amid the crowns of coconut palms while a solitary red-vented bulbul rested in a Poinciana. A golden whistler burst from shrub in a jet of yellow, and orange-breasted honeyeaters chased each other through hibiscus. Small striped skinks flicked through fallen leaves near the porch. One morning I counted nine skinks without shifting my eyes. At night geckos clung to the ceiling of the porch. On noticing me, they shimmed like cracks to the edge of the roof. Geckos also hunted insects inside the bure. One night a gecko chirped on the wall above my bed and woke me. In the day I didn't see insects in the bure, but on the last morning a centipede bit Eliza in the armpit.

Our bure was number 56, inland from the South Beach and

almost under the ridge. Walls of the bure were blocks painted white, and the roof was thatch, eight inches thick. Attached to the front of the building was a small porch on which sat three plastic chairs. Across the front of the porch stretched a clothesline attached to posts supporting the roof. The front door opened off the right side of the porch; to the left behind the chairs was a window. Inside, the bure was in effect a single room into which furniture and partitions had been fitted like box springs dropped into a bed frame. Two single beds ran head to foot along one wall of the first two-fifths of the frame. On the opposite side of the room were a plant, two chairs, a sofa, and a coffee table. Facing the door were a refrigerator and a shelf. Atop the shelf sat a coffee pot. The shelf also divided the bure, shutters above it, below wood partitioning. A door opened into the second two-fifths of the bure. In this section were a double bed, on either side of the bed tables with lamps, then a wardrobe, and a long table. At the far end of the section lay the last fifth of the bure, the bathroom, itself divided into shower, sink, and lavatory areas. No partition reached the ceiling, and ten feet above the floor, the bure was a single room. From the ceiling hung two fans, the one in Vicki's and my section turning with a soft thump. Walls of the bure rose in an arch above the bed. Covering the inside of the roof was thick paper, designs painted on it. The word KALUNI appeared often, all the N's printed backwards. Amid black and white cross-hatchings, birds, perhaps pigeons, dove toward the ground. About the birds six pointed stars flickered in pale orange. In the first portion of the bure, windows pocked walls. As a result the bure was cool and comfortable and tempted me to sleep. Sleeping, however, is something one does at home, not on vacation.

Brick walks wound between bures like veins. Beside walkways croton and philodendron grew low and fleshly; above them flourished palms; sea grape; almond, rails of yellow running through leaves; coconut; drala; paw paw, and fish poison tree, its leaves green as magnolia. I didn't recognize many trees. "Qori Qori Wai," an Indian gardener said, pointing to a tree, its flowers big as cantaloupes. "That's an Indian name, not a Fijian name," a maid said. "What's the Fijian name?" I asked. "I don't know," she said. Before breakfast gardeners raked the resort, both lawn and beach. At night toads jutted up from the grass big as faucets. The resort was shaped like a V, bures along both legs, beach and water lying outside the legs. At the point where the legs met were buildings: the main restaurant, white tables scattered over a deck built on pilings; a bar which served pizza; under the bar, the dive shop; behind the dive shop, offices and a boutique. The bar was high above the water, and some evenings Vicki and I watched the sunset from the bar. We drank concoctions with sugary names: Castaway Special, Tropical Splice, and Love on the Beach. While Tropical Splice contained Midori, Cointreau, pineapple juice, and cream, Love on the Beach was a heart-stopping caloric bomb of Baileys, Kahlúa, crème de cacao, and cream. Drinks were sweeter than they were alcoholic. Never did they turn sunset and words garish. Instead color rose soft and fruity from the lip of the sea: lemon, peach, pineapple then grape, first purple, lastly weary brown.

Behind the boutique a pool unbuttoned like a shirt. Vicki and I didn't swim in the pool, although one night on the terrace surrounding it I splashed through four ladles of kava, a Fijian drink made from pepper tree leaves. Supposedly kava is anesthetizing. I did not notice anything, but maybe that was the effect. Behind and to the side of the pool were two Ping-Pong tables. Eliza and I played four games. I won three, in the one I lost giving Eliza a fifteen-point handicap. By 9:30 every night I was asleep. During the day, however, I raced the hours, snorkeling twice a day and kayaking once. One morning Eliza parasailed, hanging beneath a yellow parachute, a smiling face painted black upon it. "Sky diving is next," Eliza said after landing on South Beach. What came next was scuba diving, lessons in the pool then four dives at Magic Island and Rainbow Forest.

Castaway was small and familial. During meals employees sang and played musical instruments: guitars, ukuleles, and bass. This last was a box with a stick in one corner. A string ran from the box to the top of the stick. When the stick stood straight or leaned, the

SAM PICKERING

string was taut. One employee sang the songs of John Lee Hooker. The man was almost as good as Hooker himself. After-dinner entertainment was simple, consisting of races, a fiddler crab race one night, another night, a frog, really toad, race. For both races an employee ran a Calcutta, auctioning runners. On the shells of the crabs, he painted numbers. Crabs represented the homelands of visitors to the resort: Japan, Italy, Australia, England, and the United States, among others. While a crab dubbed Yokohama represented Japan, Jordan, named after the basketball player Michael Jordan, represented the United States. Bidding began at five dollars. Selling for $87, the crab representing Fiji brought the highest price. Going for $16, Yokohama was the cheapest "nag," the average selling price for the ten entrants being $50.80 in Fijian, about $23 American. The course was a circle chalked on the floor of the bar. Crabs were dumped in the middle, and the first to drag itself over the chalk won the race. For the record, crabs representing Samoa and India finished second and third respectively, behind Yokohama, the winner earning its "owner," $200, second and third bringing $170 and $138. I'm not a gambler, but I bid on several runners in the toad race. I stopped bidding at $20, however, $3 under the selling price of the most inexpensive toad, Stars and Stripes, who was an "also-hopped." Though I fancied them more than the crabs, I was in the minority, the price for the average toad being $35.30.

We spent time and money in the boutique. Despite eating dessert at lunch, almost every afternoon, we purchased Magnum ice cream bars, the "Classic," vanilla ice cream smothered by dark chocolate. We also bought a duffel of souvenirs: a tape of the Castaway Islanders, the group that sang at meals; a laminated poster of the island, four by two feet, "for winter in the English department," Vicki said; then a closet of shirts and sarongs. I bought two shirts, the first short-sleeved and yellow with a black and white collar, stitches over the left breast forming a gold starfish, underneath in blue the words "Castaway Island." The second shirt was a Del-Cee product of Fiji. Hibiscus bloomed down the shirt. Suspended between flowers were surfboards, some of the boards pink with blossoms, a forest of trees white on other boards, the number *8* appearing mysteriously amid branches. Only when I make a speech do I pay attention to dress. On such occasions I appear wing-tipped and buttoned-down in a gray suit and blue and red regimental necktie. The rest of the time, my clothes, as Doreen in the English department at Connecticut put it, "make people wonder who dressed you." Still as my skin turns translucent and my hair begins to look like the ashy remnant of a fire, I dress more colorfully. "Fijian in spirit and now in shirt," I said to Vicki.

Meals structure holidays. I purchased meal plans so we could eat peacefully, never cracking teeth against coin. At 8:30 in the morning, we strolled to the restaurant, employees greeting us, smiling and forever saying the Fijian equivalent of "good morning." Breakfast was buffet, consisting of fruits, cereals, meats, vegetables, and eggs in and out of omelets. Every morning I drank a pot of coffee, buttered a croissant, and ate a bowl of sliced fruit, topping this last with paw paw. The worse the smell the tastier the paw paw. After breakfast Vicki and I snorkeled or kayaked. For the first three mornings Eliza joined us. Later scuba diving absorbed her days. At noon we met for lunch, sitting under the awning and gazing at the sea. Usually I ate a Caesar salad then seafood, squid or shrimp. Desserts were not tasty, but I sampled them all: coconut cream pie, chocolate sponge roulade, baked lime meringue pie, and macadamia nut crunch cheesecake, among others. At 7:30 we ate dinner, usually on the deck above the water. Lights bathed the shoreline, and fish wavered beneath us in silver lines. We began dinner with appetizers, for example, "sliced smoked salmon on potato roesti with an orange Dijon dressing" or "Tempura prawns and Asian mushrooms with dashi and souva noodles." For main courses I selected seafood, my favorite being barbequed sea kabobs with prawns, scallops, reef fish, and mussels served on rice with lime hollandaise sauce. Vicki and I also drank wine at dinner. Service was haphazard. Place settings were obstacles to waiters. While Eliza's setting might be missing a fork and Vicki's a spoon, mine lacked a knife and napkin. Getting dishes to the table at the same time was also a hurdle. Inevitably one main course arrived ten minutes after the other two. When blended with exercise, however, wine made us mellow and jovial. Moreover sitting above the water, sand yellow beneath us, guitars strumming, small lights opening like drills in the dark distance, we didn't fret when dishes drifted to the table. Absence from the city erased concern about schedule. Often after meals Vicki and I lingered at the table, turning empty wine glasses through our fingers. For her part Eliza returned to the bure and read Charlotte Brontë's novel *Villette*. Dallying became life. When I sauntered back to the bure, I sat outside for a while, content to watch geckos scurry after insects.

Most visitors stayed three days on the island. Vicki and I discussed extending our week. Alas changing flights proved impossible. Moreover, six days after our return to Storrs, Edward was scheduled to come home from Maine. "We must be there to greet him and set him up for college," I said to Vicki. Still on Fiji the thought of responsibility made me weary. Vacations inevitably make a person think he has squandered life, or so I thought on the porch at night. During days themselves I was so active I rarely thought. Kayaks were fiberglass and slid easily over coral. Vicki particularly liked kayaking, and twice we paddled around the island. We explored coves, and the trips took two hours. Vicki was a stronger paddler than me. Age and bone spurs have rotted the muscle in my right arm and spread caution through my life. One morning Vicki proposed paddling to Honeymoon Island, a muffin of stone and beach northwest of Castaway. To reach the island, one paddled across a pan of sea bubbling with current. To no avail I tried to dissuade Vicki, and when she set out, I followed. A boatload of picnickers greeted us on the beach. "Returning against the current is going to be tough," a man said. "No, it won't," his wife said. Both were right. Returning wore me out but not Vicki. That night she plotted a trip to a distant island. When I told her that she'd have to go alone, Eliza said, "I'll go with you Mommy." "No, you won't," I said. Vicki did not make the trip, not because of my misgivings, but because paddling sanded flesh from her backside, producing two round abrasions, each as big as a cow's eye. The way of a man with a wife of twenty years differs from that of a man with a maid. On discovering that Vicki couldn't make the trip, I opined I might paddle to the island. "My arms and legs are a bit tight," I said, "but my ass is just dandy."

Every day we walked, either hiking the woods behind the bure or strolling beaches, usually past Monkey Rock on the north side of the resort. Ghost crabs scuttled across sand, and rock crabs shuttered in and out of sight. A snake moral eel thrashed through a tidal pool. A Portuguese man of war eddied back and forth, becalmed atop a shallow ledge. Beaches beyond the resort had not been groomed, and Vicki and I collected trash, bringing it back to Castaway and dumping it into a garbage bin. Gleanings were rich. One morning we harvested bags: two green plastic; four black plastic, each with a cinch at the top; a gray cloth bag, MARSHALL SAILS LTD MADE IN FIJI stamped on the outside; then three cloth bags, the first once containing fifty kilos of long grain rice imported from Thailand; the second once full with fifty kilos of cane sugar, processed by the Fiji Sugar Corporation; lastly a forty-five-kilo bag, big enough to hold forty-five kilos of A-Grade Long Grain Sungrown Rice, milled and packed by Four Mills of Fiji, located on Leonidas Street, Walu Bay, Suva.

Along with the bags we retrieved a storeroom of boxes, among others, two boxes capable of holding four kilos of Crest Chicken "without Giblets." Stamped on the outside of the box was a chicken, atop his head a baker's cap. Collapsed against a log was a box that had held a kilo of "BII Reliable Nails, 50 mm JHD." In reeds offshore lay another box, the container for fifteen disposable diapers, Huggies, size 3, for children weighing fifteen to eighteen kilos. We did not rake up much glass, the top half of a whiskey bottle and the bottom of what appeared to be a Coca-Cola bottle. In contrast plastic flourished: a five-gallon jug, POISON impressed into the front; two Janola containers, each 750 ml, "For Tough Cleaning and Germ Killing"; the bottom half of a bottle that contained 250 grams of something mysterious, a Vanda orchid pink on the label; and eleven other plastic bottles, their labels washed off. Litterers ate M&M's and Oryx Glucose bars. They drank

Schweppes Orange and Mango Sparkling Mineral Water, Golden Circle Pineapple Juice, Lite Milk, and Fiji Export Bitter. They sucked Tuckers Kool Pops. On the wrapper a green crocodile stood on his hind legs and tail, a baseball cap akimbo on his head. In his left hand the crocodile held a pink pop, probably cherry-flavored. Litterers also tossed Styrofoam into the water where waves shattered hunks into bite-sized bits.

Despite time spent hiking, kayaking, and collecting garbage, snorkeling occupied my days. For hours I swam above the edges of coral reefs. Sometimes I drifted three hundred yards off shore. Often I stayed in the water for two hours without getting out. Beforehand I basted head and legs with sunscreen, and I always wore a shirt. Foolishly I swam alone, particularly off the North Beach. Underwater sights were elixir. No matter the currents I breasted, I didn't tire. Hedges of coral wrapped the shore, portions rising into gables and turrets; other bits, massive balls; still others thorny and sliding into plates. Sea kraits wavered through the water, refracted into black and silver wrinkles. An octopus rooted itself in coral. Giant clams winked then shut. Nudibranchs clung to coral, and black sea cucumbers slid along the ocean floor, sand so dusting them that they looked like slabs of rubber, remnants of an exploded tire. Blue sea stars lay leggy amid grasses while a chunky red star pasted itself to a coral platter. Squid hung motion-less in the water like clear glass bottles. Urchins plugged pockets in coral, and sea fans spread themselves into trellises. Beyond the reef spotted eagle rays kited the deep. Along a moat under a keep of coral, a wobbegong lay still as a gray log. From rubble a lizardfish tilted upward. Ornate pipefish wormed through sea grass, and a trumpet fish ruddered slowly, fins turning black and yellow. Schools of trevallies scooted past, giant trevallies black, others shards of silver, tipped with yellow. Fish bloomed throughout the reefs: hawkfish; groupers, the color of tomatoes; waspfish; dotty-backs; white-tailed chromis, and hump-backed snappers, fins along their spines red ridges. While dark surgeonfish fell away like waterlogged leaves, scissor-tailed sergeants schooled around me.

The more fish I recognized the more the sea seemed home.

Longfin spadefish drifted instead of swimming. When they turned sideways, they transformed themselves into cracks into which they vanished. Mullet swam past in orange and bronze showers. A warty frog fish hunkered atop a hand of coral. Families of wrasse abounded: blackedge thicklips, the lower half of their bodies black, the upper, white, blue veins spreading about their eyes; cigar; cleaner; bird, blue and green and "snouted"; sugar; and floral, brown and pink ruffling scales like tissue paper. I saw scores of parrot fish: redlip, steephead, green, and saddled, the forehead of this last swollen into a purple boulder. Damsels dotted reefs with color: black, purple, yellow, and red. Butterfly fish melted into color: the long-nosed, yellow, black, and white; others simply black and white; others splats of yellow. So great was the diversity of butterfly fish that they made underwater endlessly alluring. I floated on currents following Moorish idols and palette sur-geonfish. I hovered over black blotched porcupine fish and anemonefish. Lemon damsels lit musty corners like weak flash-lights. I watched a goatfish scratch sand with barbels. Would that I had grown up in the Pacific, I told Eliza one afternoon. "Then I would be able to recognize more fish." "You will never know many," Eliza said. "Think of them as flowers in a garden, the col-ors bright but the species beyond identification." "Monet's gar-den," Vicki said. "Right," Eliza said. By making people aware of the unexperienced, travel dissatisfies. Later that night in the bure, I muttered, "If woman had not existed, I would have wandered the oceans." "What?" Eliza said, looking up from *Villette*. "Nothing sweetheart," I said, "nothing important."

Home

We left Fiji at 11:30 at night on August 5. I am not a comfortable flyer, and to calm my nerves, I spent the morning snorkeling beyond North Beach. Because Eliza was scuba diving and Vicki kayaking, I snorkeled alone. If I didn't drown, I hoped I'd be so tired that I would sleep all the way to the United States. I had anticipated flying Air Pacific's aging 747. Instead we flew in a 767–200, the single 767 owned by Air Pacific. After takeoff I thumbed the in-flight magazine. Near the end of the magazine I read that the 767 had a range of 8,000 kilometers. On the next page the magazine stated that the distance from Nadi to Los Angeles was 8,886 kilometers. We were flying into a headwind, and the plane was loaded. Not a seat was vacant, and most passengers, I noticed in the airport, carried as much luggage as we did. I stopped a stewardess and pointed out the discrepancy between the plane's range and the distance to California. She giggled and said, "Several people have noticed this." Then she giggled again, adding afterward, "Maybe one of the numbers is a misprint." I did not giggle. Neither did I sleep. Instead I prayed the pilot would divert to Hawaii and take on more fuel. He didn't change the flight, and as we approached Los Angeles, I expected us to belly flop into the water. "No more snorkeling for me and thee," I told Vicki. "Tomorrow people will be snorkeling after us." After the plane landed, Vicki said, "All that worry for nothing." "Bullshit," I said, "worry is never for nothing. There was hardly a drop of fuel in the tanks when we landed. In fact we flew the last ten minutes on fumes alone."

Our flight to Hartford did not leave for eleven hours. In Perth I explored flying through Salt Lake City, Dallas, Nashville, Cincinnati, St. Louis, and Vancouver in hopes of finding a better connection. Better flights didn't exist. The Los Angeles airport throbbed with people. "Not the outback," Eliza said. To escape the crowd I booked a room in the Doubletree Hotel. When we checked in, the desk clerk gave us each two chocolate chip cookies. We ate them on the ride to the fifth floor. Early in the evening we returned to the airport. At ten o'clock the next morning, we arrived in Hartford. The air was humid and metallic with gas. Aaron, our house sitter, met us. He drove our Toyota to the airport, and his girlfriend drove a pickup truck. We piled our bags in the truck. An hour later we were home. George the dog looked like a mothy school satchel, the childhood possession of a grandfather, stored and long forgotten in the attic. That afternoon I wandered the yard. Nests of fall web worms hung from branches like socks. During the year the golden chain tree had grown into leggy adolescence. Gone was the weedy patch by the mailbox, eleven years of goldenrod and New England asters. Also gone were two small azaleas and a clump of Oregon holly I'd carted away from the Pharmacy School Garden one summer afternoon. "Mowed down by Edward before he went to Maine," I said.

The next morning I mailed checks to Middlebury and Princeton, slightly over seventeen thousand dollars to Middlebury and just over thirteen thousand dollars to Princeton. The amount for Francis was less because he hadn't reserved a room or signed a food contract. "That will come," Vicki assured me. Next I telephoned my accountant and said I would soon drop off materials for income tax. The battery in the Mazda was dead. "Seven years ago when you came back from Australia," Dave said, checking his records, "the battery in this car was dead." "Does anything change?" he said. "Nope," I said. Four days later Edward returned from Maine. He lounged around the house that night. The next

SAM PICKERING

evening he left home at five. He returned at 12:59 the next after-noon. "Are you going to say anything to him?" Vicki asked. "No," I said. "Gee whiz," Vicki said. "We are right where we were a year ago." "Yep," I said, "right back."

That afternoon I received a letter from Turlow Gutheridge. "Welcome home to the world of high-falutin' education," he wrote. "Thought you'd like to know that things in Carthage are pleasingly academic. Two weeks ago I ran across Cerumen Hooberry in the town library. He was reading *Beowulf*, and when he saw me, he said, 'The fellow who wrote this *Beowulf* sure can tell a story, but it's a shame he can't spell any better.'" During the past semester there been a literary tiff in Tennessee. When a pro-fessor at Austin Peay attributed Shakespeare's plays to Francis Bacon, he aroused a graduate school of criticism. The hullabaloo filtered down to Smith County. When Cropple Shanks applied for the post of English teacher in the high school at Maggart, Minnie Gossett, principal of the school, interviewed him. Near the end of the interview, she asked Cropple what he thought about the controversy. For a moment Cropple stroked his Adam's apple with his left hand, drawing his fingers forward and together as if he were pulling taffy. "Well," he eventually answered, "I've not met this Mr. Bacon, but I'll tell you right now if he didn't write Shakespeare's plays, he's done passed up the opportunity of a lifetime."

A week later on campus I heard a student begin a sentence by saying, "I'm like." The student got no farther. Her brow furrowed as she ploughed her mind for words. Finally, she said *like* again then stopped and shut her mouth. After dinner that night I went on-line and contacted Aboriginal Fine Arts in Darwin. On the gallery's web page was a long-necked turtle painted by Ivan Namirrikki. The painting including shipping to Connecticut cost $672. "I can't afford this," I thought. "College tuition has busted me." Half an hour later I purchased the painting. "You look cheery," Vicki said when I ambled into the kitchen. "I'm just happy to be home," I said. The next afternoon I jogged around

Horsebarn Hill. Behind the piggery blue birds perched on fence posts. An osprey dove into Mirror Lake and speared a carp. As the bird pulled itself aloft, the fish writhed, golden in the moment before death.